Fodor's InFocus

JAMAICA

2nd Edition

Fodor's Travel Publications   New York, Toronto, London, Sydney, Auckland

www.fodors.com

Be a Fodor's Correspondent

Your opinion matters. It matters to us. It matters to your fellow Fodor's travelers, too. And we'd like to hear it. In fact, we *need* to hear it. When you share your experiences and opinions, you become an active member of the Fodor's community. Here's how you can help improve Fodor's for all of us.

Tell us when we're right. We rely on local writers to give you an insider's perspective. But our writers and staff editors also depend on you. Your positive feedback is a vote to renew our recommendations for the next edition.

Tell us when we're wrong. We update most of our guides every year. But things change. If any of our descriptions are inaccurate or inadequate, we'll incorporate your changes in the next edition and will correct factual errors at fodors.com *immediately*.

Tell us what to include. You probably have had fantastic travel experiences that aren't yet in Fodor's. Why not share them with a community of like-minded travelers? Share your discoveries and experiences with everyone directly at fodors.com. Your input may lead us to add a new listing or a higher recommendation.

Give us your opinion instantly at our feedback center at www.fodors.com/feedback. You may also e-mail editors@fodors.com with the subject line "Jamaica Editor." Or send your nominations, comments, and complaints by mail to Jamaica Editor, Fodor's, 1745 Broadway, New York, NY 10019.

Happy Traveling!

Tim Jarrell, Publisher

FODOR'S IN FOCUS JAMAICA

Series Editor: Douglas Stallings

Editor: Douglas Stallings
Editorial Contributors: John Bigley, Paris Permenter

Production Editor: Carolyn Roth
Maps & Illustrations: David Lindroth, *cartographer*; Bob Blake and Rebecca Baer, *map editors;* William Wu, *information graphics*
Design: Fabrizio La Rocca, *creative director*; Guido Caroti, *art director*; Nora Rosansky, *designer*; Melanie Marin, *senior picture editor*
Cover Photo: (Heading toward Pelican Bar, Treasure Beach): Axiom Photographic Limited/SuperStock
Production Manager: Amanda Bullock

COPYRIGHT

2nd Edition

ISBN 978-1-4000-0446-1

ISSN 1940-3283

SPECIAL SALES

This book is available for special discounts for bulk purchases for sales promotions or premiums. Special editions, including personalized covers, excerpts of existing books, and corporate imprints, can be created in large quantities for special needs. For more information, write to Special Markets/Premium Sales, 1745 Broadway, MD 6-2, New York, NY 10019, or e-mail specialmarkets@randomhouse.com.

AN IMPORTANT TIP & AN INVITATION

Although all prices, opening times, and other details in this book are based on information supplied to us at press time, changes occur all the time in the travel world, and Fodor's cannot accept responsibility for facts that become outdated or for inadvertent errors or omissions. **So always confirm information when it matters,** especially if you're making a detour to visit a specific place. Your experiences—positive and negative—matter to us. If we have missed or misstated something, **please write to us.** We follow up on all suggestions. Contact the Jamaica editor at editors@fodors.com or c/o Fodor's at 1745 Broadway, New York, NY 10019.

PRINTED IN CHINA
10 9 8 7 6 5 4 3 2 1

CONTENTS

1 EXPERIENCE JAMAICA......9
What's Where 10
Jamaica Planner 12
Top Experiences 14
When to Go. 18
Great Itineraries 19
Weddings and Honeymoons . . .20
The Tapestry of Jamaica. 22
2 MONTEGO BAY. 25
Orientation and Planning. 26
Exploring Montego Bay. 33
Where to Eat. 40
Where to Stay. 46
Sports and the Outdoors 57
Shopping. 65
Nightlife and the Arts. 69
**3 OCHO RIOS AND
RUNAWAY BAY 71**
Orientation and Planning. 72
Exploring Ocho Rios and
Runaway Bay. 80
Where to Eat. 85
Where to Stay. 91
Beaches. 105
Sports and the Outdoors 106
Shopping. 111
Nightlife and the Arts. 113
4 PORT ANTONIO 115
Orientation and Planning. 117
Exploring Port Antonio 120
Where to Eat. 125
Where to Stay. 127
Sports and the Outdoors 133
Shopping. 135
Nightlife and the Arts. 136
**5 KINGSTON AND THE
BLUE MOUNTAINS 137**
Orientation and Planning. 139
Where to Eat. 157
Where to Stay. 159
Sports and the Outdoors 165

Shopping. 169
Nightlife and the Arts. 170
6 THE SOUTH COAST 173
Orientation and Planning. 175
Exploring the South Coast 180
Where to Eat. 184
Beaches. 189
Sports and the Outdoors 192
Nightlife and the Arts. 196
7 NEGRIL. 197
Orientation and Planning. 198
Exploring Negril 205
Where to Eat. 206
Where to Stay. 211
Beaches. 223
Sports and the Outdoors 224
Shopping. 230
Nightlife and the Arts. 231
TRAVEL SMART JAMAICA . . .233
INDEX 249
ABOUT OUR WRITERS. 256

MAPS

Montego Bay Area 28
Where to Stay and Eat in
Montego Bay. 41
Exploring Ocho Rios and
Runaway Bay. 74
Where to Stay and Eat in
Ocho Rios 86
Where to Stay and Eat in Ocho Rios
and Runaway Bay. 88
Port Antonio Area. 117
Port Antonio 123
Exploring Kingston 140
Exploring Kingston and Vicinity . .147
Where to Stay and Eat in
Kingston 156
The South Coast 176
Negril Dining. 200
Negril Lodging 213

ABOUT THIS BOOK

Our Ratings

We wouldn't recommend a place that wasn't worth your time, but sometimes a place is so experiential that superlatives don't do it justice: you just have to be there to know. These sights, properties, and experiences get our highest rating, **Fodor's Choice** indicated by orange stars throughout this book. Black stars highlight sights and properties we deem **Highly Recommended** places that our writers, editors, and readers praise again and again for consistency and excellence.

Credit Cards

AE, D, DC, MC, V following restaurant and hotel listings indicate whether American Express, Discover, Diners Club, MasterCard, and Visa are accepted.

Restaurants

Unless we state otherwise, restaurants are open for lunch and dinner daily. We mention dress only when there's a specific requirement and reservations only when they're essential or not accepted.

Hotels

Unless we tell you otherwise, you can assume that the hotels have private bath, phone, TV, and air-conditioning. We always list facilities but not whether you'll be charged an extra fee to use them, so when pricing accommodations, find out what's included.

Many Listings

★ Fodor's Choice
★ Highly recommended
⊠ Physical address
✛ Directions
🕮 Mailing address
☎ Telephone
🖷 Fax
⊕ On the Web
✍ E-mail
🖾 Admission fee
☉ Open/closed times
Ⓜ Metro stations
🖃 Credit cards

Hotels & Restaurants

🏨 Hotel
🛏 Number of rooms
⚲ Facilities
⑩ Meal plans
✕ Restaurant
⚱ Reservations
⊻ Smoking
🍺 BYOB
✕🏨 Hotel with restaurant that warrants a visit

Outdoors

⛳ Golf
⛺ Camping

Other

☜ Family-friendly
⇨ See also
⊠ Branch address
☞ Take note

Experience
Jamaica

1

WHAT'S WHERE

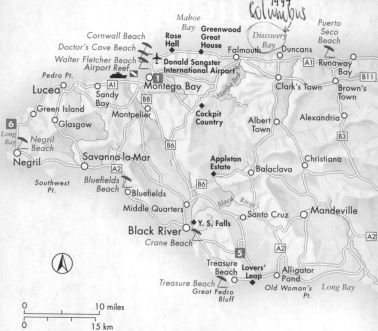

1 Montego Bay. Jamaica's main airport and busiest resort area doesn't have beaches as nice as those in Negril, but a vast array of resorts close to the airport is enticing for myriad travelers.

2 Ocho Rios and Runaway Bay. Spread out along the island's north coast are an array of resorts on nice beaches, as well as the famous Dunn's River Falls.

3 Port Antonio. More laid back than Negril, Port Antonio is best for independent travelers who don't need an all-inclusive resort to keep them entertained and who appreciate the lack of commercialism.

4 Kingston and the Blue Mountains. Jamaica's capital is not on most tourist itineraries, but it's a must-see to understand the heart and soul of the island. The Blue Mountains offer a cool escape from island heat.

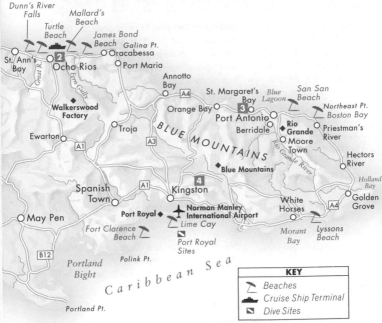

KEY

⟩	Beaches
⚓	Cruise Ship Terminal
◼	Dive Sites

Dunn's River Falls
Mallard's Beach
Turtle Beach
James Bond Beach
Galina Pt.
Oracabessa
St. Ann's Bay
2 Ocho Rios
Port Maria
Annotto Bay
A4
St. Margaret's Bay
Blue Lagoon
San San Beach
Orange Bay
3
Port Antonio
Northeast Pt.
Boston Bay
Walkerswood Factory
Berridale
Rio Grande
Priestman's River
Ewarton
Troja
B L U E   M O U N T A I N S
Moore Town
A1
A3
Rio Grande River
Hectors River
Blue Mountains
Holland Bay
Spanish Town
A1
4 Kingston
White Horses
A4
Golden Grove
May Pen
Port Royal
Norman Manley International Airport
Lime Cay
Morant Bay
Lyssons Beach
Fort Clarence Beach
Port Royal Sites
B12
Polink Pt.
Portland Bight
C a r i b b e a n   S e a
Portland Pt.

5 The South Coast. The least visited and least developed part of the island is along the southwest coast of Jamaica, where there is only one large resort and miles of wild and uncrowded beaches.

6 Negril. Jamaica's most bohemian region is being developed with larger and larger resorts, but there are still plenty of smaller independent resorts, not to mention the island's best beach.

JAMAICA PLANNER

Island Activities

Negril has the island's best **beaches,** but there are also good beaches in the southwest and in Montego Bay. Despite the conservative culture, nude sunbathing is common at some resorts.

Jamaica has some spectacular **golf courses,** the best of which are near Montego Bay.

You can go **rafting** on the slow, lazy Rio Grande, Martha Brae, or Great rivers.

Tour operators are coming up with new activities all the time. **Chukka Caribbean Adventures** operates ATV courses, canopy tours, horseback riding, and even a dog-sledding adventure.

But as many people seem to be drawn to Jamaica for the music—particularly **reggae,** which originated on the island. **Bob Marley,** one of reggae's most famous stars, is an island legend, and a pilgrimage to the places that were meaningful to him is often on the tourist's agenda.

Logistics

Getting to Jamaica: Donald Sangster International Airport (MBJ), in Montego Bay, is the island's main airport. Norman Manley International Airport (KIN), in **Kingston,** also has many international flights.

Hassle Factor: Low–high, depending on your distance from MoBay.

Nonstops: Atlanta (Delta), Baltimore (Air Jamaica), Boston (US Airways), Charlotte (US Airways), Chicago (Air Jamaica, American, United, US Airways), Dallas (American), Detroit (Northwest), Fort Lauderdale (Air Jamaica, Spirit), Houston (Continental), Memphis (Northwest), Miami (Air Jamaica), Minneapolis (Northwest), New York–JFK (Air Jamaica, American, JetBlue), New York–Newark (Air Jamaica, Continental), Orlando (Air Jamaica), Philadelphia (Air Jamaica, US Airways), Washington, DC–Dulles (United).

On the Ground

If transfers are not included for your trip, you can get shared-van service from the airport in Montego Bay to your final destination.

Renting a Car: The average traveler should not rent a car in Jamaica. Rentals are possible but are difficult to arrange on arrival, so make a reservation before your trip. You must be at least 23 years old, have a valid driver's license (from any country), and have a valid credit card. Rates are quite expensive, averaging $70 to $120 a day after the addition of the compulsory insurance, which you must usually purchase. Gas is generally more expensive than in the United States.

Where to Stay

All-Inclusive Resorts: Jamaica was the birthplace of the Caribbean all-inclusive resort, which is still the most popular vacation option here. Several of these are open only to couples.

Luxury Resorts: Jamaica has a fair number of luxury resorts that are not all-inclusive, including Half Moon and Round Hill, both in the Montego Bay area.

Small Hotels: Particularly in Negril and the south coast, you'll find smaller, more unique hotels and inns that aren't part of the big chains; they range in price from budget to luxury. The Island Outpost company operates several upscale boutique resorts all over Jamaica.

Villas: Jamaica is home to an increasing number of villas aimed at travelers looking for a home away from home experience. Discovery Bay, near Runaway Bay, is a top location for many high-end villas. Many have a one-week minimum stay.

Hotel and Restaurant Costs

Restaurant prices are for a main course at dinner. Hotel prices are per night for a double room in high season, excluding taxes and service charges.

Tips for Travelers

Jamaican cuisine is legendary. Be sure to try some of the island's famous fiery jerk barbecue; the Jamaican breakfast specialty is ackee and saltfish.

Jamaica has no minimum legal drinking age, but most resorts require you to be 18.

You can safely drink the water in Jamaica, especially in Negril. Most water in Jamaica is not desalinated seawater but derived from plentiful local groundwater.

Electricity in Jamaica is 110 volts, just like in the United States, but 50 rather than 60 cycles.

American currency is accepted almost everywhere in Jamaica, except perhaps in less visited areas along the southwest coast.

What It Costs in U.S. Dollars

	$$$$	$$$	$$	$	¢
Restaurants	over $30	$20–$30	$12–$20	$8–$12	under $8
Hotels*	over $350	$250–$350	$150–$250	$80–$150	under $80
Hotels**	over $450	$350–$450	$250–$350	$125–$250	under $125

* Indicates hotels on the European Plan (EP—with no meals), Continental Plan (CP—with a continental breakfast), or Breakfast Plan (BP—with full breakfast), ** Indicates hotels on the Modified American Plan (MAP—with breakfast and dinner), Full American Plan (FAP—including all meals but no drinks), or All-Inclusive (AI—with all meals, drinks, and most activities).

TOP EXPERIENCES

Searching for ghosts at Rose Hall

(A) Stroll the corridors of Jamaica's most legendary greathouse, Rose Hall, and you'll hear the legend of Annie, the voodoo-skilled mistress of the house who allegedly murdered several of her husbands and her slave lovers before meeting a violent end herself. Today, guided tours take visitors through the two-story home then down into the cellar, home to a pub that serves a wicked drink called the Witches Brew.

Getting out on the water

(B) Whether your idea of fun on the water means a romantic sunset sail or rowdy "booze cruise," windsurfing or sailing a hobie cat, jet skiing or water-skiing, Jamaica has plenty of options, especially along the north coast. Larger resorts have a full menu of water-sports options (often included in the basic rates at all-inclusives), and smaller resorts have local operators nearby that can supply all the water sports and water toys needed, regardless of your experience.

Watching for the green flash from Negril Beach

(C) Under the right conditions, as sunset dips behind the sea, a momentary green sizzle can appear on the horizon—and in Jamaica the conditions are best for green flash watching on Negril Beach. Every night, crowds gather at spots like Rick's Café to toast the last few rays of the day before declaring a start to the night's fun.

Dining in the Blue Mountains at Strawberry Hill

(D) Perched 3,100 feet above sea level with a view of Kingston, the

resort's open-air restaurant is a favorite of Kingstonians for special events thanks not only to its view but its menu. Gourmet dining comes with a Jamaican twist here, and you might finish with a cup of local Blue Mountain coffee and enjoy mangoes from the hotel orchard and vegetables from local farmers.

Partying at Sumfest
(E) One of the largest musical events on the island, this extravaganza draws local and international talent to Montego Bay. Rooms across the area fill up for the weeklong event held in the Freeport area of Montego Bay as both local residents and visitors arrive to watch local talent and headliners such as Third World and Ziggy Marley and the Melody Makers.

Lunching with locals at Boston Beach
Ask any Jamaican where the best jerk is found, and you'll probably be pointed to Boston Beach, a collection of jerk stands just east of Port Antonio. Here pits slowly smoke chicken, pork, goat, and fish over aromatic pimento wood to create an unforgettable meal. After a spicy meal at one of the jerk stands, take a dip in the sea, though beware of the waves, which draw surfers.

Bar-hopping on the Hip Strip
The hottest spring break spot on the island is Montego Bay's Hip Strip, which pulsates with activity pretty much any time of year. This stretch of Gloucester Avenue is lined with some of the island's top bars and clubs, most within easy

TOP EXPERIENCES

walking distance of each other for easy bar-hopping.

Kicking back at one of Jamaica's all-inclusive resorts

(F) The all-inclusive concept began in Ocho Rios (the resort that is now Couples Tower Isle) and spread across the island and across the Caribbean. Today Jamaica remains the king of the all-inclusive, resorts known for their one-price-pays-all policy. Many of these cater to a niche market, from kids to couples.

Looking for crocodiles on the Black River

(G) On the south coast, cruises up the Black River give travelers the chance to spot crocodiles. Once hunted, these now-protected reptiles remain wary and can live as long as 100 years. Along the cruise, you might also see spear fishermen with a snorkel, mask, and spear gun, swimming in the dark water stained by peat deposits.

Horseback riding in the sea

(H) What began as a way to exercise polo ponies evolved into one of the most popular activities in Jamaica: riding a horse in the sea. Chukka Caribbean offers the opportunity to hit the waves on horseback at two equestrian centers, regardless of your riding experience.

Saying "I do"—or "I do again"—on the beach

(I) Thanks to its easy marriage laws (with just a brief waiting period and no blood tests) as well as numerous professional wedding coordinators, Jamaica has become a top wedding and vow-renewal destination. Many all-inclusives even offer free wedding packages.

Teeing off in paradise

(J) The island's best courses surround Montego Bay, lying both to the east and the west of the port city. To the west, Tryall is one of the best in the Caribbean (some even say the world), built on a 19th-century sugar plantation and designed by Ralph Plummer. To the east, the White Witch course is built on the grounds of beautiful Rose Hall greathouse with 16 holes overlooking the sea.

Shopping for local goods

(K) Although Jamaica has the glittery jewelry shops and souvenir stands of other Caribbean islands, it's in the local goods that shopping really shines. Jamaica's Blue Mountain Coffee is world-class, as are its rums. The best crafts are the wood carvings made from the national tree, the lignum vitae, a blond wood so hard it takes a master wood-carver to tame. Look for both lignum vitae and mahogany carved birds, animals, and elegant busts in galleries and markets.

Feeding wild birds at Rocklands Feeding Station

Visitors to Montego Bay can make an easy visit to this feeding station, the home of the late Lisa Salmon, one of Jamaica's first amateur ornithologists. Here you can sit quietly and feed birds —including the doctor bird, recognizable by its long tail—from your hand.

WHEN TO GO

The high season in Jamaica is traditionally winter—from December 15 to April 15—when northern weather is at its worst. During this season, you're guaranteed the most entertainment at resorts and the most people with whom to enjoy it. It's also the most fashionable, the most expensive, and the most popular time to visit—and most hotels are heavily booked. You must make reservations at least two or three months in advance for the very best places (sometimes a year in advance for the most exclusive spots). Hotel prices drop 20% to 50% after April 15; airfares and cruise prices also fall. Saving money isn't the only reason to visit Jamaica during the off-season. Summer is usually one of the prettiest times of the year; the sea is even calmer, and things move at a slower pace (except for late July/early August when Montego Bay fills up for the Red Stripe Reggae Sumfest). The water is clearer for snorkeling in May, June, and July.

Climate

Weather in Jamaica is a year-round wonder. The average daily temperature is about 82°F, and there isn't much variation from the coolest to the warmest months. Rainfall averages 78 inches per year (although that varies widely depending on the part of the island). But in the tropics, rainstorms tend to be sudden and brief, often erupting early in the morning and late afternoon.

In May and June what's known as the Sahara Dust sometimes moves through, making for hazy spring days and spectacular sunsets.

Toward the beginning of summer, of course, hurricane season begins in earnest, with the first tropical wave passing by in June. Islanders pay close attention to the tropical waves as they form and travel across the Atlantic from Africa. In an odd paradox, tropical storms passing by leave behind the sunniest and clearest days you'll ever see. (And that's saying something in the land of zero air pollution.)

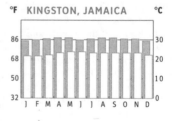

GREAT ITINERARIES

Here are a few ideas on how to spend a night (or two) celebrating all your days in Jamaica.

A Day at Negril Beach

Jamaica is dotted with good beaches, but Negril's Seven Mile Beach is a destination in itself, drawing sun lovers from around the globe. Stroll the beach as long as you like, then take a break for a lazy swim—on most days the water here is as calm as a lake. When the sun goes down, the fun continues at the many beachside restaurants (there's no need to change for dinner) and at clubs like Alfred's Ocean Palace, which pulsate to reggae into the early hours.

A Day of Exploring the South Coast

The South Coast invites travelers to get out and explore the communities of the area, whether on foot, by bike, or on tours. From hikes up Y.S. Falls (far less crowded than Dunn's River Falls) to tours of the Appleton Rum factory to visits to local rum shops for a game of dominos, properties like Jake's in the South Coast town of Treasure Beach encourage guests to meet and mingle in local communities.

A Rainy Day in Ocho Rios

Jamaica is known for its sunny days—but a quick look around at the lush vegetation, and you know that rainy days are no freak occurrence. The farther east you go on the island, the higher the incidence of rain, so it's no surprise that verdant Ocho Rios has plenty of activities when the sky turns cloudy. East of town, you can tour Noël Coward's Firefly home, still filled with belongings of the renowned playwright; to the west, in the Discovery Bay area, you can don a hardhat and head below the surface for a tour of Green Grotto, a tourist-friendly cave on the island that opens onto the sea. In town, shopping is sure way to beat the rain, whether for glittery imports or locally made crafts.

A Night of Romance in Montego Bay

Jamaica is synonymous with romance, and, for many couples, an evening of romance begins with a tranquil sunset cruise. Set sail with Dreamer Catamarans to catch the final rays of the day, then head back for a romantic dinner at Three Palms Restaurant on the grounds of historic Rose Hall. Dine by candlelight in the courtyard at this restaurant named for the three palm trees where Rose Hall mistress Annie Palmer was said to have buried her murdered husbands; Johnny Cash sang about them in a song he wrote at his Jamaica home, the neighboring Cinnamon Hill.

WEDDINGS AND HONEYMOONS

There's no question that Jamaica is one of the Caribbean's foremost honeymoon and wedding destinations. Romance is in the air here, and the white, sandy beaches and turquoise water and swaying palm trees and balmy tropical breezes and perpetual summer sunshine put people in the mood for love. A destination wedding is no longer exclusive to celebrities and the super rich. You can plan a traditional ceremony in a place of worship followed by a reception at an elegant resort, or you can go barefoot on the beach. All the large resorts have wedding planners, and some of the all-inclusive resorts even offer free weddings.

The Big Day

Choosing the Perfect Place. When choosing a location, remember that you really have two choices to make: the ceremony location and where to have the reception, if you're having one. For the former, there are beaches, bluffs overlooking beaches, gardens, private residences, resort lawns, and, of course, places of worship. As for the reception, there are these same choices, as well as restaurants. If you decide to go outdoors, remember the seasons—yes, Jamaica has seasons. If you're planning a wedding outdoors, be sure you have a backup plan in case it rains. Also, if you're planning an outdoor wedding at sunset—which is very popular—be sure you match the time of your ceremony to the time the sun sets at that time of year.

Finding a Wedding Planner. If you're planning to invite more than a minister and your loved one to your wedding ceremony, seriously consider an independent on-island wedding planner who can help select a location, help design the floral scheme and recommend a florist as well as a photographer, help plan the menu and choose a restaurant, caterer, and suggest any Jamaican traditions to incorporate into your ceremony.

Of course, all the large resorts have their own wedding planners on-site, and several of them offer a basic wedding for free. If you're planning a resort wedding, work with the on-site wedding coordinator to prepare a detailed list of the exact services they'll provide. If your idea of your wedding doesn't match their services, try a different resort.

Legal Requirements. Minimal residency and no citizenship requirements, and no blood tests or shots are required in Jamaica, and you can get married after only a 24-hour waiting period on the island if you've applied for your license and supplied all necessary forms beforehand. It's possible to get most of the legal paperwork done in advance of your arrival on-

island. You need to supply proof of citizenship (a passport or certified copy of your birth certificate signed by a notary public), written parental consent for couples under age 18, proof of divorce with the original or certified copy of the divorce decree if applicable, and copy of the death certificate if a previous marriage ended in death.

Wedding Attire. In Jamaica, basically anything goes, from long, formal dresses with trains to white bikinis. Floral sundresses are fine, too. Men can wear tuxedos or a simple pair of solid-color slacks with a nice white linen shirt. If you want formal dress and tuxedo, it's usually better to bring your formal attire with you.

Photographs. Deciding whether to use the photographer supplied by your resort or an independent photographer is an important choice. Since Jamaica is a large, well-populated island, you do have many choices in professional island-based photographers, and an independent wedding planner will know the best in the area. Look at the portfolio (many photographers now have Web sites) and decide if this person can give you the kind of memories you are looking for. If you're satisfied with the photographer that your resort uses, then make sure you see proofs and order prints before you leave the island.

The Honeymoon

Do you want champagne and strawberries delivered to your room each morning? A maze of a swimming pool in which to float? A five-star restaurant in which to dine? Then a resort is the way to go, and Jamaica offers them at many different price ranges. Whether you want a luxurious experience or a more modest one, you'll certainly find someplace romantic to which you can escape. Several of the island's resorts cater exclusively to couples, so these are ideal places for a honeymoon. On the other hand, maybe you want your own private home in which to romp naked—or maybe you want your own kitchen in which to whip up a gourmet meal for your loved one. In that case, a private vacation-rental home or condo is the answer. If you're having a destination wedding and are considering one of the many couples-only resorts in Jamaica, just remember that your wedding guests will also have to be couples.

THE TAPESTRY OF JAMAICA

Around one bend of the winding North Coast Highway lies a palatial home; around another, a shanty without doors or windows. Towns are centers of frenetic activity, filled with pedestrians, street vendors, and neighbors taking time to visit. Roads are crammed with vehicles and full of honking—not a chorus of hostility but notes of greeting or of friendly caution and just for the heck of it. Drivers wait patiently for groups of uniformed schoolchildren and housewives bearing loads on their heads to cross, and a spirit of cooperation prevails among chaos.

A Complex Culture

A sense of paradox infuses Jamaica, and the first-time visitor is likely to experience a bewildering array of extremes. The maniacal pace on the nation's highways belies a saintly patience and old-fashioned courtliness in other situations. A shockingly high crime rate is countered with open-handed generosity. Decrepit schools mask one of the highest literacy rates in the hemisphere, and the number of rum shops is surpassed only by the number of churches.

The cultural life of Jamaica is a wealthy one; its music, art, and cuisine have a spirit that's easy to sense but as hard to describe as the rhythms of reggae or an outburst of streetwise patois. Although 95% of the population traces its bloodlines to Africa, Jamaica is a stockpot of cultures, including those of other Caribbean islands, Great Britain, the Middle East, India, China, Germany, Portugal, and South America. The third-largest island in the Caribbean (after Cuba and Hispaniola), Jamaica enjoys a considerable self-sufficiency based on tourism, agriculture, and mining.

Early Colonization

The first group known to have reached Jamaica were the Arawak, who paddled their canoes from the Orinoco region of South America around AD 1000. In 1494 Christopher Columbus stepped ashore at what is now called Discovery Bay. Having spent four centuries on the island, the Arawak had little notion that his feet on their sand would mean their extinction within 50 years. What is now St. Ann's bay was established as New Seville in 1509 and served as the Spanish capital until the local government crossed the island to Santiago de la Vega (now Spanish Town). The Spaniards were never impressed with Jamaica; they found no precious metals, and they let the island fester in poverty for 161 years. When 5,000 British soldiers and sailors appeared in Kingston Harbor in 1655, the Spaniards didn't put up a fight.

The arrival of the English, and the three centuries of rule that followed, provided Jamaica with both the genteel underpinnings of its present life—and a period of history enlivened by a rousing pirate tradition that was fueled by rum. The British buccaneer Henry Morgan counted Jamaica's governor as one of his closest friends and enjoyed the protection of His Majesty's government no matter what he chose to plunder. Port Royal, once said to be the "wickedest city in Christendom," grew up on a spit of land across from present-day Kingston. Morgan and his brigands were delighted to have such a haven, and the people of Jamaica could buy pirate booty at bargain prices.

Morgan enjoyed a prosperous life; he was knighted and made lieutenant governor of Jamaica before the age of 30, and, like every other good bureaucrat, he died in bed and was given a state funeral. Port Royal fared less well. On June 7, 1692, an earthquake tilted two-thirds of the city into the sea, and the tidal wave that followed the last tremors washed away millions in pirate treasure. Port Royal simply disappeared. In recent years divers have turned up some of the treasure, but most of it still lies in the depths, adding an exotic quality to the water sports pursued along Kingston's reefs.

Plantation Economy

The very British 18th century was a time of prosperity for landholders in Jamaica. This was the age of the sugar baron, who ruled his plantation greathouse and made the island the largest sugar-producing colony in the world. Because sugar fortunes were built on slave labor, however, production became less profitable when the Jamaican slave trade was abolished in 1807 and slavery finally ended in 1838. Additional labor forces were brought in from India as well as China; wages were low and the economy further diminished. Sugar remained a major export and was later joined by bauxite, mined from the hills to be used in the production of aluminum.

Independence

The second half of the 20th century brought independence to Jamaica. On August 6, 1962, the island became an independent nation, although it remains a member of the British Commonwealth. The government is ruled by a freely elected prime minister. Two political parties, the People's National Party (PNP) and the Jamaica Labour Party (JLP), vie for the position and elections can become heated and even violent events. Election time riots in 1980 resulted in many deaths, mostly in Kingston's ghettos. More recent elections have been carefully monitored by

a contingency that has included Jimmy Carter and Colin Powell, and the mood has remained peaceful throughout most of the island, despite an economy that still suffers from high unemployment, low wages, and an interest rate that reaches 75%.

Today's Jamaica is a place where poverty is rampant and many must work at the fringes of the tourist industry as unlicensed taxi drivers, hair braiders, and vendors who walk the beaches in search of a vacationer. Hassling is one of the most common complaints of most travelers to Jamaica, and the government has increased fines and even penalties of jail time for this offense. Many problems involve attempts to sell marijuana or ganja, an illegal product.

Reggae and Jamaican Culture

The smoking of sacramental ganja and flowing dreadlocks are the most recognizable aspect of Rastafarianism, a religion that believes in the divinity of the late Haile Selassie (also known by the name Tafari), progressive emperor of Ethiopia from 1930 to 1974. Rastafarianism began in the 1930s, following the 1920s black pride and nationalist movement led by Jamaican Marcus Garvey, founder of the Universal Negro Improvement Association. Garvey's "back to Africa" message

resonated with the Rastas, who embraced Ethiopia as their chosen homeland. Although their culture gained strength in the 1960s and became internationally known through celebrities such as the late reggae singer Bob Marley, Rastas are a small sector of Jamaican population today.

Reggae rhythms are not solely a Rasta musical expression and are just one aspect of Jamaica's rich tapestry. You'll find many subtle melodies on the island, whether that be the sizzle of jerk pork on a roadside grill, the lap of waves on a sandy beach, the call of the tiny doctor bird as it flies through the trees, or the quiet whistle of a breeze through the Blue Mountains.

Montego Bay

WORD OF MOUTH

"Go to Rocklands Bird Sanctuary! It is amazing!"

—Tango

By Paris
Permenter
and John
Bigley

For many travelers, Montego Bay is synonymous with Jamaica. This northern coast community is the capital of the island's tourism industry (although Ocho Rios is quickly moving up, having already taken over the top rank in terms of cruise-ship arrivals). Most visitors arrive in Montego Bay by air, but plenty of people get here by ship.

As home of the island's busiest international airport, Montego Bay (or MoBay, as it's locally known), is the first taste most visitors have of the island. Thanks to its numerous resorts, many travelers never venture any farther.

Today many explorations of MoBay are conducted from a reclining chair—frothy drink in hand—at Doctor's Cave Beach, the city's original tourist draw, which attracted travelers who wanted to swim in what were called healing waters. Head out into the water off Doctor's Cave Beach, or any of the island's beautiful beaches, and you can find a world of undersea life awaiting exploration by snorkeling, diving, or even by venturing out in the belly of a small submarine or under your own power with the help of a high-tech dive helmet.

If you can pull yourself away from the water's edge and brush the sand off your toes, you can find some interesting colonial sights in the surrounding area. Because sugarcane plantations were an important part of the local economy for centuries, Montego Bay is home to some of the island's most famous greathouses, many open for public tours that give you a peek back at colonial days.

ORIENTATION AND PLANNING

ORIENTATION

Montego Bay has the advantage of being the closest resort area to the island's main airport—an important consideration for travelers with a short vacation (or with restless children who don't want to spend up to two hours on the road after their flight). Three-night stays in Montego Bay aren't unusual, and many travelers are willing to ignore jet noise to book a resort near the airport and maximize their vacation on the beach rather than on the bus to more distant towns.

Touring Jamaica can be both thrilling and frustrating. Rugged (albeit beautiful) terrain and winding (often potholed) roads make for slow going. Before you set off to explore the island by car, *always* check conditions prior to heading out, but especially in the rainy season from May through October, when roads can easily be washed out. Primary roads that loop around and across the island have been recently improved along the North Coast; beyond the main highway, other roads are not particularly well marked. Numbered addresses are seldom used outside major townships (or, for that matter, even within towns), locals drive aggressively, and people and animals seem to have a knack for appearing on the street out of nowhere. That said, Jamaica's scenery shouldn't be missed. To be safe and avoid frustration, stick to guided tours and licensed taxis.

PLANNING

WHEN TO GO

Like the rest of Jamaica, Montego Bay experiences high season from mid-December through mid-April, a time when the balmy breezes are a sharp contrast to the cold winds of the north. During that period, prices hit the roof at the end of the December and the beginning of January, dropping a bit after the holidays and rising again by late January as the pre-Valentine's crowds begin to arrive. Prices fall during the shoulder season that begins in mid-April (after Easter week) then fall further in late summer as hurricane season reaches its peak. During mid-July, however, expect higher prices in Montego Bay as demand rises during the annual Red Stripe Reggae Sumfest, a weeklong music festival.

Spring break for college students, generally falling in late March and early April, can mean a busy time for properties along Gloucester Avenue (known as the "Hip Strip"). The higher rates of the all-inclusive resorts discourage that crowd. You will find a big demand for flights during those weeks, especially with charter air companies.

GETTING HERE AND AROUND

BY AIR

Jamaica's busiest airport is the Sangster International Airport (MBJ) in Montego Bay. Most vacationers going to Negril, Ocho Rios, and Runaway Bay also land here. Many hotels offer shuttles to pick you up at the airport. The airport's new arrivals hall is home to hotel lounges for Sandals, Beaches, SuperClubs, Couples, Sunset, and Half Moon resorts; check in at the desk and relax until the bus leaves. If your hotel does not offer a shuttle (or if your tour operator didn't include one in the price of your

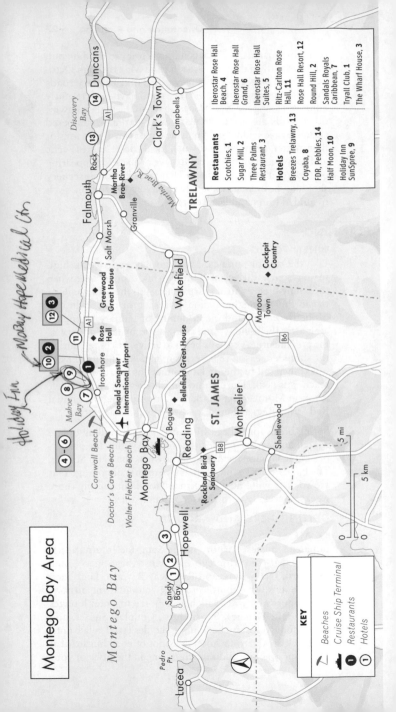

TOP REASONS TO GO

Dancing the Night Away: Montego Bay's "Hip Strip" has a string of bars and clubs that appeal to anyone waiting to bust a move.

Pursuing Phantoms: The haunted halls of the legendary Rose Hall may be enough to make you believe in ghosts.

Riding the River: There's nothing like gliding down the smooth and gentle Martha Brae River atop a traditional bamboo raft.

Driving a Hard Bargain: Perfect your haggling skills to get the best possible price at one of Montego Bay's lively craft markets.

Getting Teed Off: The Tryall Club, which is just south of MoBay, has few rivals in the Caribbean, which is why this is a golfer's mecca.

vacation package to Jamaica), the best way into the city is by taxi. The authorized airport taxi desk is just beyond the exit past Customs.

Montego Bay is well served by major airlines with nonstop flights from cities including Atlanta (Delta), Baltimore (Air Jamaica), Boston (US Airways), Charlotte (US Airways), Chicago (Air Jamaica, American, United, US Airways), Dallas (American), Detroit (Northwest), Fort Lauderdale (Air Jamaica, Spirit), Houston (Continental), Memphis (Northwest), Miami (Air Jamaica), Minneapolis (Northwest), New York–JFK (Air Jamaica, American, JetBlue), New York–Newark (Air Jamaica, Continental), Orlando (Air Jamaica), Philadelphia (Air Jamaica, US Airways), Washington, DC–Dulles (United).

TimAir offers charter service from Montego Bay's Sangster International Airport to airports in Port Antonio, Ocho Rios, Runaway Bay, Kingston, and Negril. Scheduled service is available on Skylan Airways between Montego Bay and Kingston. Charter helicopter service is provided by Captain John's Island Hoppers to Ocho Rios.

Airport Information Sangster International Airport (✉ Rte. A1, 1½ mi (2½ km) east of Montego Bay city center ☎ 876/952–3124 ⊕ www.mbjairport.com).

BY BUS

If you need to get to Kingston or Ocho Rios and have a limited budget, one option for transportation from Montego Bay is the **Knutsford Express** (☎ 876/971–1822 ⊕ www. knutsfordexpress.com).

Menu at Scotchies famous jerk stand

BY CAR

Driving in Jamaica can be extremely frustrating. You must constantly be on guard—for enormous potholes, people and animals darting out into the street, and aggressive drivers. With a narrow road encircling the island, local drivers are quick to pass other cars. Sometimes two cars will pass simultaneously, inspiring the UNDERTAKERS LOVE OVERTAKERS signs seen throughout the island. Driving in Jamaica is on the left, British-style.

Because many car renters are returning Jamaicans, the breakdown between high season and low season for car rentals is different than the high and low hotel seasons. Car-rental prices are highest over the winter holidays, Easter, and July and August. To rent a car you must be between the ages of 23 (with at least one year possessing a valid driver's license) and 70. Many companies require you to purchase insurance in Jamaica, and rental rates are expensive.

Car Rental Contacts **Alex's Car Rentals and Tours** (☎ 876/971–2615). **Avis Rent a Car** (☎ 876/952-0762 ⊕ www.avis.com.jm). **Budget** (☎ 876/952-3838 ⊕ www.budgetjamaica.com). **Fiesta Car Rentals** (☎ 876/684-9444 ⊕ www.fiestacarrentals.com). **Hertz** (☎ 876/979-0438 ⊕ www.hertz.com). **Island Car Rentals** (☎ 876/952-7225 ⊕ www.islandcarrentals.com). **Jamaica Car Rental** (☎ 876/952-5586).

BY CRUISE SHIP

Montego Bay is one of three Jamaican cruise ports (along with the very busy Ocho Rios and the very quiet Port Antonio). Ships dock at the Montego Cruise Terminal. West of Montego Bay, the cruise terminal has five berths and accommodates both cruise and cargo shipping. The terminal includes specialty shops, a communications center, a visitor information booth, and a taxi stand supervised by the Jamaica Tourist Board.

The Montego Cruise Terminal is a short ride from town. The Freeport Shopping Centre is within walking distance of the docks. If you just want to visit a beach, then Doctor's Cave Beach is a good nearby option, and it's right in town.

From the terminal, both taxis and buses shuttle passengers to downtown. Taxi service is about US$10 each way to downtown. Expect to pay $2 per person each way by shuttle bus to the City Centre Shopping Mall or $3 each way to Doctor's Cave Beach.

BY TAXI

Some, but not all, of Montego Bay's taxis are metered. If you accept a driver's offer of his services as a tour guide, be sure to agree on a price before the vehicle is put into gear. Taxis are expensive in Jamaica. A one-day tour should run about $150 to $180, in U.S. dollars, depending on distance traveled. All licensed taxis display red Public Passenger Vehicle (PP) plates. Cabs can be summoned by phone or flagged down on the street. Rates are per car, not per passenger, and 25% is added to the metered rate between midnight and 5 AM. Licensed minivans are also available and bear the red PP plates. JUTA is the largest taxi franchise and has offices in all resort areas.

Contacts JCAL Taxi (☏ 876/952-7574 ⊕ www.Jcaltours.com). **JUTA Montego Bay** (☏ 876/952-0813 ⊕ www.jutatours.info).

RESTAURANTS

As Jamaica's second-largest city, Montego Bay has its fair share of fast-food joints. Don't worry—it is home to plenty of authentic eateries as well. Restaurants range from elegant dining rooms with white-glove service to casual beach bars a stone's throw from the surf. Reservations are required at a few of the top eateries (especially during high season from mid-December through mid-April) but generally are not necessary. Many all-inclusive resorts offer evening passes for nonguests who would like to eat at one of their restaurants. They often don't include all of a resort's restaurants, so ask before you buy.

HOTELS

As the first of the developed resort areas in Jamaica, Montego Bay is home to many older (and now less-expensive) properties, most in the hills above the city with fine views of the sea. The beachfront has the area's largest and nicest resorts; the grandest of these are east of Montego Bay in the Rose Hall area and west of the city near Hopewell. Although Ocho Rios was the birthplace of the all-inclusive resort, Montego Bay has taken the concept to a higher level. Sandals has more locations here than anywhere else; other all-inclusive resorts cater to the adults-only and family markets.

The all-inclusive market is especially strong with couples and honeymooners. To maintain a romantic atmosphere (no Marco Polo games in the pool), some resorts have minimum age requirements ranging from 14 to 18. Other properties court families with tempting supervised kids' programs, family-friendly entertainment, and in-room amenities especially geared to young travelers.

WHAT IT COSTS IN DOLLARS				
¢	$	$$	$$$	$$$$
RESTAURANTS				
under $8	$8–$12	$12–$20	$20–$30	Over $30
HOTELS*				
under $80	$80–$150	$150–$250	$250–$350	Over $350
HOTELS**				
under $125	$125–$250	$250–$350	$350–$450	Over $450

*EP, BP, CP; **AI, FAP, MAP; restaurant prices are per person for a main course at dinner and do not include the 15% V.A.T. and 10% service charge. Hotel prices are per night for a double room in high season, excluding 15% V.A.T. and 10% service charge.

ESSENTIALS

BANKS AND CURRENCY EXCHANGE

Currency exchange is available at Sangster International Airport (just past immigration) as well as in hotels, banks, and exchange offices. NCB ATMs dispense U.S. dollars using debit or credit cards; these machines are at the Montego Bay Cruise Ship Terminal and Half Moon Resort. Cool Cash ATMs provide U.S. currency; in the Montego Bay area, you can find these machines at Rose Hall Resort, Holiday Inn, Iberostar, Coral Cliff, Sunset Beach Resort, City Centre Shopping Plaza, and four locations at Sangster International Airport.

EMERGENCIES

Outside of Kingston, Montego Bay is home to the island's most extensive medical facilities. For travelers, the major hospital is the MoBay Hope Medical Center on the grounds of the Half Moon Resort.

INTERNET

Internet service is becoming far more common, and most hotels offer at least limited service, either at public terminals (sometimes free at the all-inclusive resorts) or wireless service.

Internet Cafés Cyber Haus (⊠ *35 Gloucester Ave., Montego Bay* ☎ *876/971–9548*).

VISITOR INFORMATION

The Jamaica Tourist Board has a full office in downtown Montego Bay filled with visitor information, maps, and brochures; the office is open weekdays 8:30 to 4:30 and Saturday 9 to 1. At the city's Sangster International Airport, arriving passengers will find a JTB booth in the customs hall. The airport information desk is open 6 AM to 10 PM daily.

Information Jamaica Tourist Board (⊠ *18 Queens Dr., Montego Bay* ☎ *876/952–4425* ⊕ *www.visitjamaica.com*).

EXPLORING MONTEGO BAY

You can find at least three days' worth of activity right along MoBay's boundaries; you should also consider a trip to the lush resort area of Ocho Rios if you have the time. Day trips from Montego Bay to Negril also give you the opportunity to experience that community's 7-mi- (11-km-) long beach and watch the sunset from the island's westernmost point.

IF YOU LIKE

COLONIAL ARCHITECTURE

Rose Hall is undoubtedly Jamaica's most famous greathouse, thanks to its scenic backdrop, titillating legend, and excellent renovation, but it's just one of many in the Montego Bay area. The area's longtime plantation history meant expansive farms were administered by greathouses, which once numbered 80 across the island.

GOLF

Jamaica is one of the Caribbean's top golf destinations and Montego Bay is the capital of the courses. The Tryall Club is one of the most prestigious, since the pros come here to play. East of town, along what's nicknamed the "Elegant Corridor," Half Moon and the White Witch Course vie for top honors. Neighboring Cinnamon Hill Ocean Course is on the grounds of a greathouse that was once home to Johnny Cash.

SOFT ADVENTURE

With its popular canopy tours and horseback rides, Montego Bay offers a wide selection of activities accessible to most travelers. From white-water rafting on the Great River to bouncy jeep tours across the countryside, you'll find plenty of half-day options for a little off-the-beach fun.

WHAT TO SEE

When Columbus arrived in the New World, he first named this region the Gulf of Good Weather, a description that remains true today. Later, the Spanish named this Bahía de Manteca, or Lard Bay. Why? The Spanish once shipped hogs from this port city. Jamaican tourism began here in 1924, when the first resort opened at Doctor's Cave Beach so that health-seekers could "take the waters." Properties first built up near Doctor's Cave Beach and up on the Queen's Highway, a roadway high above the city that takes advantage of cooling breezes as well as excellent views.

With plenty of attractions and activities to fill a short vacation, Montego Bay makes a good home base for exploring the island. Day-trips can take you to interesting communities like Negril and Ocho Rios. Remember that although distances appear short on the map, heavy traffic, frequent road construction, and, poor road conditions (at least away from the main North Coast Highway) can mean that destinations 50-mi (80-km) away easily take two hours to

Bob Marley Mausoleum, Nine Mile

reach, however. The North Coast Highway–improvement project has improved access to both Ocho Rios and Negril, about 90 minutes to either community.

Bellefield Great House. Since 1735 this imposing greathouse has stood on the Barnett Estate, a 3,000-acre plantation owned by the Kerr-Jarrett family for generations and still growing mangoes, sugarcane, and coconuts. Visitors on the 90-minute morning tour are greeted with a traditional Planter's Punch, then led on a tour that includes the sugar mill, boiler house, rum cellar, and jerk grill. Afternoon tours feature a four-course tea on the greathouse's spacious veranda. Transportation from Montego Bay hotels is included in the tour. ⊠ *Granville Main Rd., Montego Bay* ☎ *876/952–2382* ⊕ *www.bellefieldgreathouse.com* ☜ *$10 for house tour, $56 including lunch and transportation* ☉ *Tours Tues.–Thurs.*

BOB MARLEY CENTRE AND MAUSOLEUM. The famous reggae star's birthplace is in Nine Mile, south of Runaway Bay, and it's a don't-miss side-trip for true fans. Although you can drive there in a rental car from Montego Bay, Nine Mile is actually closer to Ocho Rios, from where most guided tours are conducted, and we recommend one of these tours to help you avoid some of Jamaica's most aggressive hustlers, who will approach you on arrival. *See* ⇨ *Chapter 3, Ocho Rios for more information.*

Cockpit Country. About 15 mi (24 km) inland from MoBay is one of the most untouched areas in the West Indies: a terrain of pitfalls and potholes carved by nature in limestone. For nearly a century after 1655 it was known as the Land of Look Behind, because British soldiers nervously rode their horses through here on the lookout for the guerrilla freedom fighters known as Maroons. Former slaves who refused to surrender to the invading English, the Maroons eventually won their independence. Today their descendants populate this area, untaxed and virtually ungoverned by island authorities. Although the area sees relatively few visitors, most of the visitors who do come here make a stop in Accompong, a small community in St. Elizabeth Parish. You can stroll through town, take in the historic structures, and learn more about the Maroons—considered Jamaica's greatest herbalists.

★ **Greenwood Great House.** Unlike Rose Hall, Greenwood has no spooky legend to titillate, but it's much better than Rose Hall at evoking life on a sugar plantation. The Barrett family, from whom the English poet Elizabeth Barrett Browning descended, once owned all the land from Rose Hall to Falmouth; on their vast holdings they built this and several other greathouses. (The poet's father, Edward Moulton Barrett, "the Tyrant of Wimpole Street," was born at nearby Cinnamon Hill, later the estate of country singer Johnny Cash.) Highlights of Greenwood include oil paintings of the Barretts, china made for the family by Wedgwood, a library filled with rare books from as early as 1697, fine antique furniture, and a collection of exotic musical instruments. There's a pub on-site as well. It's 15 mi (24 km) east of Montego Bay. ⌂ *Greenwood* ☎ *876/953–1077* ⊕ *www.greenwoodgreathouse.com* ✉ *$14* ⊙ *Daily 9–6 (last tour at 5).*

Martha Brae River. This gentle waterway about 25 mi (40 km) southeast of Montego Bay takes its name from an Arawak woman who killed herself because she refused to reveal the whereabouts of a local gold mine. According to legend, she agreed to take her Spanish inquisitors there and, on reaching the river, used magic to change its course, drowning herself and the greedy Spaniards with her. Her *duppy* (ghost) is said to guard the mine's entrance. Rafting on this river is a very popular activity.

NEED A BREAK? Grab a gelato—in island flavors such as passion fruit, guava, soursop, or papaya–or a free sample of the famous

The Leeward Maroons

2

Southeast of Montego Bay lies one of the island's most rugged regions, Cockpit Country. Since the mid-1700s this area has been the home of the Leeward Maroons, much as the Portland area was home to the Windward Maroons. Both groups made up the island's Maroon population, a name derived from *Cimarron,* meaning "wild" in Spanish. The Maroons, descendants of escaped slaves, were fierce fighters who took to the hills and stayed there, never to again be recaptured.

The Windward Maroons were led by an Ashanti priestess named Nanny; her brothers Cudjoe and Accompong each took a group west. Cudjoe settled in today's St. James parish, while Accompong took his group south to St. Elizabeth parish. Both were in Cockpit Country, a land of steep hills, impenetrable vegetation, and terrain pocked with sinkholes and caves.

When the British took the island, they called Cockpit Country the "land of look behind." Soldiers rode two to a horse, one facing forward and one back, to guard against an ambush. After years of fighting, the British and the Leeward Maroons eventually signed a peace treaty, later joined by the Windward Maroons.

Today the Maroons are self-governing, with their own elected officials. The most visited community in Cockpit Country is Accompong. Tours often depart for this unique region. The Maroons, who for so long lived a completely self-sustained existence, are still known as the island's greatest herbalists.

Tortuga Rum Cakes at Calypso Gelato (⊠ *North Coast Hwy. [Reading Main Rd.], Montego Bay* ☎ 876/979–9381). The facility, open daily, houses a 10,000-square-foot baking facility for the famous cakes as well as an ample gift shop.

★ **Rocklands Bird Sanctuary and Feeding Station.** A great place to spot birds in the MoBay area is this private sanctuary south of Montego Bay. The station was the home of the late Lisa Salmon, one of Jamaica's first amateur ornithologists. Here you can sit quietly and feed birds—including the doctor bird, recognizable by its long tail—from your hand. A visit costs $15. Not recommended for families with young children (they'll scare the birds), this memorable attraction, which is open daily from 10:30 to 5:30, offers Jamaica's

easiest bird-watching. ⊠ *Anchovy* ☎ *876/952–2009* ☉ *Daily 10:30–5:30* ☜ *$15.*

★ **Fodor's** Choice **Rose Hall.** In the 1700s it may well have been the greatest of greathouses in the West Indies. Today it's popular less for its architecture than for the legend surrounding its second mistress, Annie Palmer. As the story goes, Annie was born in 1802 in England to an English mother and Irish father. When she was 10, her family moved to Haiti, and soon her parents died of yellow fever. Annie was adopted by a Haitian voodoo priestess and soon became skilled in the practice of voodoo. Annie moved to Jamaica, married, and built Rose Hall, an enormous plantation spanning 6,600 acres with more than 2,000 slaves. There's a pub on-site. It's across the highway from the Rose Hall Resort & Country Club, A Hilton Resort. ⊠ *North Coast Hwy., St. James, 15 mi (24 km) east of Montego Bay* ☎ *876/953–2323* ☜ *$20* ☉ *Daily 9:15–5:15.*

WHERE TO EAT

As the birthplace of the island's tourism industry, Montego Bay is home to many restaurants. Reservations are often necessary during high season. Some restaurants require you get a bit dressed up, but you can also find plenty of casual eateries with a straight-from-the-beach dress code.

$–$$ ✕ **The Groovy Grouper Beach Bar and Grill.** *Jamaican.* Located on Doctor's Cave Beach at the Beach Club, this casual eatery may be a tourist favorite due to its location, but it offers a menu of genuine Jamaican and other Caribbean dishes. Sit outside beneath the thatched roof and start with Jamaican fish tea (a local soup) or conch fritters then move on to a grouper burger, fish and bammy, escoveitch fish (fish topped with a vinegar and Scotch bonnet pepper mixture), or the signature dish, an 8-ounce grouper filet dusted with jerk spices. Steaks and burgers round out the menu options. ⊠ *Gloucester Ave., Montego Bay* ☎ *876/952–8287* ▭ *MC, V.*

$–$$ ✕ **Jamaican Bobsled Café.** *Eclectic.* The trials and triumphs of Jamaica's Olympic bobsled team, inspiration for the 1993 film *Cool Runnings,* are remembered at this Hip Strip eatery. Offerings like the barbecue burger and the barbecue chicken pizza make up the family-friendly menu. A percentage of the café's profits go toward supporting the team. ⊠ *69 Gloucester Ave., Montego Bay* ☎ *876/940–7009* ▭ *D, MC, V.*

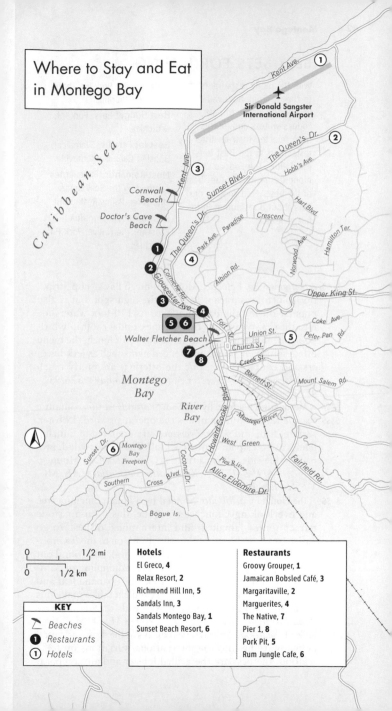

Where to Stay and Eat in Montego Bay

Sir Donald Sangster International Airport

Kent Ave.

The Queen's Dr.

Hobb's Ave.

Sunset Blvd.

Cornwall Beach

Doctor's Cave Beach

Park Ave. Paradise

Crescent

Hart Blvd.

Norwood Ave.

Hamilton Ter.

Caribbean Sea

Albion Rd.

Upper King St.

Coke Ave.

Peter Pan Rd.

Walter Fletcher Beach

Fort St.

Union St.

Church St.

Creek St.

Barnett St.

Mount Salem Rd.

Montego Bay

River Bay

Montego River

Howard Cooke Blvd.

West Green

Pres River

Alice Eldemire Dr.

Fairfield Rd.

Montego Bay Freeport

Sunset Dr.

Coconut Dr.

Coconut Blvd.

Southern Cross Blvd.

Bogue Is.

| 0 | 1/2 mi |
| 0 | 1/2 km |

KEY
- Beaches
- ● Restaurants
- ① Hotels

Hotels
El Greco, **4**
Relax Resort, **2**
Richmond Hill Inn, **5**
Sandals Inn, **3**
Sandals Montego Bay, **1**
Sunset Beach Resort, **6**

Restaurants
Groovy Grouper, **1**
Jamaican Bobsled Café, **3**
Margaritaville, **2**
Marguerites, **4**
The Native, **7**
Pier 1, **8**
Pork Pit, **5**
Rum Jungle Cafe, **6**

BEST BETS FOR DINING

With the many restaurants to choose from, how will you decide where to eat? Fodor's writers and editors have selected their favorite restaurants in the Best Bets lists below. The Fodor's Choice properties represent the "best of the best." Find specific details about a restaurant in the full reviews.

Fodor's Choice Pork Pit; Three Palms Restaurant.

Best Budget Eats: Pork Pit; Scotchies.

Best for Families: Jamaican Bobsled Café; Margaritaville.

Most Romantic: Marguerites Seafood by the Sea; Sugar Mill; Three Palms Restaurant.

Best for Local Jamaica Cuisine: The Native; Pork Pit; Scotchies.

$-$$ ✕**Margaritaville.** *Eclectic.* Along Montego Bay's "Hip Strip," this colorful restaurant is a favorite nightspot, but is also popular during the day thanks to its 110-foot waterslide into the sea, two water trampolines, and a rooftop whirlpool tub. When it's time to settle down for lunch, the menu offers some Caribbean-influenced items such as jerk burgers and conch fritters, but the offerings are pretty much all-American. ⊠ *Gloucester Ave., Montego Bay* ☎ *876/952–4777* ▭ *AE, MC, V.*

$$$– ✕**Marguerites Seafood By the Sea.** *Seafood.* At this romantic
$$$$ seaside restaurant, flambé is the operative word. Lobster, shrimp, fish, and several desserts are prepared in dancing flames as you sip an exotic cocktail. The Caesar salad, prepared table-side, is also a treat. ⊠ *Gloucester Ave., Montego Bay* ☎ *876/952–4777* ⚠ *Reservations essential* ▭ *AE, MC, V* ◷ *No lunch.*

$-$$ ✕**The Native.** *Caribbean.* Shaded by a large poinciana tree and overlooking Gloucester Avenue, this open-air stone terrace serves Jamaican and international dishes. To go native, start with smoked marlin, move on to the *boonoo-noonoos* platter (a sampler of local dishes), and round out with coconut pie or *duckanoo* (a sweet dumpling of cornmeal, coconut, and banana wrapped in a banana leaf and steamed). Live entertainment and candlelit tables make this a romantic choice for dinner on weekends. ⊠ *29 Gloucester Ave., Montego Bay* ☎ *876/979–2769* ▭ *AE, D, MC, V.*

$$-$$$ ✕**Pier 1.** *Seafood.* After tropical drinks at the deck bar, you'll be ready to dig into the international variations on fresh seafood; the best are the grilled lobster and any prepara-

CLOSE UP

Jamaican Bobsled Team

Ice is a rare sight in Jamaica—except in the cocktails enjoyed at many beach bars. But in the 1980s, the idea of founding an Olympic bobsled team wasn't as crazy as it seemed. After all, a Jamaican pushcart derby uses many of the same moves as bobsledding. The team that debuted at the Calgary Olympics in 1988 drew worldwide attention; in the 1992 Winter Olympics in Albertville, France, the team finished in 14th place. The team inspired the 1993 movie *Cool Runnings*. What became of the team? It continues to train in Evanston, Wyoming. Proceeds come from the Jamaica Bobsled Café, on Montego Bay's Hip Strip and at the Sangster International Airport.

2

---

tion of island snapper. Several party cruises leave from the marina here, and on Friday night the restaurant is mobbed by locals who come to dance. ⊠ *Off Howard Cooke Blvd., Montego Bay* ☎ *876/952–2452* ⊟ *MC, V.*

★ **Fodor's** Choice ✕ **Pork Pit.** *Jamaican.* A favorite with many
¢–$ MoBay locals, this no-frills eatery serves Jamaican specialties including some fiery jerk—note that it's spiced to local tastes, not watered down for tourist palates. Many get their food to go, but you can also find picnic tables just outside. ⊠ *27 Gloucester Ave., Montego Bay* ☎ *876/940–3008* ⊟ *D, MC, V.*

$–$$ ✕ **The Royal Stocks.** *British.* In Half Moon's Shopping Village, this pub brings a slice of jolly old England to Jamaica, from its dark decor to its menu featuring shepherd's pie, bangers and mash, and plenty of fish-and-chips. Umbrella-shaded tables out in the courtyard are the most popular, except on the hottest of days, when visitors retreat to the dark-panel pub. ⊠ *Half Moon Shopping Village, North Coast Rd., 7 mi (11 km) east of Montego Bay* ☎ *876/953–9770* ⊟ *AE, MC, V.*

$$–$$$ ✕ **Rum Jungle Restaurant.** *Caribbean.* Decorated like an indoor jungle, this expansive restaurant in the Coral Cliff entertainment center is casual and fun. Large buffets feature Caribbean dishes ranging from escoveitch fish to jerk chicken, while the large bar pours from a selection of Caribbean and worldwide rums. Sunday brunch is popular. ⊠ *Coral Cliff, 165 Gloucester Ave., Montego Bay* ☎ *876/952–4130* ⊟ *D, MC, V.*

Jamaican Cuisine

Jamaican cuisine, like its people, is a product of a mix of cultures from around the world. Spanish, English, Chinese, East Indian, and other groups each brought their own tastes to the island.

Ackee: A red fruit that's poisonous until ripe

Alligator pear: A local name for an avocado

Bammy: Fried bread made from cassava flour

Bun: Spicy bread eaten with cheese

Callaloo: A leafy vegetable that resembles spinach

Cho-Cho: A member of the squash family

Cut cake: A sweet cake made with diced coconut and ginger toffee

Dasheen: A root vegetable used like a potato; some Jamaicans call it coco yam

Duckanoo: A dessert of African origin made with cornmeal, coconut, spices and brown sugar, tied up in a banana leaf and slowly cooked in boiling water

Escovitch: A style of cooking using vinegar, onions, and spices brought to Jamaica by the Spanish Jews

Festival: A bread similar to hush puppies served with jerk

Fish tea: A spicy fish bouillon

Garden egg: The local name for an eggplant

Gizzada: A coconut tart

Grater cake: A grated coconut and sugar confection

Janga: Crayfish cooked and sold as hot peppered shrimp by the women of Middle Quarters on the South Coast

Jerk: Jamaican barbecue

Mannish water: A spicy soup— a reported aphrodisiac—made from goat's head

Matrimony: A dessert using the star apple; usually served during the holidays

Otaheiti Apple: An apple that looks like a small, red pear

Pawpaw: Local name for papaya

Pepperpot soup: A peppery callaloo soup

Pimento: Called allspice in other parts of the world; the wood from these trees gives jerk its distinctive taste

Red pea soup: Made with kidney beans

Rice and peas: Rice and red kidney beans, an omnipresent lunch and dinner dish

Rundown: Pickled fish cooked in seasoned coconut milk

Solomon gundy: An appetizer made of pickled fish

Spinners: Twisted dumplings used in soup

Stamp and go: Small fish fritters

Swimming at Margaritaville on the Hip Strip

¢–$ ✕ Scotchies. *Jamaican.* Many call this open-air jerk eatery the best in Jamaica, but the new Scotchies Too in Ocho Rios certainly makes it a tough decision. Like its sister restaurant, Scotchies serves up genuine jerk—chicken, pork, fish, sausage, and more—with fiery sauce and delectable side dishes including festival (similar to a Southern hush puppy) and rice and peas. This restaurant is a favorite with Montego Bay residents; on a typical day, you're likely to see a slap-the-table game of dominoes. ⊠ *North Coast Hwy., across from Holiday Inn SunSpree, 10 mi (16 km) east of Montego Bay* ☎ *876/953–3340* ▤ *MC, V.*

$$$$ ✕ Sugar Mill. *Eclectic.* Seafood is served with flair at this terrace restaurant on the Half Moon golf course. Caribbean specialties, steak, and lobster are usually offered in a pungent sauce that blends Dijon mustard with Jamaica's own Pickapeppa sauce. Otherwise, choices are the daily à la carte specials and anything flame-grilled. Live music and a well-stocked wine cellar round out the experience. ⊠ *Half Moon, North Coast Rd., 7 mi (11 km) east of Montego Bay* ☎ *876/953–2228* ⚐ *Reservations essential* ▤ *AE, MC, V.*

★ Fodor's Choice ✕ Three Palms Restaurant. *Jamaican.* This fine-dining enclave serves Jamaican as well as Continental cuisine with a gourmet twist. Within Cinnamon Hill's Ocean Course Clubhouse, the restaurant includes both indoor and alfresco dining options. Dishes range from herb-crusted snapper to seafood rundown, a take on a traditional Jamaican seafood dish made with coconut milk and lemongrass.

BEST BETS FOR LODGING

Fodor's offers a selective listing of quality lodging experiences, from the island's best boutique hotel to its most luxurious beach resort. Here, we've compiled our top recommendations based on the different types of lodging found on the island. The very best properties—in other words, those that provide a particularly remarkable experience—are designated in the listings with the Fodor's Choice logo.

Fodor's Choice

Half Moon; Sandals Royal Caribbean Resort & Private Island.

Best Budget Stay: El Greco; Relax Resort.

Best Boutique Hotel: Sandals Inn.

Best All-Inclusive Resort: Sandals Royal Caribbean Resort & Private Island; Sunset Beach Resort & Spa.

Best for Honeymooners: Half Moon; Round Hill Hotel & Villas; Sandals Royal Caribbean Resort & Private Island; Tryall Club.

Best for Families: Breezes Resort & Spa Trelawny; FDR, Pebbles; Holiday Inn.

SunSpreeResort, Rose Hall Resort & Country Club, A Hilton Resort; Sunset Beach Resort & Spa.

⊠ *Rose Hall Resort & Spa, North Coast Hwy., St. James, 15 mi (24 km) east of Montego Bay* ☎ *876/953–2650* ⊕ *www.hilton.com* ⚲ *Reservations essential* ⊟ *AE, D, DC, MC, V* ⊗ *No lunch.*

WHERE TO STAY

Montego Bay has miles of hotels and resorts ranging from inexpensive properties in town and in the hills overlooking town to larger hotels and all-inclusive resorts west and east of town. Montego Bay has the added advantage of being the closest resort area to the island's main airport.

$$$ **⊡ Breezes Resort and Spa Trelawny.** *Resort.* This all-inclusive
ⓒ resort (formerly Starfish Trelawny) is operated by Super-Clubs and is a favorite with families. For beach lovers, the best option would be the garden-level cottages (especially popular with larger groups), which are just off the beach, but most guest rooms are found in high-rise towers. The resort is family-friendly from its restaurants to its nightly entertainment, although the late-night disco is aimed at adults. The resort has a rock-climbing wall, a circus workshop, "ice-skating" on a special plastic surface, and trapeze

2

sessions. **Pros:** good value; excellent children's program; numerous activities. **Cons:** high-rise balconies can be scary with small children; may not have much appeal to guests not traveling with children. ⊠ *North Coast Hwy., Falmouth* ☎ *876/954–2450* ⊕ *www.superclubs.com* ⬅ *350 rooms* ☌ *In-room: safe, Internet, Wi-Fi (some). In-hotel: 5 restaurants, room service, bars, tennis courts, pools, gym, spa, beachfront, diving, water sports, children's programs (ages 6 months–12), Wi-Fi hotspot* ⊟ *AE, D, DC, MC, V* ⬅ *3-night minimum* ⍥ *AI.*

$$$$ ⌶ **Coyaba Beach Resort and Club.** *Resort.* Privately owned and operated, this intimate property offers a relaxing, welcoming ambience. From the plantation-style greathouse to the guest rooms, which are decorated with colonial prints and hand-carved mahogany furniture, you feel the graciousness and comforting atmosphere reminiscent of a country inn but with the amenities of a larger resort. **Pros:** quiet atmosphere of an inn; excellent restaurants; good-size private beach. **Cons:** located directly on North Coast Highway; fairly small pool; climb to third-floor rooms can be difficult without elevator. ⊠ *Little River* ☎ *876/953–9150* ⊕ *www. coyabaresortjamaica.com* ⬅ *50 rooms* ☌ *In-room: safe, refrigerator (some), Wi-Fi. In-hotel: 3 restaurants, room service, bars, tennis court, pool, gym, spa, beachfront, water sports, laundry service, Internet terminal* ⊟ *AE, D, MC, V* ⍥ *EP.*

$–$$ ⌶ **El Greco.** *Hotel.* For visitors who don't have to be on the beach, El Greco is a budget-friendly option. Thanks to an elevator, there's direct service from the hilltop hotel to Doctor's Cave Beach. Somewhat bare bedrooms are air-conditioned, although they also have glass doors and usually an ample breeze. An on-site restaurant serves lunch and dinner (a full breakfast is included), and full kitchens make it easy to prepare your own meals. **Pros:** good value; near many dining and nightlife options; kitchens in rooms. **Cons:** no private beach; bland room decor. ⊠ *11 Queens Dr.* ☎ *876/940–6116* ⊕ *www.elgrecojamaica.com* ⬅ *96 suites* ☌ *In-room: a/c, safe, kitchen, refrigerator, Internet. In-hotel: restaurant, room service, bar, tennis courts, pool, laundry service, Internet terminal* ⊟ *AE, MC, V* ⍥ *BP.*

$$$$ ⌶ **FDR Pebbles.** *Resort.* A slightly more grown-up version of ☋ its sister resort, FDR, Pebbles bills itself as a soft-adventure experience for families. Although you're still assigned a vacation nanny for personalized babysitting if you have young kids, the family experience is taken a step further here with many more supervised programs for teens, includ-

ing campouts. Thirty minutes east of Montego Bay, the resort has the feel of a campground, with wooden room blocks, which are not as big or as amenity-filled as those at FDR, Franklyn D. Resort. Each junior suite is paneled with cedar and pine, highlighted with trim in tropical colors. Up to three children under age 16 can share a room with two parents; kids under six stay and eat free when sharing a room with parents. **Pros:** individual nannies for families; good supervised kids program; good selection of activities for older children. **Cons:** may not pack appeal for travelers without kids; far from local attractions and activities; property can be noisy. ⊠ *Main St., Falmouth* ☎ *876/617–2509* ⊕ *www.fdrholidays.com* ⤳ *96 junior suites* ⌂ *In-room: refrigerator, Wi-Fi. In-hotel: 4 restaurants, bar, tennis court, pool, gym, spa, beachfront, water sports, bicycles, children's programs (ages newborn–16), laundry service, Internet terminal, Wi-Fi hotspot* ⊟ *AE, D, MC, V* ⊚ *AI.*

★ **Fodor's** Choice ⊞ **Half Moon.** *Resort.* With its many room cat-
$$$$ egories, massive villas (with three to seven bedrooms),
⟳ shopping village, hospital, school, dolphin swims, golf course, and equestrian center, Half Moon almost seems more like a town than a mere resort. What started out in 1954 as a group of private beach cottages offered for rent during off-season months has blossomed into one of Jamaica's most extensive resorts. Those beach cottages are still available and—just steps away from the sand as well as public areas—remain a great choice. The resort is also home to Fern Tree—the Spa at Half Moon, which opened in 2007 as the island's largest. **Pros:** huge beach; many room categories including villas; numerous on-site activities. **Cons:** some accommodations are a long walk from public areas, some activities are not within walking distance; some accommodations are more recently renovated than others. ⊠ *North Coast Hwy., 7 mi (11 km) east of Montego Bay* ⌖ *Box 80, Montego Bay* ☎ *876/953–2211* ⊕ *www. halfmoon.com* ⤳ *34 rooms, 164 suites, 33 villas* ⌂ *In-room: safe, kitchen (some), refrigerator, Internet, Wi-Fi (some). In-hotel: 6 restaurants, room service, bars, golf course, tennis courts, pools, gym, spa, beachfront, diving, water sports, bicycles, children's programs (ages infants–17), laundry service, Internet terminal, Wi-Fi hotspot* ⊟ *AE, D, DC, MC, V* ⊚ *EP.*

$$–$$$ ⊞ **Holiday Inn SunSpreeResort.** *Resort.* Family fun is tops here,
⟳ although many couples and singles are also drawn to the moderate prices and good location, 6 mi (10 km) east of

the airport. You can find seven-room blocks spread along the long beach and large public areas that can, at times, feel a bit overrun with kids and the noise they produce. Adults can find some peace in the quiet pool, which has its own swim-up bar. On the other side of the grounds, a lighted 9-hole miniature golf course offers night play. Shoppers will be happy with the moderately priced shopping mall directly across the street. Children 12 and under stay and eat free. **Pros:** good family atmosphere; easy access to shopping area; complimentary self-serve laundry. **Cons:** numerous children mean some areas can be noisy; only nonmotorized water sports included in rates; hotel located directly beside North Coast Highway. ⊠ *North Coast Hwy., 10 mi (16 km) east of Montego Bay* ☎ *Box 480, Montego Bay* ☎ *876/953–2485* ⊕ *www.caribbeanhi.com* ⇗ *524 rooms, 27 suites* ⚶ *In-room: safe, Internet, Wi-Fi (some). In-hotel: 4 restaurants, room service, bars, tennis courts, pools, beachfront, diving, water sports, children's programs (ages 6 months–12), laundry facilities, laundry service* ⊟ *AE, D, DC, MC, V* ⊙*AI.*

$$$– **▥ Iberostar Rose Hall Beach.** *Resort.* Twenty minutes east of
$$$$ the Montego Bay airport, this all-inclusive resort, which
☾ opened in 2007, was the first (and least expensive) of three adjacent Ibersotar properties. An extensive array of dining options (including three à la carte restaurants that require reservations) and activities are offered, although motorized water sports and scuba diving incur an additional fee. Operated by a European company, the resort has some of the same feel as the brand's popular Mexico properties, which are noted for the Mexican atmosphere with thatch-roof poolside palapas, Spanish lessons, tropical dance lessons, and around-the-clock action. **Pros:** numerous on-site activities; easy access to airport and into Montego Bay; complimentary minibar. **Cons:** high-rise setup can mean elevator wait; more limited all-inclusive program than some others. ⊠ *North Coast Hwy., 8 mi (13 km) east of Montego Bay city center* ☎ *876/680–0000* ⊕ *www.iberostar.com* ⇗ *336 rooms, 34 suites* ⚶ *In-room: safe, refrigerator (some), Internet. In-hotel: 4 restaurants, room service, bars, pools, gym, spa, beachfront, diving, water sports, children's programs (ages 4–12), laundry service* ⊟ *AE, D, MC, V* ⊙*AI.*

$$$$ **▥ Iberostar Rose Hall Suites.** *Resort.* This all-suites all-inclusive is the middle-range property among the three adjacent Iberostar resorts in Montego Bay. Welcoming guests with an expansive marble lobby and sweeping grand staircase, the resort is a clear step up the price scale with a lobby punc-

Sandals Royal Caribbean Resort & Private Island

tuated by red velvet couches and giant brass chandeliers; rooms take a quiet, almost minimalist look with soothing green and brown tones. **Pros:** numerous dining options; round-the-clock activities; use of facilities at Iberostar Rose Hall Beach. **Cons:** expansive complex can be tiring; bars can be crowded. ⊠ *North Coast Hwy., 8 mi (13 km) east of Montego Bay city center* ☎ *876/680–0000* ⊕ *www.iberostar. com* ↪ *273 suites, 46 suites* ⌂ *In-room: safe, refrigerator, DVD. In-hotel: 7 restaurants, room service, bars, tennis courts, pools, gym, spa, beachfront, diving, water sports, children's programs (ages 4–12), laundry service, Internet terminal* ⊟ *AE, D, MC, V* ⧖⧙ *AI.*

$$$$ ⬚ **Iberostar Rose Hall Grand Hotel.** *Resort.* The most upscale of the three adjacent Iberostar resorts, this property differentiates itself with its adults-only policy. The all-inclusive also provides butler service and a level of exclusivity; guests from the other two properties may not use the Grand Hotel's facilities although Grand Hotel guests may dine and play at both the Beach Hotel and Rose Hall suites. **Pros:** larger suites than those found at the other Iberostar properties; one complimentary round of golf at Cinnamon Hill per stay; guests can dine at the other two Iberostar resorts in the complex. **Cons:** some sports such as golf and scuba not included in all-inclusive rates; extremely large hotel complex. ⊠ *North Coast Hwy., 8 mi (13 km) east of Montego Bay city center* ☎ *876/680–0000* ⊕ *www. iberostar.com* ↪ *295 suites* ⌂ *In-room: safe, refrigerator,*

DVD. *In-hotel: 6 restaurants, room service, bars, tennis courts, pools, gym, spa, beachfront, diving, water sports, laundry service, Internet terminal, no kids under 18* ⊟ *AE, D, MC, V ☞ 3-night minimum* ⊚ *AI.*

$–$$ ⚏ **Relax Resort.** *Hotel.* This family-owned hotel is a budget-friendly option for travelers who don't mind not being on the beach (although a complimentary shuttle is available). Simple rooms have tile floors and balconies, but the best bargains are the studios and apartments; these have kitchens that can be stocked with the groceries you've requested in advance. Only the bedrooms of the apartments are air-conditioned. **Pros:** good value; access to transportation; family-friendly atmosphere. **Cons:** not on the beach; not all rooms have air-conditioning; limited on-site activities. ⊠ *26 Hobbs Ave., Montego Bay* ☎ *876/979–0656* ⊕ *www.relax-resort.com* ☞ *36 rooms* ☖ *In-room: a/c (some), safe, kitchen (some), refrigerator. In-hotel: restaurant, room service, bar, pool, gym, laundry service, Internet terminal* ⊟ *AE, MC, V* ⊚ *EP.*

$ ⚏ **Richmond Hill Inn.** *Inn.* This hilltop inn—a 200-year-old greathouse originally owned by the Dewars clan—has spectacular views of the Caribbean and a great deal of peace. The decor tends toward the dainty, frilly lace curtains and doilies, lots of lavenders and mauves, and crushed-velvet furniture here and there. A free shuttle takes you to shops and beaches about 10 minutes away. **Pros:** good value; eye-popping view; delicious dining. **Cons:** somewhat dated decor; not on the beach; not within walking distance of attractions. ⊠ *Union St., Montego Bay* ☎ *876/952–3859* ⊕ *www.richmond-hill-inn.com* ☞ *20 suites* ☖ *In-room: refrigerator (some), Internet. In-hotel: restaurant, room service, bar, pool, laundry service* ⊟ *MC, V* ⊚ *EP.*

$$$$ ⚏ **Ritz-Carlton Golf & Spa Resort, Rose Hall.** *Resort.* A favorite with conference groups, golfers, and anyone demanding the highbrow service for which the chain is known, this expansive resort lies across the road from the historic Rose Hall estate. Although the luxury hotel is elegant and has solid service, little here sets the mood of a Caribbean resort except its beachfront location and water-sports offerings. High tea is offered daily. Along with a full-service spa, there's a fully supervised children's club, making it a popular choice for families. **Pros:** excellent meeting and business travel facilities; great golf; good children's program. **Cons:** generic decor gives no sense of Jamaica; atmosphere small beach; somewhat formal for a family-friendly resort. ⊠ *1 Ritz Carlton Dr., St. James, 15 mi (24 km) east of Mon-*

tego Bay ☎ 876/953–2800 ⊕ www.ritzcarlton.com ⇨ 427 rooms ♿ In-room: safe, refrigerator, Internet. In-hotel: 5 restaurants, bars, golf course, tennis courts, pool, gym, spa, beachfront, diving, water sports, children's programs (ages 5–12), Internet terminal, Wi-Fi hotspot ▭ AE, D, DC, MC, V 🍽 EP.

$$$ **Rose Hall Resort & Country Club, A Hilton Resort.** *Resort.* Popular with conference groups as well as families, this self-contained resort 4 mi (6 km) east of the airport is on the grounds of the 400-acre Rose Hall Plantation. Kids love the huge water park, complete with lagoons and lazy rafting river, while golfers head across the street to the course. The lack of a good swimming beach is the biggest drawback; the waters here are sometimes better for sailing. However, the expansive pool and water-park complex is a good alternative. **Pros:** extensive renovation in 2007; family-friendly dining and pool area; easy access to golf. **Cons:** beach is not as good as others in the area; kid-filled pool can be noisy; some activities located across highway. ✉ *North Coast Hwy., St. James, 15 mi (24 km) east of Montego Bay* ✉ *Box 999, Montego Bay ☎ 876/953–2650 ⊕ www.rosehallresort.com ⇨ 488 rooms, 14 suites ♿ In-room: safe, Internet, Wi-Fi. In-hotel: 5 restaurants, room service, bars, golf course, tennis courts, pools, gym, beachfront, diving, water sports, children's programs (ages 4–12), Internet terminal, Wi-Fi hotspot ▭ AE, D, DC, MC, V 🍽 AI.*

$$$$ **Round Hill Hotel & Villas.** *Resort.* A favorite of celebrities thanks to its private and elegant villas, this peaceful resort 8 mi (13 km) west of MoBay also offers 36 traditional hotel rooms in the Pineapple House. The hotel rooms are decorated in a refined Ralph Lauren style—done by the designer himself, who owns one of the 27 villas that dot the resort's 98 acres. Each villa includes a personal maid and a cook to make your breakfast, and most have private pools. It's a fairly quiet place, with a small beach and limited dining options, but most guests return again and again because of the personal service and excellent management. **Pros:** personal service; stylish accommodations; quiet atmosphere. **Cons:** somewhat remote location; costly; some villas do not have pools. ✉ *North Coast Hwy., 8 mi (13 km) west of Montego Bay ☎ 876/956–7050 ⊕ www.roundhilljamaica.com ⇨ 36 rooms, 27 villas ♿ In-room: safe, kitchen (some), refrigerator (some), DVD (some), no TV (some), Internet, Wi-Fi. In-hotel: 2 restaurants, room service, bar, tennis courts, pools, gym, spa, beachfront, diving, water sports,* *children's programs (ages 3–11), laundry service, Internet terminal, Wi-Fi hotspot* ⊟*AE, D, DC, MC, V* ⦿*EP.*

$$$$ ⌨ **Sandals Inn.** *Hotel.* If you can forego a private beach at your doorstep (there's a public one across the street, and an hourly shuttle that takes you to other Sandals properties), you can stay here for much less than at the other Sandals resorts. Managed more as a small hotel than a large resort, this property is intimate and relatively quiet. The charming rooms are compact; most have balconies that face the small pool area. Although the hotel has fewer on-site facilities than its sister properties, it does have the added benefit of 24-hour room service. The in-town location puts you close to shops and sights, a bonus if you like to get out and explore. Like others in the Sandals chain, this property is for couples only (but no longer restricted to male–female duos). **Pros:** less expensive than other Sandals resorts; complimentary shuttle to sister properties; convenient location. **Cons:** no private beach; small pool; limited on-site dining options. ⊠*Kent Ave., Montego Bay* ☏*876/952–4140* ⦿*www.sandals.com* ⊷*52 rooms* ⌂*In-room: safe, Internet. In-hotel: 2 restaurants, room service, bars, tennis court, pool, laundry service, Internet terminal, no kids under 18* ⊟*AE, D, DC, MC, V* ⦿*AI.*

$$$$ ⌨ **Sandals Montego Bay.** *Resort.* The largest private beach in Montego Bay is the highlight of this Sandals—one of the most popular upscale resorts in the Caribbean. It's one big party, despite the planes that zoom overhead (the airport is minutes away, making it a good option for quick departures). Rooms are done in tropical colors and have four-poster beds; for top-notch luxury the rooms and suites in the Bay Roc Villa Suites are the resort's nicest. The pricier rooms offer butler service and 24-hour room service. **Pros:** good beach; convenient to transportation; butler service in some rooms. **Cons:** airport noise; not walking distance to other restaurants; some rooms need upgrading. ⊠*N. Kent Ave., 1½ mi (2½ km) east of Montego Bay city center* ☏*876/952–5510* ⦿*www.sandals.com* ⊷*251 rooms* ⌂*In-room: safe, refrigerator (some), Internet. In-hotel: 5 restaurants, room service (some), bars, tennis courts, pools, gym, spa, beachfront, diving, water sports, laundry service, Internet terminal, no kids under 18* ⊟*AE, D, DC, MC, V* ⦿*AI.*

★ **Fodor's**Choice ⌨ **Sandals Royal Caribbean Resort & Private Island.**
$$$$ *Resort.* Four miles (6 km) east of the airport, this elegant resort—the most upscale of the three Sandals properties in MoBay—consists of Jamaican-style buildings arranged

in a semicircle around attractive gardens. Less boisterous
than Sandals Montego Bay, it offers a few more-civilized
touches, including afternoon tea. In the evenings, a colorful
"dragon boat" transports you to Sandals' private island
for meals at a gourmet Thai restaurant. **Pros:** numerous
room categories; offshore dining; complimentary airport
shuttle and shuttle to other Sandals resorts in Montego
Bay. **Cons:** some guests might feel the resort is too quiet;
smaller beach than Sandals Montego Bay; couples-only
policy means some guests can't stay here. ⊠ *North Coast
Hwy., 6 mi (9 km) east of Montego Bay city center ⊕ Box
167, Montego Bay* ☎ *876/953–2231* ⊕ *www.sandals.com*
⇨ *176 rooms, 14 suites* ⌂ *In-room: safe, refrigerator, Wi-Fi.
In-hotel: 5 restaurants, room service (some), bars, tennis
courts, pools, gym, spa, beachfront, diving, water sports,
laundry service, Internet terminal, Wi-Fi hotspot, no kids
under 18* ⊟ *AE, D, MC, V* ☞ *2-night minimum* ⍵ *AI.*

$$$– ⊡ **Sunset Beach Resort & Spa.** *Resort.* Often packed with
$$$$ charter groups, this expansive resort is a very good value
☉ if you don't mind mass tourism. With one of Jamaica's best
(and most-used) lobbies, a water park, a teen center, and
excellent beaches on a peninsula jutting out into the bay,
the facilities here help to redeem the motel-basic rooms. You
can choose among three beaches (one clothing-optional) or,
when it's time to take a break from the sun, hit the spa or
slots-only casino. **Pros:** excellent beaches; good restaurants;
numerous on-site activities. **Cons:** can be crowded; high-rise
setup means lines for the elevator; somewhat remote loca-
tion if you want to explore Montego Bay. ⊠ *Freeport, 5 mi
(8 km) west of Montego Bay on Rte. A1* ☎ *876/979–8800*
⊕ *www.sunsetbeachresort.com* ⇨ *430 rooms, 15 suites* ⌂ *In-
room: safe, Internet, Wi-Fi. In-hotel: 5 restaurants, bars,
tennis courts, pools, gym, spa, beachfront, water sports,
children's programs (ages 2–12), laundry service, Internet
terminal, Wi-Fi hotspot* ⊟ *AE, MC, V* ⍵ *AI.*

$$$$ ⊡ **Tryall Club.** *Resort.* Well known among golfers, Tryall
is west of MoBay. The sumptuous villas—each with a
private pool—and pampering staff lend a home-away-
from-home atmosphere. The beautiful seaside golf course
is considered one of the toughest in the world and hosts
big-money tournaments. Golfers are more than willing to
accept the relative isolation for easy access to the great
course, but this resort is even farther out than Round Hill.
Pros: excellent golf; villa experience with the conveniences
of a resort; good family program. **Cons:** nonmember guests
must become temporary members of Tryall Club for $100

Feeding a hummingbird with sugar water, Rocklands Bird Sanctuary

per person per week fee; shared public facilities; somewhat formal atmosphere. ⊠ *North Coast Hwy., Sandy Bay, 15 mi (24 km) west of Montego Bay* ☎ *876/956–5660* ⊕ *www. tryallclub.com* ⤶ *56 villas* ♿ *In-room: kitchen. In-hotel: restaurant, bars, golf course, tennis courts, pool, gym, spa, beachfront, water sports, children's programs (ages 5–12)* ⊟ *AE, D, DC, MC, V* ⏲️ *EP.*

PRIVATE VILLAS

$$$$ ▣ **The Wharf House.** *Vacation rental.* A short drive from Round Hill, this stylish 18th-century home is comprised of five buildings connected by walkways. The main house includes the living and dining rooms as well as two bedrooms sharing a bath; two other bedrooms are in private cottages. A play cottage welcomes young visitors with a wealth of toys and games while a fifth building offers a Ping-Pong table and a bar. The house (which can also be rented as just a two-bedroom) includes membership at nearby Round Hill and includes complimentary access to that resort's beach and fitness center. **Pros:** excellent facilities for families; beautiful decor; good location. **Cons:** need car to get around; layout not good for families with small children no a/c in some rooms. ⊠ *Rte. A1, 5 mi (8 km) west of Montego Bay city center* ☎ *876/940–0030* ⊕ *wharf-house.net* ⤶ *4 bedrooms, 2 baths* ♿ *In-villa: a/c (some), safe, kitchen, refrigerator, Internet, daily maid service, cook,*

on-site security, fully staffed, pool, beachfront, water toys, laundry facilities ⏹️ *EP.*

BEACHES

Most of the resorts in Montego Bay have their own private beaches. Some of these, such as the one at the Half Moon Resort, are long and extensive. Others, such as the one at the Ritz-Carlton, are rather small and unimpressive. In general some of this areas' best beaches are the ones closest to the city of Montego Bay. These are protected by offshore reefs and are mostly composed of white sand. In addition to Half Moon, other MoBay resorts with premium beaches include Sandals Montego Bay and Sunset Beach Resort which boasts four separate beaches, each with a distinct personality ranging from family-friendly to clothing-optional. As the name suggests, in the Ironshore area east of the city beaches tend to be composed of as much rock as sand. This has led some properties, such as Rose Hall Resort, to invest in extensive pool areas.

★ **Doctor's Cave Beach.** Montego Bay's tourist scene has its roots right on the Hip Strip, the bustling entertainment district along Gloucester Avenue. Here a sea cave whose waters were said to have healing powers drew travelers from around the world. Although the cave was destroyed by a hurricane generations ago, the beach is always busy and has a perpetual spring-break feel. It has the best facilities in Jamaica, thanks to the plantation-style clubhouse with changing rooms, showers, gift shop, restaurant, and Internet café. There's a $5 fee for admission; beach chairs and umbrellas are also for rent. Its location within the Montego Bay Marine Park—where there are protected coral reefs and plenty of marine life—makes it a good spot for snorkeling. More active travelers can opt for parasailing, glass-bottom boat rides, or jet skiing. ⊠ *Gloucester Ave., Montego Bay.*

Walter Fletcher Beach. Although it's not as pretty (or as tidy) as Doctor's Cave Beach, Walter Fletcher Beach is home to Aquasol Theme Park, which offers a large beach (with lifeguards and security personnel), glass-bottom boats, snorkeling, tennis, go-kart racing, a disco at night, a bar, and a restaurant. The park is open daily 9–6; admission is $5 with à la carte pricing for most activities. Several times a week Aquasol throws a beach bash with live reggae performances. Near the center of town, the beach has unusually fine swimming; the calm waters make it a good bet for children. ⊠ *Gloucester Ave., Montego Bay* ☎ *876/979–9447*

SPORTS AND THE OUTDOORS

BIRD-WATCHING

Jamaica is a major bird-watching destination, thanks to its various natural habitats. The island is home to more than 200 species, some seen only seasonally or in particular parts of the island. Many bird-watchers flock here for the chance to see the vervain hummingbird (the world's second-smallest bird, larger only than Cuba's bee hummingbird) or the Jamaican tody (which nests underground). The early-morning and late-afternoon hours are usually the best time for spotting birds. Rocklands Bird Sanctuary and Feeding Station, which is in Anchovy south of Montego Bay, is a great place to go if you want an easy bird-watching experience (*see* ⇨ *Exploring Montego Bay, above*).

CANOPY TOURS

There are many ways to see Jamaica's thick tropical forests, but perhaps none quite as exciting as by zip line. Following a short introductory lesson, you climb platforms, hook up to steel cables strung between trees and, with the help of local operators, literally zip throughout the canopy of trees. First offered in Costa Rica, these attractions have spread throughout the world and are found in several places in Jamaica.

From its operation west of Montego Bay, **Chukka Caribbean Adventures** (⊠ *Sandy Bay, Hanover* ☎ *876/972–2506* ⊕ *www.chukkacaribbean.com*) offers a canopy tour over the Great River. Nine lines traverse the trees, at times buzzing you through the canopy at 35-mi (56-km) per hour. On the tour you can catch a glimpse of a 150-year-old dam. The three-hour tour is $89 per person and is open to those ages 10 and up. Chukka Caribbean Adventures also offers a second zip-line tour at Rose Hall; the "Flight of the White Witch" runs two hours and is available for ages eight and up. The attraction is priced at $89 per person.

DIVING AND SNORKELING

Jamaica isn't a major dive destination, but you can find a few rich underwater regions, especially off the north coast. Montego Bay, known for its wall dives, has **Airport Reef** at its southwestern edge. The site is known for its coral caves,

Doctor's Cave Beach Club

tunnels, and canyons. The first marine park in Jamaica, the **Montego Bay Marine Park** was established to protect the natural resources of the bay; a quick look at the area and it's easy to see the treasures that lie beneath the surface. The north coast is on the edge of the Cayman Trench, so it boasts a wide array of marine life.

Prices on the island range from $55 to $80 for a one-tank dive. All the large resorts have dive shops, and the all-inclusive places sometimes include scuba diving in their rates. To dive, you need to show a certification card, though it's possible to get a small taste of scuba diving and do a shallow dive—usually from shore—after taking a one-day resort diving course, which almost every resort with a dive shop offers.

Scuba Jamaica (⊠ *Half Moon Resort, North Coast Hwy., Montego Bay* ☎ *876/381–1113* ⊕ *www.scuba-jamaica.com*) offers serious scuba facilities for dedicated divers. This PADI and NAUI operation also offers Nitrox diving and instruction as well as instruction in underwater photography, night diving, and open-water diving. There's a pickup service for the Montego Bay, Runaway Bay, Discovery Bay, and Ocho Rios areas.

DOGSLED TOURS

First popularized at its Ocho Rios location, **Chukka Caribbean Adventures** (✉ *Sandy Bay, Hanover* ☎ *876/972–2506* ⊕ *www.chukkacaribbean.com*) now offers dogsled tours from its Montego Bay headquarters as well. The 90-minute tour ($140) for ages six and older takes two rides and a musher on a wheeled sled powered by dogs rescued by the Jamaica SPCA. The tour includes a ride through many of the areas used to film the Steve McQueen movie, Papillion.

DOLPHIN SWIM PROGRAMS

Although not to everyone's liking, dolphin swim programs are nevertheless popular activities in Jamaica, and there are a few operations on the island. Under the same management as the public Dolphin Cove in Ocho Rios, Montego Bay is home to one private dolphin experience, **Dolphin Lagoon Half Moon** (✉ *Half Moon Resort, North Coast Hwy., 7 mi (11 km) east of Montego Bay* ☎ *876/953–2211* ⊕ *www. dolphinswimjamaica.com*), which is open only to guests of Half Moon resort. The Beach Encounter ($89) allows you to interact briefly with dolphins in shallow water. The 35-minute Deep Water Encounter ($155) for ages eight and over and the 40-minute Swim Encounter ($199) for ages 10 and over are better for stronger swimmers. Private swims ($400) and trainer for a day programs ($890) are also available.

FISHING

Deep-sea fishing is excellent in the Montego Bay area; anglers have the opportunity to go out and try to land yellowfin tuna, kingfish, wahoo, marlin, sailfish, and more. Many of the larger resorts offer deep-sea fishing; several operators in town also provide half- and full-day excursions.

The **Glistening Waters Marina** (✉ *North Coast Hwy., Falmouth* ☎ *876/954–3229* ⊕ *www.glisteningwaters.com*) offers charter trips from the Falmouth area. Thirty boats moored at the Glistening Waters Marina offer deep-sea fishing charters; the marina also has nighttime boat tours for a look at the lagoon, whose iridescence is caused by microscopic dinoflagellates that become luminescent when they move.

Charter fishing excursions are available aboard the *No Problem* and *Reel E'zee* (☎ *876/381–3229*). Half- and full-day excursions take anglers in search of big catch. Plan on about $550 for a half-day charter and $1,100 for a full-day on the seas; fees includes drinks and equipment.

GOLF

Golfers appreciate both the beauty and the challenges offered by Jamaica's courses, and those in the Montego Bay area are among the most prestigious on the island. Caddies are almost always mandatory. Cart rentals costs $20 to $40.

★ **Golf at Half Moon** (✉ *Half Moon Resort, North Coast Hwy., 7 mi (11 km) east of Montego Bay* ☎ *876/953–2560* ⊕ *www. halfmoongolf.com*), a Robert Trent Jones–designed 18-hole course, is the home of the Red Stripe Pro Am. Green fees are $105 for guests, $150 for nonguests. In 2005 the course received an upgrade from Jones protégé Roger Rulewich and once again draws international attention. The course is also home of the Caribbean headquarters of the David Leadbetter Golf Academy, which offers one-day sessions, multiday retreats, and hour-long private sessions.

★ The newest course in Jamaica, which opened in January 2001, is the **White Witch** course at the **Ritz-Carlton Golf & Spa Resort, Rose Hall** (✉ *1 Ritz Carlton Dr., Rose Hall, St. James* ☎ *876/518–0174*). The green fees at this 18-hole championship course are $175 for resort guests, $185 for nonguests, and $109 for a twilight round. Designed by Robert von Hagge and Rick Baril, it is literally on the grounds of historic Rose Hall greathouse.

Rose Hall Resort & Country Club, A Hilton Resort (*North Coast Hwy., St. James, 15 mi [24 km] east of Montego Bay* ☎ *876/953–2650*), 4 mi (6 km) east of the airport, hosts several invitational tournaments. Green fees run $159 for guests, $169 for nonguests, and $99 for a twilight round of nine holes at the 18-hole championship **Cinnamon Hill Ocean Course**. The course was designed by Robert von Hagge and Rick Baril (the designers of the White Witch course at the Ritz-Carlton) and is adjacent to historic Cinnamon Hill.

SuperClubs Ironshore Golf & Country Club (✉ *Ironshore, 9 mi [15 km] east of Montego Bay city center* ☎ *876/953–3681*), just east of the Montego Bay airport, is an 18-hole links-style course. Green fees are $50 for nonguests of Super-Clubs resorts. Designed by Robert Moote, the course also includes a restaurant, pro shop, and bar.

★ **Fodor's Choice** Probably the best-known golf course in Jamaica is the course at **Tryall Club** (✉ *North Coast Hwy., Sandy Bay* ☎ *876/956–5681* ⊕ *www.tryallclub.com*), 15 mi (24 km) west of Montego Bay. The 18-hole championship course is on the site of a 19th-century sugar plantation. The famous 7th hole tees off between the stone pillars of an historic aqueduct; the adjacent waterwheel has been the subject of many photos. The course was designed by Ralph Plummer and is an official PGA tour–approved course, having hosted events such as the Johnnie Walker World Championship. Green fees are $70 for guests, $110 for nonguests.

GUIDED TOURS

Montego Bay offers a wide array of guided tours, and most of the large resorts have tour desks where you can book a wide number of excursions and activities. Guided plantation and countryside visits are also popular. Almost all tour operators will pick you up if you are staying in one of the large resorts.

The **Croydon Plantation Tour** (✉ *Box 1348, Montego Bay* ☎ *876/979–8267* ⊕ *www.croydonplantation.com*) visits the birthplace of Jamaican hero Sam Sharpe, who led the rebellion that helped put an end to slavery on the island.

Glamour Tours (✉ *2 Gloucester and Kent Aves., Montego Bay* ☎ *876/940–3277* ⊕ *www.glamourtoursdmc.com*) large tour operators, has a wide selection of guided visits to Rose Hall and Greenwood Great House.

The eight-hour **Hilton High Day Tour** (✉ *Box 162, Reading* ☎ *876/605–5197* ⊕ *www.jamaicahiltontour.com*) takes visitors 45 minutes into the hills for a country-style breakfast followed by a visit to the German-immigrant-founded Seaford Town, and a Jamaican buffet lunch.

Island Routes (☎ *877/768–8370* ⊕ *www.islandroutes.com*) was established by Sandals Resorts International in 2009 so the company could offer its own luxury tours of the island. Tours are available to both guests and nonguests of Sandals resorts, and the company offers group and private guided tours of the island.

John's Hall Adventure Tour (✉ *26 Hobbs Ave., Montego Bay* ☎ *876/971–6958* ⊕ *www.johnshalladventuretour.com*) visits a plantation near the town of John's Hall in Cockpit Country to taste fresh fruit and enjoy a barbecue lunch. The John's Hall Adventure Tours company also leads visits to

Negril and Ocho Rios and organizes "Jamaica Rhythm," an evening of folk dancing and dinner.

JUTA (✉ *Box 1155, Montego Bay* ☎ *876/952–0813* ⊕ *www. jutatours.info*), the island's largest tour operator, offers a greathouse tour and a rafting tour, as well as tours to other parts of the island like Black River, Negril, and Ocho Rios.

HELICOPTER TOURS

Departing from the domestic terminal of Montego Bay's Sangster International Airport, **Captain John's Island Hoppers** (☎ *876/974–1285* ⊕ *www.jamaicahelicopterservices.com*) offers three helicopter tours of the Montego Bay area. The longest is the hour-long Western Showcase ($1,280 for up to four persons), which flies as far away as Negril. The 30-minute Memories of Jamaica tour ($640 for up to four persons) travels west over the cruise pier and over Round Hill. On the 20-minute Montego Bay Ecstasy Tour ($440 for up to four persons) you fly east over Rose Hall.

HORSEBACK RIDING

Although it doesn't have quite the long history of horse-back rides as Ocho Rios (which began offering horseback swims at Chukka Cove after visitors saw the polo ponies being exercised in the sea), Montego Bay has a growing number of horseback options for both beginning and experienced riders.

In the Braco area near Trelawny, between Montego Bay and Ocho Rios, **Braco Stables** (✉ *Duncans* ☎ *876/954–0185* ⊕ *www.bracostables.com*) offers guided rides. Two estate rides are offered a day for $70, and riders are matched to horses based on riding ability. The trip also includes complimentary refreshments served poolside at the Braco greathouse. Experienced riders can also opt for a mountain ride ($100) for a more-rugged two-hour tour.

From its location west of Montego Bay, **Chukka Caribbean Adventures** (✉ *Sandy Bay, Hanover* ☎ *876/972–2506* ⊕ *www. chukkacaribbean.com*) offers tours for beginning riders. You travel through rain forest and open countryside before heading to the sea for an exhilarating ride through the surf. The three-hour excursion ($73) is available for riders six and older.

Half Moon Equestrian Centre (✉ *Half Moon Resort, North Coast Hwy., 7 mi [11 km] east of Montego Bay* ☎ *876/953– 2286* ⊕ *www.horsebackridingjamaica.com*) offers horse-back rides for all ages and abilities. From 9 to noon and

The Tryall Club

2 to 5, the Pony Park offers short pony rides for children under six. The cost is $10 per ride and $10 per accompanying person entering the park. Those six and older can join in the 45-minute beginner's ride ($60) that starts with an introductory lesson before progressing to the trails. The 90-minute beach ride ($80), available for ages eight and up, includes a romp in the sea.

DID YOU KNOW? The thermometer may say the temperatures are in the 80s, but combined with the high humidity days in Jamaica are hot, hot, hot. You'll need to take extra precautions. Since temperatures don't vary that much over the course of the year, it's a good idea to plan strenuous activities in the cooler morning hours year-round.

JEEP AND ATV TOURS

Open-air jeeps and ATVs are an exciting way for travelers to combine the experience of a guided tour with the thrills of an amusement-park ride. The fairly rugged landscape around Montego Bay adds to the fun.

From its location outside Montego Bay, **Chukka Caribbean Adventures** (⊠ *Sandy Bay, Hanover* ☎ *876/972–2506* ⊕ *www. chukkacaribbean.com*) offers ATV tours. There's a minimum age of 16 on the ATV tours $75). The noisy ATVs jostle and splash their way along trails at Rose Hall Estate through the hills. The company also offers four-hour jeep trips ($73) across the countryside. The bouncy ride can be enjoyed by those six and older. Another bouncy ride is available on Chukka's Dune Buggy Adventure ($76). Available to passengers age six and up and to licensed drivers age 18 and up, the 2-hour, 15-minute ride travels across the grounds of the 1600s sugar plantation before crossing a river and heading up into the mountains.

SAILING

Dreamer Catamaran Cruises (✉ *10 Queens Dr., Montego Bay* ☎ *876/979–0102* ⊕ *www.dreamercatamarans.com*) offers sails on three catamarans ranging from 53 to 65 feet. The cruise ($65) includes a snorkel stop and a visit to Margaritaville before the final leg of the cruise. There are foot massages for women, followed by dance instruction for all. Children are allowed on only the morning cruise.

TENNIS

Many hotels have tennis facilities that are free to their guests, but a few will allow nonguests to play for a fee. Court fees generally run $5 to $8 per hour for nonguests; lessons generally run $30 to $65 per hour.

The most extensive tennis center in the area, **Half Moon Resort** (✉ *North Coast Hwy., 7 mi [11 km] east of Montego Bay* ☎ *876/953–2211*) offers tennis buffs the use of 13 courts lighted for night play. There's also a resident pro and a pro shop. You need to buy a membership card if you're not a guest; a day pass is $40.

WHITE-WATER RAFTING

Cruising down the rivers of Jamaica aboard bamboo rafts had its start in Port Antonio—first with loads of bananas and later with tourists—but it has definitely caught on in Montego Bay. Today's travelers have their choice of lazy floats or energetic white-water excursions.

If you're looking for a more rugged adventure, then consider a white-water rafting trip with **Caliche Rainforest** (☎ *876/940–1745* ⊕ *www.whitewaterraftingmontegobay. com*). Two tours, both offered in inflatable rafts, traverse the waters of the Great River. The Grade II Rainforest Rafting Tour glides along with stops for a swim; ages four and up can participate. The Canyon White Water Rafting tour traverses rapids up to Grade IV; travelers must be at least 14. In most cases you will be picked up at your hotel, and the tour price includes the transfer cost.

Chukka Caribbean Adventures (✉ *Sandy Bay, Hanover* ☎ *876/972–2506* ⊕ *www.chukkacaribbean.com*) offers a 2½-hour white-water tubing experience ($63) on the Great River, a mild trip that doesn't require any previous rafting experience. Rafters travel in a convoy along the river and through some gentle rapids. Also on the Great River, the 2-mi Ultimate Kayak Experience ($64) is available for beginners age 12 and up; the excursion lasts two and half hours.

Jamaica Tours Limited (✉ *Providence Dr., Montego Bay* ☎ *876/953–3700* ⊕ *www.jamaicatoursltd.com*) conducts trips down the River Lethe, approximately 12 mi (19 km) southwest of MoBay (a 50-minute trip); the four-hour excursion costs about $54 per person, includes lunch, and takes you through unspoiled hill country. Bookings can also be made through hotel tour desks.

River Raft Ltd. (✉ *66 Claude Clarke Ave., Montego Bay* ☎ *876/952–0889* ⊕ *www.jamaicarafting.com*) leads trips down the Martha Brae River, about 25 mi (40 km) from most hotels in MoBay. The cost is $45 per person for the 1½-hour river run, including transportation from your hotel.

SHOPPING

Shopping is not one of Jamaica's high points, though you will certainly be able to find things to buy. Good choices include Jamaican handicrafts, which range from batik fabrics to woven baskets. Wood carvings are one of the top purchases; the finest carvings are made from Jamaica's national tree, the lignum vitae, or tree of life, a dense wood that requires a talented carver to transform the hard, blond wood into dolphins, iguanas, or fish. Bargaining is expected with crafts vendors.

Naturally, Jamaican rum is another top souvenir—there's no shortage of opportunities to buy it at gift shops and liquor stores—as is Tia Maria, the Jamaican-made coffee liqueur. Coffee (both Blue Mountain and the less-expensive High Mountain) is sold at every gift shop on the island. The cheapest prices are found at the local grocery stores, where you can buy either whole beans or ground coffee. As one of two major cruise ports on the island, Montego Bay has some good duty-free shops as well. Fine jewelry and watches are top buys in the duty-free shops.

The Man in Black

Jamaica has been home to many famous foreigners—Ian Fleming and Noël Coward in Ocho Rios, Errol Flynn in Port Antonio. Montego Bay had Johnny Cash, the "man in black" himself.

Cash found a home away from home in Jamaica, coming to the island for nearly 30 years to his winter residence at the Cinnamon Hill greathouse near Rose Hall. "Jamaica has saved and renewed me more times than I can count," wrote the famous musician in his autobiography. The country singer enjoyed fishing in local streams, visiting the markets for fresh fruits and vegetables, and being surrounded by the country atmosphere that reminded him of his boyhood home.

Cash and his wife June were very active in the establishment of an S.O.S. Children's Village for orphaned and abandoned children in Barrett Town, just east of Montego Bay. The duo worked to finance the first family home, performing concerts at nearby Rose Hall to raise funds for the project. Cash later wrote "The Ballad of Annie Palmer," a song about the legendary occupant of Rose Hall. All the profits, of course, fund the children's home.

AREAS AND MALLS

The most serious shopping in town is along what's called the Elegant Corridor, home to some of the area's most
★ upscale resort. This stretch of road is home to **Half Moon Village** (✉ *Half Moon Resort, North Coast Hwy., 7 mi [11 km] east of Montego Bay*), east of Half Moon resort. The bright yellow buildings are filled with the finest and most expensive wares money can buy, but the park benches and outdoor pub here make the outdoor mall a fun stop for window-shoppers as well.

The Shoppes at Rose Hall (✉ *Rose Hall Resort & Country Club, North Coast Hwy.St. James, 15 mi [24 km] east of Montego Bay*) an upscale shopping center designed to resemble an old-fashioned main street. The center, across the highway from Rose Hall, includes jewelry, cosmetics, and designer-apparel shops. Some hotels offer free shuttle service to this open-air mall.

Less serious shopping takes place at the **Holiday Inn Shopping Centre** (✉ *Holiday Inn SunSpree Resort, North Coast Hwy., 10 mi [16 km] east of Montego Bay*) directly across the

Crafts Market, Montego Bay

street from the Holiday Inn Sunspree. The casual shopping area has jewelry, clothing, and crafts stores.

Unless you have an extremely early flight, you'll find plenty of shopping in the new terminal of the **Sangster International Airport,** which has the largest shopping mall in Jamaica.

SPECIALTY ITEMS

ART

Gallery of West Indian Art (⊠ *11 Fairfield Rd., Montego Bay* ☎ *876/952–4547*) is the place to find Jamaican and Haitian paintings. A corner of the gallery is devoted to hand-turned pottery (some painted) and beautifully carved and painted birds and animals.

HANDICRAFTS

In Montego Bay, the largest crafts market is on **Market Street,** a compendium of stalls, each selling pretty much the same thing. Come prepared to haggle over prices and to be given the hard sell; if you're in the right mood, though, the whole experience can be a lot of fun and a peek into Jamaican commerce away from the resorts.

Things Jamaican (⊠ *Sangster International Airport, Montego Bay* ☎ *876/979–1929* ⊠ *Devon House, 26 Hope Rd., Kingston* ☎ *876/926–1961*) sells some of the best Jamaican crafts—from carved wooden bowls and trays to reproductions of silver and brass period pieces.

Akon performs at Sumfest in Montego Bay

LIQUOR AND TOBACCO

As a rule, only rum distilleries, such as Appleton's and Sangster's, have better deals than the airport stores. Best of all, if you buy your rum at the airport, you don't have to tote all those heavy, breakable bottles around. Remember that if you purchase rum (or other liquids, such as perfumes) outside the airport, you'll need to place them in your checked luggage when returning home. If you purchase liquids inside the secured area of the airport, you may board with your liquids. (If you connect to another flight once you land in the United States, however, you will need to check the bottles for the next leg of the trip.) The most extensive liquor stores in the airport are Jamaica Farewell and Sunshine Liquor.

Fine handmade cigars are available at the Montego Bay airport or at one of the area's cigar stores. You can also buy Cuban cigars almost everywhere, but remember that they can't legally be brought back to the United States. The Cigar Hut, the Tobacco Shop, and Jamaica Farewell sell a wide selection of cigars.

A Splash of Reggae

Since its birth in the 1960s, reggae has been the cultural heartbeat of Jamaica. Each summer, the pulsating rhythm reverberates as the genre's top performers take the microphone at the **Reggae Sumfest**. Not to be confused with the now-defunct Reggae Sunfest in Kingston, Sumfest is held in Montego Bay and includes a week of performances.

This bash, billed as the world's premier reggae event, draws more than 30,000 fans. The festival's message of "promoting music, the universal force" is spread at the main concert, as well as through a series of minitours held throughout the Caribbean.

Reggae Sumfest has broadened its musical horizons since its launch in 1992, embracing a wider spectrum of music. Reggae stars like Ziggy Marley and the Melody Makers, Burning Spear, and Beenie Man now share the same bill with performers like Kanye West, 50 Cent, G-Unit, Jay-Z, Ja Rule, and Sean Paul.

NIGHTLIFE AND THE ARTS

This island is all about music. For starters there's reggae, popularized by the late Bob Marley and performed today by his son, Ziggy Marley, as well as Jimmy Tosh (the late Peter Tosh's son), Gregory Isaacs, Jimmy Cliff, and many others. If your experience with Caribbean music has been limited to steel drums and Harry Belafonte, then the political, racial, and religious messages of reggae may set you on your ear; listen closely and you just might hear the heartbeat of the people. Dancehall is another island favorite type of music, as is soca.

ANNUAL EVENTS

★ **Fodor's**Choice Those who know and love reggae should visit Montego Bay between mid-July and August for the **Reggae Sumfest** (⊕ *www.reggaesumfest.com*). This weeklong concert—at the Bob Marley Performing Arts Center in the Freeport area—attracts such big-name performers as Third World and Ziggy Marley and the Melody Makers. Tickets are sold for each night's performances or by multi-event passes.

BARS AND CLUBS

The liveliest late-night happenings throughout Jamaica are in the major resort hotels, with the widest variety of spots probably in Montego Bay. Some of the all-inclusive resorts offer a dinner and disco pass from $50 to $100. Call ahead to check availability and bring photo identification. Pick up a copy of the *Daily Gleaner,* the *Jamaica Observer,* or the *Star* for listings on who's playing when and where.

With its location right on what's deemed Montego Bay's Hip Strip, the colorful **Margaritaville Caribbean Bar & Grill** (✉ *Gloucester Ave., Montego Bay* ☎ *876/952–4777*) boasts a spring-break crowd during the season with a fun-loving atmosphere any night of the year.

The adjacent **Blue Beat** (✉ *Gloucester Ave., Montego Bay* ☎ *876/952–477*) moves to a jazz groove every night. Thursday and Saturday brings live shows; other nights feature a DJ. Every night the club is popular as a sophisticated spot for a nightcap.

The Twisted Kilt (✉ *Gloucester Ave., Montego Bay* ☎ *876/952–9488*). Especially popular with sports lovers for its big-screen TVs, this waterfront nightspot also serves fish and chips and pub grub.

CASINOS

You won't find massive casinos in Jamaica, although a growing number of resorts have slots-only gaming rooms. In Montego Bay, the largest of these is the **Coral Cliff** (✉ *165 Gloucester Ave., Montego Bay* ☎ *876/952–4130*). Right on the Hip Strip, it has more than 120 slot machines. Weekly slot tournaments and complimentary drinks keep you in the mood. The gaming room is open 24 hours daily.

Ocho Rios and Runaway Bay

WORD OF MOUTH

"'Ochi' offers the white sands and clear water expected of a Caribbean island, complete with waterfalls and rain forests."

—jjsmith

By Paris
Permenter
and John
Bigley

Picture the Jamaica of travel brochures—the towering waterfalls, the colorful flowers, the ferns so thick they form a canopy—and you'll be envisioning Ocho Rios. Located 67 mi (111 km) east of Montego Bay, Ocho Rios (often just Ochi) is favored by honeymooners and other romantic types for its natural beauty. Often called the garden center of Jamaica, this community is perfumed by flowering hibiscus, bird of paradise, bougainvillea, and other beautiful blooms throughout the year. (All that tropical growth, of course, means more rain than most other locations in Jamaica, but more on that later.)

Ocho Rios is where you can find one of the island's most famous attractions: Dunn's River Falls, where travelers climb up in daisy-chain fashion behind a sure-footed guide. This spectacular sight is actually a series of waterfalls cascading from the mountains to the sea. Dunn's River Falls is just one of several eye-popping natural wonders in the region. Several botanical gardens invite you to enjoy a few hours surrounded by tropical beauty.

Ocho Rios is a popular destination, so you won't be wandering through those gardens on your own. But it's easy to escape the crowds. Many people take advantage of the many rivers and go kayaking or white-water rafting. Ocho Rios is also home to a growing number of land-based adventure companies, so you can also go mountain biking, take a trip in an all-terrain vehicle, or whiz through the rain forest on a zip line.

In quiet contrast to Ocho Rios is Runaway Bay, the smallest of Jamaica's resort areas. About 12 mi (19½ km) west of Ocho Rios and 50 mi (80 km) east of Montego Bay, Runaway Bay is home to a few all-inclusive resorts and an 18-hole golf course. It has little of the tropical lushness for which Ocho Rios is known.

ORIENTATION AND PLANNING

ORIENTATION

The Ocho Rios area can be explored on a guided excursion, on a tour with a licensed taxi driver, or even by rental car (although the latter is not recommended due to poor road conditions). When planning an itinerary, the distance can be misleading; plan for almost twice as long as you think it should take to get from one place to another. For example, although Ocho Rios is 67 mi (111 km) from Montego Bay, the drive can take up to two hours. The North Coast Highway (west toward Montego Bay, east toward Port Antonio) is a faster route than it was years ago, but traffic delays are something to keep in mind when visiting the surrounding area. South of Ocho Rios, the roads wind into the hills, with some of the prettiest (and, in some places, some of the slowest) drives you can take in Jamaica.

PLANNING

WHEN TO GO

Like the rest of Jamaica, Ocho Rios has a peak season that runs from mid-December through mid-April, although it also sees a surge in business during the increasingly popular Ocho Rios Jazz Festival in June. Another timing consideration: all that lush, tropical growth hints at the precipitation the area receives. The rainiest months are May and October, when the usual afternoon showers can stretch longer.

Travelers visiting Nine Mile, the hometown of Bob Marley, should note that on February 6, the anniversary of his birth, fans from around the world congregate here for concerts.

GETTING HERE AND AROUND

BY AIR

There is no regular scheduled airline service to Ocho Rios, though you can take a charter flight by airplane from either Montego Bay or Kingston or charter helicopter service from Montego Bay to Boscobel Aerodrome, 10 mi (14 km) east of Ocho Rios.

Most visitors to Ocho Rios arrive via Montego Bay's Sangster International Airport. Many of the area's larger hotels arrange for shuttle service, so you don't have to worry about transportation. JCAL Tours, Jamaica Tours, and Clive's Transport Service provide round-trip transportation for about $60 to $80 per person.

Some people choose to fly into Kingston's Norman Manley International Airport, but Ocho Rios hotels do not operate shuttles service there. Clive's Transport Service will provide service for $280 per person round-trip.

Contacts Clive's Transport Service (☎ 876/956–2615 or 876/869–7571 ⊕ www.clivestransportservicejamaica.com). **Island Hoppers** (☎ 876/974–1285 ⊕ www.jamaicahelicopterservices.com). **Jamaica Tours** (☎ 876/953–3700 ⊕ www.jamaicatoursltd.com). **JCAL Tours** (☎ 876/952–7574 ⊕ www.jcaltours.com).

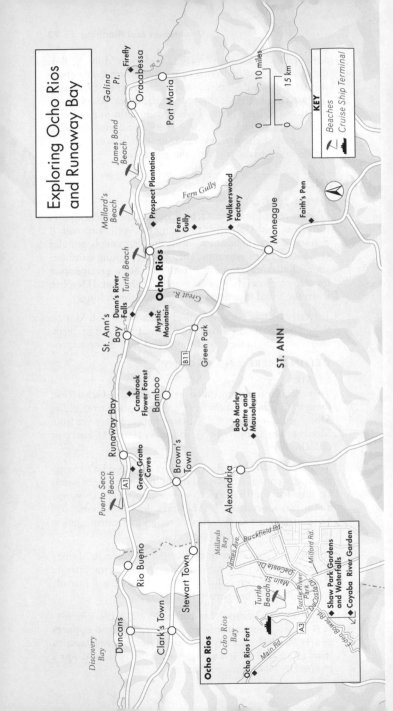

Exploring Ocho Rios and Runaway Bay

KEY

⚊ Beaches
⛴ Cruise Ship Terminal

0 ___ 10 miles
0 ___ 15 km

ST. ANN

Galina Pt.
Firefly
Oracabessa
Port Maria
James Bond Beach
Prospect Plantation
Fern Gully
Walkerswood Factory
Faith's Pen
Mallard's Beach
Fern Gully
Moneague
Ocho Rios
Turtle Beach
St. Ann's Bay
Dunn's River Falls
Mystic Mountain
Great R.
Green Park
B11
Runaway Bay
Cranbrook Flower Forest
Bamboo
Brown's Town
Bob Marley Centre and Mausoleum
Alexandria
Puerto Seco Beach
Green Grotto Caves
A1
Rio Bueno
Stewart Town
Clark's Town
Duncans
Discovery Bay

Ocho Rios

Ocho Rios Bay
Millards Bay
Buckfield Rd.
James Ave.
Main St.
DaCosta Dr.
Milford Rd.
Turtle River Park
Turtle Beach
Ocho Rios Fort
Main Rd.
A3
Shaw Park Gardens and Waterfalls
Coyaba River Garden
Eden Bower Rd.

TOP REASONS TO GO

Falling for the Falls: Form a human daisy chain and climb up Dunn's River Falls, one of Jamaica's most popular attractions.

Chills and Thrills: Live out your "Cool Runnings" fantasies on the bobsled ride at Mystic Mountain in Ocho Rios.

Remembering a Legend: Pay tribute to reggae great Bob Marley at his final resting place at Nine Mile.

Horsing Around: Splash through the waves—on horseback—at Chukka Cove, just west of Ocho Rios.

Getting Close to Nature: Swim with the dolphins, stingrays, and sharks at Dolphin Cove, just west of Ocho Rios.

3

BY BUS

One budget-minded option for transportation to Ocho Rios is **Knutsford Express** (☎ *876/971–1822* ⊕ *www.knutsfordexpress.com*), an air-conditioned bus with scheduled service. For about $15, the bus company offers service to Ocho Rios from Montego Bay and Kingston three times daily.

BY CAR

Ocho Rios, like most of the island, is plagued by poor roads and daredevil drivers. Renting a car is not recommended, especially when you consider the island's extremely high auto fatality rate—the third-highest in the world. If you do opt to rent a car, consider taking a taxi the first day or two to get accustomed to being on the left side of the road.

Car travel in downtown Ocho Rios can be very slow, especially on cruise-ship days. Traveling out of Ocho Rios is now speedier, thanks to the newly improved North Coast Highway. Note that some car-rental agencies, such as Avis, do not have a local office but will deliver cars to hotels in Ochos Rios from Montego Bay (*see* ⇨ *"By Car" in Chapter 2, Montego Bay, for more information*).

Car-Rental Contacts **Budget** (⊠ *Couples Ocho Rios, Tower Isle* ☎ *876/975–4986*). **Caribbean Car Rentals Limited** (⊠ *99 A Main St., Ocho Rios* ☎ *876/974–2513* (⊠ *Salem Crescent, Runaway Bay* ☎ *876/973–5188*).

BY CRUISE SHIP

Ocho Rios has quickly become the island's busiest cruise port. On many days the number of ships exceeds the capacity of the two-berth Turtle Bay Pier, so some ships will dock at Reynolds Pier.

BY TAXI

Taxi service is readily available in Ocho Rios, but take care to hire a licensed taxi, indicated by the red PP license plate. The largest taxi operator is JUTA, and their taxis can be called if necessary. Agree on a price before departure, as most taxis are not metered.

Contacts JUTA (☎ 876/974–2292).

RESTAURANTS

Although it's the setting for many all-inclusive resorts where guests take advantage of on-site restaurants, Ocho Rios is also home to many excellent stand-alone eateries. The city boasts a wide array of restaurants ranging from take-out jerk stands to sit-down dining rooms perched in the hills overlooking the city. During peak season, reservations are required at the most elegant establishments; otherwise, dining is a casual affair.

WHAT IT COSTS IN DOLLARS				
¢	$	$$	$$$	$$$$
RESTAURANTS				
under $8	$8–$12	$12–$20	$20–$30	Over $30
HOTELS*				
under $80	$80–$150	$150–$250	$250–$350	Over $350
HOTELS**				
under $125	$125–$250	$250–$350	$350–$450	Over $450

*EP, BP, CP; **AI, FAP, MAP; restaurant prices are per person for a main course at dinner and do not include the 15% V.A.T. and 10% service charge. Hotel prices are per night for a double room in high season, excluding 15% V.A.T. and 10% service charge.

HOTELS

With so much tropical beauty, Ocho Rios is the capital of Jamaica's couples-only and adults-only resorts. All-inclusive resorts claim the lion's share of hotel rooms—not surprising, as Ocho Rios was the birthplace of the Caribbean's all-inclusive movement. Although these sprawling resorts are the most visible (and often the most expensive) option in Ocho Rios, there are also standard hotels and a growing number of villas, complete with maid and chef service. The smaller Runaway Bay area is home to primarily all-inclusive resorts. Just beyond Runaway Bay, Discovery Bay is increasingly popular for its villas.

ESSENTIALS

BANKS AND CURRENCY EXCHANGE

Ocho Rios travelers can exchange money at hotels (usually with a less favorable exchange rate) or local banks. Many travelers, however, opt to use U.S. dollars throughout their trip. Some local ATMs give you the option of obtaining U.S. or Jamaican dollars. Cool Cash ATM machines offer U.S. cash.

EMERGENCIES

The area's largest medical facility is St. Ann's Bay Hospital, west of Ocho Rios.

INTERNET

Outside the major resort hotels, Internet service is somewhat limited in Ocho Rios. You can find a few Internet cafés, however. Expect to pay about $2 for 20 minutes of high-speed access.

Internet Cafés Jerkin (✉ *Taj Mahal Centre, Main St. and Da Costa Dr., Ocho Rios* ☎ *876/974–7438*) offers numerous terminals for staying in touch while traveling.

VISITOR INFORMATION

The main Jamaica Tourist Board offices on the island are in Montego Bay, Port Antonio, and Kingston. There's a Tourism Product Development Company office in Ocho Rios, however. The hours for this office are Monday through Thursday 8:30 to 5 and Friday 8:30 to 4.

Contacts Ocho Rios Information Office (✉ *Ocean Villa Plaza, Main St., Ocho Rios* ☎ *876/974–2582*).

EXPLORING OCHO RIOS AND RUNAWAY BAY

Ocho Rios isn't the prettiest town, but the surrounding area has several worthwhile attractions, including the very popular (and very touristy) Dunn's River Falls, located west of the city. When cruise ships are docked, the town can be incredibly crowded during the day. Evening, however, restores a calm feeling to the town of about 36,000 people.

In contrast, Runaway Bay is almost always a quiet getaway, a place where many travelers remain at their all-inclusive resort until they head back to the airport.

WHAT TO SEE

★ **Bob Marley Centre and Mausoleum.** Travelers with an interest in Bob Marley won't want to miss Nine Mile, the community where the reggae legend was born and is buried. Today his former home is a shrine to his music and values. Tucked behind a tall fence, the site is marked with green and gold flags. Tours are led by Rastafarians, who take visitors through the house and point out the single bed that Marley wrote about in "Is This Love." Visitors also step inside the mausoleum where the singer is buried with his guitar. The site includes a restaurant and gift shop. Visitors from Ocho Rios can arrange transport by taxi, but the round-trip fare is about $175; a less-expensive option is a guided tour with Chukka Caribbean. We strongly recommend a guided tour here since the hustlers that meet you outside the Bob Marley Centre are some of the most aggressive in Jamaica. ⊠ *Rhoden Hall, Nine Mile* ☎ *876/843–0498* ⌑ *$15* ☉ *Daily 9–4.*

★ **Coyaba River Garden & Museum and Mahoe Waterfalls.** Jamaica's national motto is "Out of Many, One People," and here you can see exhibits on the many cultural influences that have contributed to the creation of the one. The museum covers the island's history from the time of the Arawak Indians up to the present day. A guided 45-minute tour through the lush 3-acre garden, which is 1½ mi (2½ km) south of Ocho Rios, introduces you to the flora and fauna of the island. The complex includes a crafts and gift shop and a snack bar. ⊠ *Shaw Park Estate, Shaw Park Ridge Rd., Ocho Rios* ☎ *876/974–6235* ⊕ *www.coyabagardens. com* ⌑ *$10* ☉ *Daily 8–5.*

★ **Cranbrook Flower Forest and River Head Adventure Trail.** You can enjoy the north-coast rivers and flowers without the crowds at this botanical reserve filled with blooming orchids, ginger, and ferns. This park is the private creation of Ivan Linton, who has pampered the plants of this former plantation since the early 1980s. Today Linton proudly points out the birds-of-paradise, croton, ginger, heliconia, and begonias as if they were his dear children. The grounds are perfect for a picnic followed by a hike alongside shady Laughlin's Great River. The path climbs high into the hills to a waterfall paradise. Donkey rides, picnicking, croquet, wading, and volleyball are also available here. The complex has a snack shop and restrooms. ⌧ *5 mi (8 km) east of Runaway Bay, 1 mi (2 km) off North Coast Hwy.* ☎ *876/610–6509* ⊕ *www.cranbrookff.com* ⌧ *$10* ☉ *Daily 9–5.*

★ **Fodor'sChoice Dunn's River Falls.** One of Jamaica's most popular attractions is an eye-catching sight: 600 feet of cold, clear mountain water splashing over a series of stone steps to the warm Caribbean. The best way to enjoy the falls is to climb the slippery steps: don a swimsuit, take the hand of the person ahead of you, and trust that the chain of hands and bodies leads to an experienced guide. The leaders of the climbs are personable fellows who reel off bits of local lore while telling you where to step; you can hire a guide's service for a tip of a few dollars. After the climb, you exit through a crowded market, another reminder that this is one of Jamaica's top tourist attractions. If you can, try to schedule a visit on a day when no cruise ships are in port. ⚠ Always climb with a licensed guide at Dunn's River Falls. Freelance guides might be a little cheaper, but the experienced guides can tell you just where to plant each footstep— helping you prevent a fall. ⌧ *Off Rte. A1, between St. Ann's Bay and Ocho Rios, Ocho Rios* ☎ *876/974–4767* ⊕ *www. dunnsriverfallsja.com* ⌧ *$15* ☉ *Daily 8:30–5.*

Faith's Pen. If you want to combine a cultural experience with lunch, stop by Faith's Pen. Rows of stalls with names like Johnny Cool No. 1 and Shut's Night and Day offer local specialties with home-cooked taste. For just a few dollars, buy a lunch of jerk chicken, curried goat, or roasted fish and enjoy it at one of the nearby picnic table. An unusual treat is the mannish water (a soup—and reported aphrodisiac—made from a goat's head). Faith's Pen is on Route A1, 12 mi (19½ km) south of Ocho Rios. ⌧ *Rte. A1, about 4 mi (6½ km) south of Rte. A3.*

Fern Gully. Don't miss a drive through Fern Gully, a natural canopy of vegetation that sunlight barely penetrates. (Jamaica has the world's largest number of fern species, with more than 570 types.) The 3-mi (5-km) stretch of fern-shaded forest includes many walking paths as well as numerous crafts vendors. Most tours through the area include a drive through Fern Gully, but to experience the damp, shady forest, stop and take a walk. ⊠ *Rte. A3, south of Ocho Rios.*

★ **Firefly.** About 20 mi (32 km) east of Ocho Rios near Port Maria, Firefly was once Sir Noël Coward's vacation home and is now maintained by the Jamaican National Heritage Trust. Although the setting is Eden-like, the house is surprisingly spartan, considering that he often entertained jet-setters and royalty. He wrote *High Spirits, Quadrille,* and other plays here, and his simple grave is on the grounds next to a small stage where his works are occasionally performed. Recordings of Coward singing about "mad dogs and Englishmen" echo over the lawns. Tours include a walk through the house and grounds where Coward is buried. The view from the house's hilltop perch is one of the best on the north coast, making Firefly well worth the price of admission. ⊠ *Port Maria* ☎ *876/725–0920* ⊒ *$10* ⊙ *Mon.–Thurs. and Sat. 9–5.*

Green Grotto Caves. A good choice for rainy days, these caves offer 45-minute guided tours that include a look at a subterranean lake. The cave has a long history as a hiding place for everyone from fearsome pirates to runaway slaves to the Spanish governor (he was on the run from the British at the time). It's a good destination if you want to see one of Jamaica's caves without going too far off the beaten path. You'll feel like a spelunker, since you must wear a hard hat throughout the tour. ⊠ *North Coast Hwy., 2 mi (3 km) east of Discovery Bay* ☎ *876/973–2841* ⊕ *www.greengrottocavesja.com* ⊒ *$20* ⊙ *Daily 9–4.*

DID YOU KNOW? Green Grotto Caves are the most popular caves in Jamaica—but they are by no means the only spelunking options. With porous limestone making up much of island, more than 1,100 caves have been discovered on the island. Some are open for guided tours; others are explored primarily by adventure travelers that hire local guides. One of the top resources on the subject is *Jamaica Underground,* published by the University of the West Indies Press.

CLOSE UP

Getting Hitched

With its lush tropical backdrop and wide selection of romantic resorts, Ocho Rios is one of the island's top wedding spots. Weddings are big business, so your hotel will be happy to offer all the assistance you'll need for your special day.

Several all-inclusive resorts, including Couples and Sandals, offer free wedding packages. These typically include a ceremony and small reception, although you'll pay for other expenses like the marriage license. All the major resorts have wedding coordinators that handle all the paperwork that will be needed before your arrival.

Getting married in Jamaica is easy and inexpensive, with just a 24-hour waiting period after you arrive on the island. No blood tests are required. You'll need to bring along a proof of citizenship, including a certified copy of your birth certificate. If applicable, you'll also need a proof of divorce, a copy of a deceased partner's death certificate, or a parent's written consent if you're under 21.

3

Mystic Mountain. This is Ocho Rios' newest attraction, covering 100 acres of mountain-side rainforest near Dunn's River Falls. Visitors board the Rainforest Sky Explorer, a chair lift that soars through and over the pristine rain forest to the apex of "Mystic Mountain." On top, there is a restaurant with spectacular views of Ocho Rios, arts and crafts shops, and the attraction's signature tours, the Rainforest Bobsled Jamaica ride and the Rainforest Zipline Tranoply ride. Custom-designed bobsleds, inspired by Jamaica's Olympic bobsled team, run downhill on steel rails with speed controlled by the driver, using simple push-pull levers. Couples can run their bobsleds in tandem. The zip-line tours streak through lush rain forest under the care of an expert guide who points out items of interest. The entire facility was built using environmentally friendly techniques and materials so as to leave the native rain forest undisturbed. ⊠ *Balmoral Rd., Ocho Rios* ☎ *876/ 974–3990* ⊕ *www. rainforestbobsledjamaica.com* ⊠ *$42 (tram only); $62 (tram and bobsled); $104 (tram and zip line); $124 (tram, bobsled, and zip line)* ⊙ *Daily 7:30–5.*

Ocho Rios Fort. There's not much left of the 17th-century Ocho Rios Fort besides a wall and four cannons that still look out to the sea. Two of the cannons were brought here to protect the bay from the French, and the other two once

A Malay apple blossom at Prospect Plantation

protected nearby Mammee Bay (where the French did attack). ⊠ *Main St. next to Reynolds Pier, Ocho Rios* ☎ *No phone* ⊕ *www.jnht.com* ⊟ *Free* ⊙ *Open 24 hrs.*

Prospect Plantation. To learn about Jamaica's agricultural heritage, a trip to this working plantation, just east of town, is a must. It's not just a place for history lovers, however. Everyone enjoys the views over the White River Gorge and the tour in a tractor-pulled cart. The grounds are full of exotic flowers and tropical trees, some planted over the years by such celebrities as Winston Churchill and Charlie Chaplin. The estate includes a small aviary with free-flying butterflies. You can also saddle up for horseback rides and camel safaris on the plantation's 900 acres, but the actual tour times are usually geared toward the cruise-ship schedule, so call ahead. ⊠ *Rte. A1, 4 mi (3.2 km) east of Ocho Rios* ☎ *876/994–1058* ⊕ *www.prospectplantationtours.com* ⊟ *$32* ⊙ *Daily 8–5; tour times vary.*

Shaw Park Gardens and Waterfalls. Originally used for growing sugarcane and later oranges, this estate became the original site of the exclusive Shaw Park Hotel (today relocated to the beach). The owner's daughter, appropriately named Flora, worked to create the lush gardens, which now fill the 25-acre site with flame flowers, birds of paradise, and orchids. ⊠ *Shaw Park Rd., Ocho Rios* ☎ *876/974–2723* ⊕ *www.shawparkgardens.com* ⊟ *$10* ⊙ *Daily 8–4.*

Walkerswood Factory. To learn more about Jamaican cuisine (as well as the island's bountiful supply of herbs, fruits, and spices), visit the source of many sauces and seasonings. Walkerswood Factory produces everything from jerk sauces to jams and pepper sauces. A one-hour guided tour provides a look at herb gardens, a visit to a re-created hut to learn more about historic countryside life, a jerk marinade demonstration, and sampling Walkerswood products. The site includes a gift shop and snack bar featuring local dishes. Tours are based on cruise-ship schedules, so call ahead. ⊠ *About 6 mi (10 km) south of Ocho Rios on A3 in Walkerswood, St. Ann's Bay* ☎ *876/917–2318* ☜ *$15* ☺ *Tour times vary.*

WHERE TO EAT

Although Ocho Rios is a hub of all-inclusive activity, travelers find a wide variety of independent dining options in the area as well, from jerk stands to fine-dining restaurants to familiar burgers-and-fries eateries. The area within walking distance of the cruise terminal is home to many casual restaurants that are especially popular for lunch; dinner options can range from seaside restaurants to open-air establishments high in the hills overlooking the city lights.

\$\$–\$\$\$ ✕**Almond Tree.** *Eclectic.* A longtime favorite in Ocho Rios, this restaurant is named for the massive tree growing through the roof. For many diners, the evening starts with a drink at the terrace bar overlooking the sea. Dinner, which can be enjoyed on the terrace or in the dining room, begins with pumpkin and pepperpot soup before moving on to such entrées as fresh fish, veal piccata, and fondue. The service can be somewhat slow, so for many diners this is the evening's activity. ⊠ *Hibiscus Lodge Hotel, 87 Main St., Ocho Rios* ☎ *876/974–2813* ☴ *AE, MC, V.*

¢–\$ ✕**Bumperee Jerk Centre and Rest Stop.** *Jamaican.* This open-air eatery, a popular stop for travelers headed out to Bob Marley's house in Nine Mile, is also a favorite with locals who come by for tasty jerk and spicy patties. Pork and chicken take center stage here, accompanied by rice and peas and tasty festival. A separate bar, housed in a colorful rondoval, serves drinks and expensive sodas. Jerk is available Monday to Saturday; on Sunday you can only order the patties. ⊠ *Claremont* ☎ *No phone* ☴ *No credit cards.*

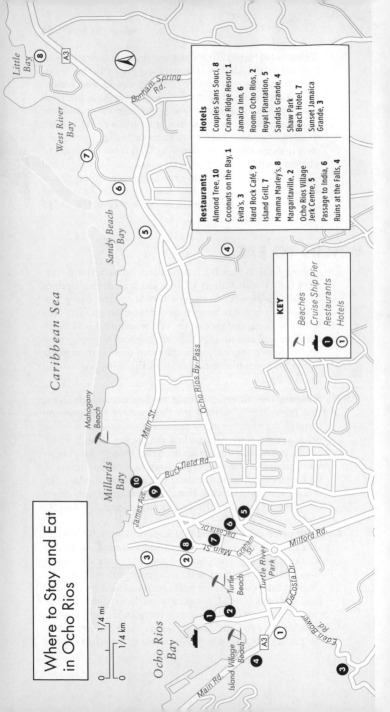

Where to Stay and Eat in Ocho Rios

Caribbean Sea

Little Bay

West River Bay

Sandy Beach Bay

Mahogany Beach

Millards Bay

Ocho Rios Bay

Island Village Beach

Turtle Beach

A3

Bonham Spring Rd.

Ocho Rios By-Pass

Main St.

Buckfield Rd.

James Ave.

DaCosta Dr.

Graham St.

Milford Rd.

Turtle River Park

Eden Bower Rd.

Main Rd.

0   1/4 mi
0   1/4 km

Hotels

Couples Sans Souci, **8**
Crane Ridge Resort, **1**
Jamaica Inn, **6**
Rooms Ocho Rios, **2**
Royal Plantation, **5**
Sandals Grande, **4**
Shaw Park
Beach Hotel, **7**
Sunset Jamaica
Grande, **3**

Restaurants

Almond Tree, **10**
Coconuts on the Bay, **1**
Evita's, **3**
Hard Rock Café, **9**
Island Grill, **7**
Mamma Marley's, **8**
Margaritaville, **2**
Ocho Rios Village
Jerk Centre, **5**
Passage to India, **6**
Ruins at the Falls, **4**

KEY

🏖 Beaches
⚓ Cruise Ship Pier
■ Restaurants
① Hotels

BEST BETS FOR DINING

With the many restaurants to choose from, how will you decide where to eat? Fodor's writers and editors have selected their favorite restaurants in the Best Bets lists below. The Fodor's Choice properties represent the "best of the best." Find specific details about a restaurant in the full reviews.

Fodor's Choice

Evita's Italian Restaurant; Scotchie's Too.

Best Budget Eats: Margaritaville; Scotchie's Too.

Best for Families: Margaritaville; R2.

Most Romantic: Evita's Italian Restaurant; Toscanini's.

Best for Local Jamaican Cuisine: Ocho Rios Village Jerk Centre; Scotchie's Too.

$$-$$$ ✕ **Coconuts on the Bay.** *Jamaican*. This casual eatery, opposite the cruise pier, offers slightly upscale versions of local specialties. Start with jerk chicken wings or conch and shrimp fritters before moving on to specialties like tamarind shrimp or lobster served grilled, curried, or creole style. Complimentary transportation from local hotels is available. ⊠ *Turtle Beach Rd., Ocho Rios* ☎ *876/795–0064* ⊟ *AE, MC, V.*

★ **Fodor's**Choice ✕ **Evita's Italian Restaurant.** *Eclectic*. Just about
$$-$$$ every celebrity who has visited Ocho Rios has dined at this hilltop restaurant, and Evita has the pictures to prove it. Guests feel like stars themselves, with attentive waitstaff helping to guide them through a list of about 30 kinds of pasta, ranging from lasagna Rastafari (vegetarian) and fiery jerk spaghetti to *rotelle colombo* (crabmeat with white sauce and noodles). Kids under 12 eat for half-price, and light eaters will appreciate half-portions. The restaurant offers free transportation from area hotels. ⊠ *Mantalent Inn, Eden Bower Rd., Ocho Rios* ☎ *876/974–2333* ⊟ *AE, D, MC, V.*

$-$$ ✕ **Hard Rock Café.** *Eclectic*. Within walking distance of the cruise pier, this popular eatery is filled with music memorabilia, including Bob Marley's handwritten lyrics for "Jammin'" and a guitar he used in the recording of "Kaya." The menu features the usual fare, including burgers, ribs, and fajitas. ⊠ *Taj Mahal Shopping Centre, 4 Main St., Ocho Rios* ☎ *876/974–3333* ⊟ *AE, D, MC, V.*

¢ ✕ **Island Grill.** *Jamaican*. With several locations across the island, Island Grill is Jamaica's version of fast food. Jerk,

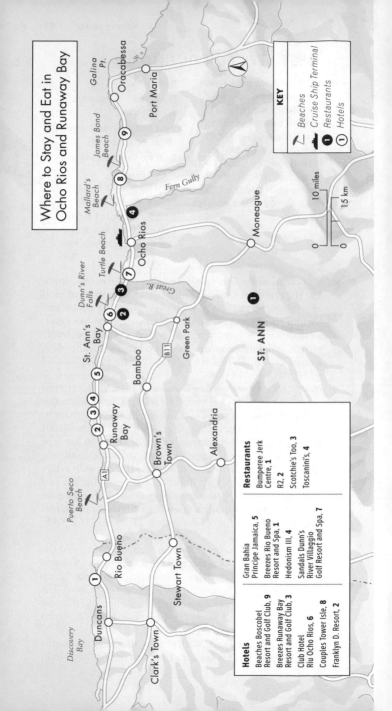

Where to Stay and Eat in Ocho Rios and Runaway Bay

KEY

↙ Beaches
⚓ Cruise Ship Terminal
🍴 Restaurants
① Hotels

Discovery Bay

Puerto Seco Beach

Duncans

Rio Bueno

Stewart Town

Clark's Town

Runaway Bay

Brown's Town

Bamboo

Alexandria

St. Ann's Bay

Turtle Beach

Dunn's River Falls

Ocho Rios

Moneague

Great R.

Fern Gully

Mallard's Beach

James Bond Beach

Galina Pt.

Oracabessa

Port Maria

Green Park

ST. ANN

A1
B11

0   10 miles
0   15 km

Hotels
Beaches Boscobel Resort and Golf Club, **9**
Breezes Runaway Bay Resort and Golf Club, **3**
Club Hotel Riu Ocho Rios, **6**
Couples Tower Isle, **8**
Franklyn D. Resort, **2**

Gran Bahia Principe Jamaica, **5**
Breezes Rio Bueno Resort and Spa, **1**
Hedonism III, **4**
Sandals Dunn's River Villaggio Golf Resort and Spa, **7**

Restaurants
Bumperee Jerk Centre, **1**
R2, **2**
Scotchie's Too, **3**
Toscanini's, **4**

Abundant local seafood is widely available

patties, rice and peas—all spiced for the local palate—fill the menu of this eat-in or take-out restaurant about a block from the main tourist area. ⊠ *59 Main St., Ocho Rios* ☎ *876/974–8725* ▭ *MC, V.*

$–$$ ✕ **Mamma Marley's Jammin' Bar and Grill.** *Jamaican.* The influence of the late Cedella Booker, Bob Marley's mother, remains the force behind this popular eatery across from the largest crafts market in Ocho Rios. Cedella's recipes include some of her son's favorite dishes. You'll find jerk on the menu, but look for other local dishes like ackee and saltfish, coconut curried vegetables, and grilled lobster tails. Bob Marley memorabilia is for sale, of course. ⊠ *52 Main St., Ocho Rios* ☎ *876/974–0197* ▭ *MC, V.*

$–$$ ✕ **Margaritaville Caribbean Bar and Grill.** *Eclectic.* Part of the popular chain (you can also find branches in Montego Bay and Negril), this easygoing restaurant and bar is especially popular with cruise-ship passengers because of its location near the pier. You can find jerk burgers and conch fritters but, for the most part, the menu is all-American. The large bar in the center of the restaurant is packed, especially during the evening hours. ⊠ *Island Village, Turtle Beach Rd., Ocho Rios* ☎ *876/675–8800* ▭ *AE, D, MC, V.*

¢–$ ✕ **Ocho Rios Village Jerk Centre.** *Jamaican.* This blue-canopied, open-air eatery is a good place to park yourself for frosty Red Stripe beer and fiery jerk pork, chicken, or seafood. Milder barbecued meats, also sold by weight (typically, ¼ or ½ pound makes a good serving), turn up on the fresh daily chalkboard menu posted on the wall. It's lively at lunch, especially when passengers from cruise ships swamp the place. ⊠ *Da Costa Dr., Ocho Rios* ☎ *876/974–2549* ▭ *D, MC, V.*

$$ ✕ **Passage to India.** *Indian.* With a downtown location convenient both to cruise passengers looking for a midday meal and vacationers headed to dinner, Passage to India is Ocho Rios's most popular Indian eatery. Start with savory chicken tikka (a rich stew) or samosas (mutton- or vegetable-filled dumplings), then work your way to minced mutton with green peas or shrimp with sweet peppers. All the dishes are flavored to satisfy the local craving for spicy food. ⊠ *15A Soni's Plaza, 50 Main St., Ocho Rios* ☎ *876/795–3182* ▭ *AE, D, MC, V.*

$-$$ ✕ **R2.** *Eclectic.* Perched high above Ocho Rios, R2 is part of the Mystic Mountain entertainment area. Serving contemporary Caribbean cuisine with an emphasis on healthy choices, the menu includes the Health Basket, a roasted turkey breast on ciabatta bread, and stir-fried vegetables with tofu, as well as more traditional Jamaican dishes such as jerk or escovitch fish. R2 also offers a separate kid's menu. The spectacular view of Ocho Rios and the cruise harbor is an added attraction. ⊠ *Balmoral Rd., Ocho Rios* ☎ *876/974–3990* ⊕ *www.rainforestbobsledjamaica.com* ▭ *D, MC, V* ⊗ *No dinner.*

$-$$ ✕ **The Ruins at the Falls.** *Asian.* Just as the name suggests, this restaurant is perched beside a waterfall. Tables sit at the base of the 40-foot cascade, making this a romantic spot for lunch or dinner. The menu here is diverse, with Asian specialties such as lotus lily lobster joining Jamaican favorites like curried goat. There are even a few vegetarian dishes. This place is popular for weddings and other big events, so call ahead. ⊠ *17 Da Costa Dr., Ocho Rios* ☎ *876/974–8888* ▭ *AE, D, MC, V.*

★ **Fodor's**Choice ✕ **Scotchie's Too.** *Caribbean.* The Ocho Rios
¢–$ branch of the longtime Montego Bay favorite has already been lauded by international chefs for its excellent jerk. The open-air eatery offers plates of jerk chicken, sausage, fish, pork, and ribs, all accompanied by *festival* (a rolled bread similar to a Southern hush puppy), *bammy* (fried cassava bread), and some fire-breathing hot sauce. Be sure to step over to the kitchen to watch the preparation of the jerk over the pits. ⊠ *North Coast Hwy., Drax Hall, Ocho Rios* ☎ *876/794–9457* ▭ *MC, V.*

$$–$$$ ✕ **Toscanini's.** *Italian.* At Harmony Hall, this longtime favorite offers seating in the dining room and on the garden

Bond, James Bond

Jamaica was a seductive muse for author Ian Fleming, who penned every line of his 13 James Bond novels at his Oracabessa residence, Goldeneye. The beauty of the island played a starring role in more than one of Agent 007's on-screen adventures, so it's easy to retrace the footsteps of Sean Connery and Roger Moore.

Bikini-clad Ursula Andress sang "Under the Mango Tree" as she emerged from the cobalt-blue ocean at **Laughing Waters Beach** in *Dr. No*, 007's first foray in film. Known today as the original James Bond Beach, this Ocho Rios oasis is known for its golden sand. Link hands with fellow travelers as you

climb nearby **Dunn's River Falls,** where the secret agent and Honey Ryder enjoyed a seductive swim.

The sound of Paul McCartney singing "Live and Let Die" in the opening credits will ring in your head much like the echo of footsteps that reverberate inside **Green Grotto Caves,** which served as a stalagmite-filled sanctuary for Bond's adversary Dr. Kananga in the 1973 film of the same name.

The spy showed his softer side in the same installment of the movie franchise with a picnic scene filmed on the grounds of The **Ruins at the Falls** restaurant.

veranda. The menu features classic Italian dishes prepared with Jamaican flair. Start with the savory minestrone soup, but save room for the main courses: grilled snapper filet, chicken breast simmered in tomatoes, and veal cutlets with fontina cheese and proscuitto sautéed in butter and wine. Delicious desserts like tiramisu and chocolate and amaretto cheesecake end meals with a flourish. If you're staying in an Ocho Rios hotel, call for complimentary shuttle. ✉ *Harmony Hall, North Coast Hwy., Ocho Rios* ☎ *876/975–4785* ⊟ *AE, MC, V.*

WHERE TO STAY

Ocho Rios area hotels are along a 40-mi (64-km) span of Jamaica's central North Coast and can be found in several different communities. From west (closer to Montego Bay) to east (Ocho Rios and beyond), these regions and towns include Trelawny, Rio Bueno, Discovery Bay, Mammee Bay, Runaway Bay, St. Ann's Bay, Ocho Rios, Oracabessa, and St. Mary. All of these communities are located on or adjacent to the North Coast Highway, A1.

OCHO RIOS AND VICINITY

$$$$ ⚅ **Beaches Boscobel Resort & Golf Club.** *Resort.* Although this
☾ resort is for anyone—including singles and couples—it's
best suited for families, whose children enjoy supervised
activities in one of five kids' clubs divided by age, from
infants to teens. Some rooms have pull-out sofas, and there
are also connecting rooms for large families. Children under
age two stay free, and special rates cover children under
age 16 sharing a room with a parent. The all-inclusive program here is extensive (including golf and a golf school)
and includes activities for all members of the family as well
as nightly activities. **Pros:** excellent children's program;
numerous dining options; good options for adults including spa. **Cons:** long drive from the airport; beach is a long
walk (or an elevator ride) from the rooms; resort is distant
from Ocho Rios attractions. ⊠ *North Coast Hwy., Box 63,
St. Ann's Bay* ☎ *876/975–7777* ⊕ *www.beaches.com* ⇆ *123
rooms, 100 suites* ☖ *In-room: safe, kitchen (some), refrigerator (some), DVD (some), Internet, Wi-Fi. In-hotel: 5
restaurants, room service, bars, tennis courts, pools, gym,
spa, beachfront, diving, water sports, children's programs
(ages infant–17), laundry service, Internet terminal, Wi-Fi
hotspot* ⊟ *AE, D, MC, V* ⇆ *2-night minimum* ⦿ *AI.*

$$$– ⚅ **ClubHotel Riu Ocho Rios.** *Resort.* This sprawling resort, built
$$$$ in two U-shape wings each overlooking a pool, is presently
the largest in Jamaica. Rooms are generously sized and well
maintained, although there are long walks to public areas.
All rooms come with an all-inclusive package, but suites
include such extras as 24-hour concierge service. Some
activities including billiards and scuba diving (except for
an introductory lesson in the pool) are not part of the all-
inclusive package. **Pros:** numerous dining options; large
rooms; expansive beach. **Cons:** long walk to beach; some
public areas feel cramped; all-inclusive package is lim-
ited. ⊠ *North Coast Hwy., Mammee Bay* ☎ *876/972–2200*
⊕ *www.riu.com* ⇆ *478 rooms, 378 suites* ☖ *In-room: safe,
refrigerator. In-hotel: 7 restaurants, bars, tennis courts,
pools, gym, spa, beachfront, diving, water sports, children's
programs (ages 4–12), laundry service, Internet terminal,
Wi-Fi hotspot* ⊟ *AE, DC, MC, V* ⦿ *AI.*

$$$$ ⚅ **Couples Sans Souci Resort and Spa.** *Resort.* This classy all-
inclusive encourages its guests to check their cares at the
entrance and indulge in some soul-nurturing pampering.
Rooms—all of which are suites—are soothing, with tile
floors, plush linens, large balconies, and a style more Medi-

BEST BETS FOR LODGING

Fodor's offers a selective listing of quality lodging experiences, from the island's best boutique hotel to its most luxurious beach resort. Here, we've compiled our top recommendations based on the different types of lodging found on the island. The very best properties—in other words, those that provide a particularly remarkable experience—are designated in the listings with the Fodor's Choice logo.

Fodor's Choice

Breezes Runaway Bay; Jamaica Inn; Royal Plantation.

Best Budget Stay: Rooms Ocho Rios; Shaw Park Beach Hotel & Spa; Sunset Jamaica Grande Resort and Spa.

Best Boutique Hotel: Jamaica Inn; Royal Plantation.

Best All-Inclusive Resort: Breezes Runaway Bay; Couples Tower Isle; Sunset Jamaica Grande Resort and Spa.

Best for Honeymooners: Couples Tower Isle; Jamaica Inn.

Best for Families: Beaches Boscobel Resort & Golf Club; Rooms Ocho Rios; Sunset Jamaica Grande Resort and Spa.

3

terranean than Caribbean. Bathrooms are particularly large and luxurious. Romantic oceanfront suites have oversized whirlpool tubs. Guests have their choice of beaches (one clothing-optional), though both have pebbly sand, and neither is as appealing as the pools. Though the resort is open to couples only, they do not have to be male-female couples. **Pros:** excellent spa; upscale accommodations; property is spacious and feels uncrowded. **Cons:** no reciprocal privileges with Couples Tower Isle; public areas and some guest rooms are a long walk from some rooms; beaches are not as good as others in area. ⊠ *North Coast Hwy., 2 mi (3 km) east of Ocho Rios, Mammee Bay* ☎ *876/994–1206* ⊕ *www. couples.com* ⇌ *150 suites* ⚐ *In-room: safe, refrigerator, Wi-Fi (some). In-hotel: 4 restaurants, room service, bars, tennis courts, pools, gym, spa, beachfront, diving, water sports, laundry service, Wi-Fi hotspot, no kids under 18* ⊟ *AE, D, DC, MC, V* ⚏ *3-night minimum* ⊚ *AI.*

$$$$ ⊡ **Couples Tower Isle.** *Resort.* Renovations in 2004 and 2008 spiffed up the guest rooms of Jamaica's first all-inclusive resort. Though similar to a Sandals in its creation of a romantic, cozy atmosphere, this Couples resort isn't quite as upscale and tends to draw a somewhat older repeat clientele. Connected by long hallways, rooms are a short walk from the beach; a handful of villa suites are tucked

Breezes Runaway Bay—beach and boats

Jamaica Inn

back in the gardens with private plunge pools or hot tubs. The resort is on a nice stretch of beach, and there's also a private island where you can sunbathe in the buff if you want. Weddings are included in the package, as are several off-site excursions. **Pros:** free weddings; excellent beach facilities; expansive all-inclusive package. **Cons:** long distance from Montego Bay airport; does not include reciprocal privileges with Couples Sans Souci. ⊠ *Tower Isle, 5 mi (8 km) east of Ocho Rios on A1, Box 330, St. Mary* ☎ *876/975–4271* ⊕ *www.couples.com* ➪ *200 rooms, 17 suites* ⚹ *In-room: safe, refrigerator (some), Wi-Fi (some). In-hotel: 6 restaurants, bars, tennis courts, pools, gym, spa, beachfront, diving, water sports, Wi-Fi hotspot, no kids under 18* ⊟ *AE, D, MC, V* ⚲ *3-night minimum* ⊚ *AI.*

$–$$ 🏨 **Crane Ridge Resort.** *Hotel.* In the hills west of the city center, Crane Ridge Resort is a good option for travelers who don't demand a beachfront property or all the bells and whistles of an all-inclusive. A complimentary shuttle takes you to the beach, but you might prefer the on-site pool. The lemon-tinted building consists primarily of one- and two-bedroom suites with private balconies (standard guest rooms share balconies). **Pros:** good value; spacious rooms; convenient location. **Cons:** no beach; limited on-site dining; dated decor. ⊠ *17 Da Costa Dr., Ocho Rios* ☎ *876/974–8056* ⊕ *www.craneridge.net* ➪ *30 rooms, 60 suites* ⚹ *In-room: safe, kitchen (some), refrigerator, Internet. In-hotel: restaurant, room service, bar, tennis courts, pool, gym* ⊟ *AE, D, MC, V* ⊚ *EP.*

$$$$ 🏨 **Gran Bahia Principe Jamaica.** *Resort.* Somewhat bare grounds surround this massive property, one of the island's newest resorts. Guest rooms, decorated in muted tropical tones, are a good value for travelers who don't mind some dining restrictions (and plenty of fellow travelers at the buffet line). All in all, this is one of the island's most economical all-inclusives. A special Club Golden Principe offers separate check-in, concierge service, room service, and some exclusive facilities. **Pros:** numerous on-site activities; expansive pool areas; good value. **Cons:** limited dining options; lack of landscaping; long walks to public areas. ⊠ *North Coast Hwy., Runaway Bay* ☎ *876/973–7000* ⊕ *www.bahia-principe.com* ➪ *700 suites* ⚹ *In-room: safe, refrigerator. In-hotel: 5 restaurants, room service (some), bars, tennis courts, pools, gym, spa, beachfront, diving, water sports, children's programs (ages 4–12), Internet terminal, Wi-Fi hotspot* ⊟ *AE, D, MC, V* ⊚ *AI.*

★ **Fodor's Choice** 🖫 **Jamaica Inn.** *Hotel.* Start a conversation about

$$$$ elegant Jamaican resorts, and this quietly sophisticated hotel will surely be mentioned. A historic favorite with the rich and famous (one suite is named for guest Winston Churchill), this pricey, genteel resort is known for its attentive staff. Each suite has its own veranda (larger than most hotel rooms) on the private cove's powdery, champagne-color beach. The cliff-top spa is known for its ayurveda and Fijian treatments. This small resort is not very child-friendly. **Pros:** elegant accommodations; exceptional service; good spa. **Cons:** some travelers may feel it's too quiet; too traditional and stiff for some visitors; no in-room TV. ⊠ *North Coast Hwy., 2 mi (3.2 km) east of Ocho Rios, Box 1* ☎ *876/974–2514* ⊕ *www.jamaicainn.com* 🛏 *47 suites* ⚖ *In-room: no TV, Internet (some), Wi-Fi (some). In-hotel: restaurant, room service, bars, pool, gym, spa, beachfront, water sports, laundry service, Internet terminal, no kids under 12* ☐ *AE, D, MC, V* ⎮◎⎮ *AI.*

$–$$ 🖫 **Rooms Ocho Rios.** *Hotel.* Adjacent to Sunset Jamaica Grande Resort, this SuperClubs-owned hotel, as its name suggests, has a room-only plan (only continental breakfast is included). Formerly Club Jamaica, the family-friendly hotel offers Wi-Fi service throughout. It's favored by business travelers and vacationers who plan to explore the region rather than make a resort their primary destination. Rooms have ocean views and all the basics, decorated in tropical tones. It's an economical choice for independent-minded travelers who would rather sample the town's many restaurants than be tied to an all-inclusive plan. **Pros:** good value; good beach; good location from which to explore Ocho Rios. **Cons:** small pool area; limited on-site dining options; limited activities. ⊠ *Main St., Ocho Rios* ☎ *876/974–6632* ⊕ *www.roomsresorts.com* 🛏 *92 rooms, 5 suites* ⚖ *In-room: safe, Internet, Wi-Fi. In-hotel: restaurant, bar, pool, gym, beachfront, diving, water sports, laundry facilities, Internet terminal* ☐ *AE, D, MC, V* ⎮◎⎮ *CP.*

★ **Fodor's Choice** 🖫 **Royal Plantation.** *Resort.* Dating back to the

$$$$ 1950s, when it was a getaway for Hollywood names, this small, adults-only resort was purchased in 2007 by Butch Stewart of Sandals and Beaches fame, but this boutique resort operates independently. More exclusive than any of its sister properties, the resort puts an emphasis on personal service, fine dining, and a refined atmosphere. Built high atop a bluff, it has a feel of exclusivity; all rooms, which are suites, have ocean views, not to mention luxurious bedding, fully stocked in-room bars, CD players, mahogany furniture, and marble baths, many with whirlpool tubs. The most expensive suites have special check-in and luggage services; optional butler service is also available. Steps lead to twin beaches, where the luxury continues with the services of a beach butler. **Pros:** accommodations are expansive and stylish; good dining; room service offered. **Cons:** guest rooms and beach are on different levels; small pool; small beach. ⊠ *Main St., Box 2, Ocho Rios* ☎ *876/974–5601* ⊕ *www.royalplantation.com* ⟿ *74 suites* ⚬ *In-room: safe, refrigerator, DVD, Internet, Wi-Fi. In-hotel: 3 restaurants, room service, bars, tennis courts, pool, gym, spa, beachfront, diving, water sports, laundry service, Internet terminal, Wi-Fi hotspot, no kids under 18* ⊟ *AE, MC, V* ⟿ *2-night minimum* ⑩ *EP.*

$$$$ ☲ **Sandals Grande Ocho Rios Beach and Villa Resort.** *Resort.* This sprawling resort began years ago as two separate properties, and today it continues to have a split personality. The "Riviera" section sits right on the ocean; its lush grounds are a shady alternative to the sunny beach. Across the road (accessible by shuttle or tunnel), the "Manor" side is home to both traditional hotel rooms in the faux greathouse and suites in primarily four-unit villas that share a common pool. Some villas are a quite distance from the public areas and the beach. **Pros:** airport shuttle; lots of privacy; numerous swimming options; romantic dining options. **Cons:** villas a long way from the beach; some rooms removed from public areas; long wait for the shuttle. ⊠ *Main St., Ocho Rios* ☎ *876/974–2691* ⊕ *www. sandals.com* ⟿ *529 rooms* ⚬ *In-room: safe, kitchen (some), refrigerator (some), Internet. In-hotel: 11 restaurants, room service, bars, tennis courts, pools, gym, spa, beachfront, diving, water sports, laundry service, Internet terminal, no kids under 18* ⟿ *2-night minimum* ⊟ *AE, D, DC, MC, V* ⑩ *AI.*

$$ ☲ **Shaw Park Beach Hotel & Spa.** *Resort.* With its hospital-green corridors and motel-style rooms, the Shaw Park won't win any awards for its design. But it just might be the friendliest place around. The staff at this smaller property makes up for any shortcomings. Guest rooms have either a patio or balcony overlooking a long stretch of beach that ends near the White River. Most guests opt for dining on the open-air terrace, where excellent local and international dishes are featured. Meals are served at specified hours (not around the clock, as at larger all-inclusives). For an additional fee, you can opt for meals at the gourmet restaurant. A nightclub and casino are quiet

during the week but busy Friday and Saturday night. **Pros:** beachfront rooms; excellent food; friendly staff. **Cons:** very basic rooms; limited on-site dining options; limited activities. ⊠ *Cutlass Bay, Ocho Rios* ☎ *876/974–2552* ⊕ *www. shawparkbeachhotel.com* ⇌ *94 rooms, 12 suites* ⚹ *In-room: safe, Internet. In-hotel: 2 restaurants, room service, bars, pool, gym, spa, beachfront, water sports, laundry service* ▭ *AE, MC, V* ⱓ⡏⡒*AI.*

$$$ 🏨 **Sunset Jamaica Grande Resort and Spa.** *Resort.* Jamaica's
ⓒ largest conference hotel, which is right in Ocho Rios, bustles with groups thanks to its expansive conference center (although it also welcomes a large percentage of leisure travelers). Rooms, brightened with tropical colors, are divided between two high-rise towers; the best views are found in the north tower. Many guests spend their time at the pool complex, which includes a meandering river and a lighthouse slide. Kids are kept busy in the complimentary Club Mongoose activity program, and parents can play in an 80-machine slot and video blackjack room. Teens can head to the Jamrock Teen Center. **Pros:** nice pool complex; good location for exploring Ocho Rios; good sunset views from some rooms. **Cons:** mix of leisure and convention clientele; some restaurants feel crowded; rooms are basic. ⊠ *Main St., Box 100, Ocho Rios* ☎ *876/974–2200* ⊕ *www.sunsetjamaicagrande.com* ⇌ *730 rooms, 12 suites* ⚹ *In-room: safe, refrigerator (some), Internet. In-hotel: 6 restaurants, bars, tennis courts, pools, gym, spa, beachfront, water sports, children's programs (ages 2–12), laundry facilities, laundry service, Internet terminal* ▭ *AE, D, DC, MC, V* ⱓ⡏⡒*AI.*

RUNAWAY BAY AND VICINITY

$$$$ 🏨 **Breezes Rio Bueno Resort and Spa.** *Resort.* Fifteen minutes west of Runaway Bay, the resort is built around a "village" complete with a town square. You can also find the island's largest clothing-optional facilities, which include a pool, hot tub, grill, and tennis courts. The beach—both clothed and clothing-optional sides—is expansive, although not Jamaica's best strip of sand; the large pool complex provides a popular option. Rooms have all the basic amenities but are not very large. Active vacationers find plenty of options including an on-site golf course as well as complimentary transfers and green fees at SuperClubs Golf Club at Runaway Bay Golf Course and SuperClubs Ironshore Golf & Country Club, the latter east of Montego Bay. **Pros:**

Waiters will serve your tropical drink right on the beach

upscale all-inclusive; complimentary manicure/pedicure and dry cleaning; 18-hole executive golf course within walking distance of rooms; separate clothing-optional facilities, from beach to tennis courts to grill. **Cons:** pebbly beach; somewhat remote for exploring Ocho Rios attractions. ⊠ *North Coast Hwy., between Duncans and Rio Bueno, Trelawny* ☐ *Rio Bueno P.O., Trelawny* ☎ *876/954–0000* ⊕ *www.superclubs.com* ↝ *226 rooms, 58 suites* ⚄ *In-room: safe, refrigerator. In-hotel: 7 restaurants, room service (some), bars, golf course, tennis courts, pools, gym, spa, beachfront, diving, water sports, bicycles, Internet terminal, Wi-Fi hotspot, no kids under 16* ▤ *AE, D, DC, MC, V* ↝ *3-night minimum* ⏻ *AI.*

★ **Fodor's Choice** ⌾ **Breezes Runaway Bay.** *Resort.* This moderately
$$$–
$$$$ priced SuperClubs resort, which underwent an extensive renovation and expansion in 2007, emphasizes an active, sports-oriented vacation—including golf (at the resort's own course), a circus workshop, tennis, and an array of water sports. Expert instruction and top-rate equipment are part of the package. Guests—often European and Japanese—flock here to dive and snorkel around the reef off the beach, which also makes the bay superbly smooth for swimming. There's also a good golf school. **Pros:** extensive sports and water sports options; complimentary airport shuttle; low-rise room blocks mean easy beach access. **Cons:** some public areas can feel crowded; small spa; some restaurants are too small to accommodate demand. ⊠ *North Coast*

Hwy., Box 58, 58 Main St., Runaway Bay ☎ *876/973–6099* ⊕ *www.superclubs.com* ⤶ *220 rooms, 46 suites* ♿ *In-room: safe, Wi-Fi. In-hotel: 6 restaurants, bars, golf course, tennis courts, pools, gym, spa, beachfront, diving, water sports, Internet terminal, no kids under 14* ⊟ *AE, D, DC, MC, V* ⚲ *3-night minimum* ⎮◎⎮*AI.*

$$$$ ⚏ **FDR, Franklyn D. Resort.** *Resort.* A favorite for families
ↄ with very young children, this relaxed resort goes a step beyond the usual supervised kids' programs, assigning you a professional caregiver who will assist you throughout your stay. Kids can take part in a supervised club, but a nanny also assists with in-room help from washing out bathing suits to supervising naps. Guests enjoy spacious one-, two-, and three-bedroom suites. Children under six stay and eat free when staying in a room with their parents. **Pros:** good supervised kids' programs; nanny program especially good for young families; spacious accommodations. **Cons:** not appealing to travelers without children; small pool area; rooms need updating. ✉ *Main Rd., Box 201, Runaway Bay* ☎ *876/973–4591* ⊕ *www.fdrholidays.com* ⤶ *77 suites* ♿ *In-room: safe, kitchen, refrigerator, Internet. In-hotel: 4 restaurants, bars, tennis court, pool, gym, beachfront, diving, water sports, bicycles, children's programs (ages newborn–16), laundry facilities, laundry service* ⊟ *AE, D, MC, V* ⎮◎⎮*AI.*

$$$– ⚏ **Hedonism III.** *Resort.* Like its more spartan cousin in Negril,
$$$$ Hedonism III is an adults-only resort for travelers looking for uninhibited fun that includes a waterslide (through the disco, no less). Unlike its Negril equivalent, however, Hedonism III offers luxurious rooms and Jamaica's first swim-up rooms. The guest rooms, each with mirrored ceilings, have Jacuzzis and CD players. The beach is divided into "nude" and "prude" sides, although a quick look shows that most people leave the suits at home. Scheduled activities include nude body painting and volleyball; the resort even holds Jamaica's only nude weddings. **Pros:** swim-up guest rooms; rooms more upscale than Hedonism II; around-the-clock activities. **Cons:** spring-break-for-adults–type atmosphere; beach is not as good as others in area; not for travelers looking for a quiet getaway. ✉ *Main Rd., Runaway Bay* ✉ *Box 250, Ocho Rios* ☎ *876/973–4100* ⊕ *www.superclubs.com* ⤶ *210 rooms, 15 suites* ♿ *In-room: safe. In-hotel: 4 restaurants, bars, tennis courts, pools, gym, spa, beachfront, diving, water sports, Internet terminal, no kids under 18* ⊟ *AE, D, DC, MC, V* ⚲ *3-night minimum* ⎮◎⎮*AI.*

PRIVATE VILLAS

Ocho Rios is filled with private villas, especially in the Discovery Bay area. In Jamaica, most luxury villas come with a full staff including a housekeeper, cook, butler, gardener, and often a security guard. Many can arrange for a driver, either for airport transfers, for daily touring, or for a prearranged number of days for sightseeing.

The island's villas were once mostly smaller homes, but recent years have seen an increased demand for larger, more luxurious properties. Numerous villas have five or more bedrooms spread around different parts of the building—or in different buildings altogether—for extra privacy.

3

Most villas come fully stocked with linens. You can often arrange for the kitchen to be stocked with groceries upon your arrival. Air-conditioning, even in the most luxurious villas, is typically limited to the bedrooms.

A four-night minimum stay is average for many villas although this can vary by season and property. Gratuities, usually split among the staff, typically range from 10% to 15%. Several private companies specialize in villa rentals, matching up vacationers with accommodations of the right size and price range.

VILLA-RENTAL AGENTS

Since 1967, the **Jamaica Association of Villas and Apartments** (✉ *2706 W. Agatite, 2nd fl., Chicago, IL* ☎ *800/845–5276* ⊕ *www.villasinjamaica.com*) has handled villas, cottages, apartments, and condos across the island.

Jamaica Villas by Linda Smith (✉ *8029 Riverside Dr., Cabin John, MD* ☎ *301/229–4300* ⊕ *www.jamaicavillas.com*) offers more than 60 fully staffed villas on the island. **Luxury Retreats International** (✉ *5530 St. Patrick St., Suite 2210, Montréal, Quebec, Canada* ☎ *877/993–0100* ⊕ *www. luxuryretreats.com*) offers numerous luxury villa rentals in Negril, Montego Bay, Ocho Rios (including the Discovery Bay area), and Port Antonio.

PRIVATE VILLAS

$$$$ ⚈ **A Summer Place.** *Vacation Rental.* More economical than many of the villas in the Fortlands Road neighborhood, this slightly older home can sleep more than a dozen people in its seven bedrooms. (One more private bedroom is housed in a garage conversion.) Just outside the living area awaits a pool and a yard that leads to a 100-foot private beach. **Pros:**

good value; nice beach; private bedroom good for those looking for more privacy. **Cons:** dated decor; few water toys; need car to get around. ⊠ *Fortlands Rd., Discovery Bay* ⊕ *www.luxuryretreats.com* ⤴ *7 bedrooms, 7 baths* ⚹ *In-villa: a/c (some), safe (some), dishwasher, DVD, Internet, daily maid service, cook, on-site security, pool, beachfront, water toys, laundry facilities* ⊟ *AE, MC, V* ⦿*EP.*

$$$$ 🏨 **Blue Harbour.** *Vacation Rental.* This complex of three beachfront villas includes Noël Coward's original Jamaica home, the two-bedroom Villa Grande. The complex also includes the playwright's former art studio, the three-bedroom Villa Rose, and the former guest quarters, now the one-bedroom Villa Chica. Villa Grande, where Coward entertained stars like Marlene Dietrich, Katherine Hepburn, and Patricia Neal, includes some original furnishings, including a sleigh bed in the main bedroom. Downstairs, the kitchen and veranda are shared by other guests at Blue Harbour, just as they were in Coward's day. You'll also share a small saltwater pool and the beach on the half-moon cove. You can opt for an all-inclusive meal plan for $120 per person daily; it does not include alcoholic beverages. The entire complex can be rented as a single unit or separately. **Pros:** private beach; interesting history; good value. **Cons:** dated accommodations; shared public facilities; need car to get around. ⊠ *North Coast Hwy. between Oracabessa and Port Maria* ☎ *575/586–1244* ⊕ *www.blueharb.com* ⤴ *3 villas* ⚹ *In-villa: no a/c, safe, daily maid service, cook, on-site security, pool* ⊟ *No credit cards* ⦿*AI.*

$$$$ 🏨 **Goldenfoot.** *Vacation Rental.* This stylish Oracabessa getaway is perfect for travelers seeking luxury accommodations without a budget-busting price tag. You're welcomed at the bamboo bar for a taste of the Goldenfoot Jamosa, a blend of white wine and the island's Ting soda. Each day you're served two meals—breakfast and either lunch or dinner, depending on your schedule. Bedrooms, like the rest of the property, are painted in subtle tropical shades and have an island ambience; the main bath includes its own bamboo-screened outdoor bath. Unlike most Jamaican villas, this property is wheelchair-accessible (although there are stairs leading down to the pool). **Pros:** good value; stylish decor; wheelchair accessible. **Cons:** too quiet for some travelers; need car to get around; long distance from airport. ⊠ *Off Rte. A3, Oracabessa* ☎ *876/842–1237* ⊕ *www. agoldenfootvilla.com* ⤴ *2 bedrooms, 3 baths* ⚹ *In-villa: a/c (some), DVD, daily maid service, cook, on-site security, fully staffed, pool* ⊟ *AE, MC, V* ⦿*MAP.*

CLOSE UP

Mad Dogs and Englishmen

A two-week vacation led to a lifelong love affair for Noël Coward. After visiting Jamaica in 1944, the playwright and songwriter would return four years later to claim an 8-acre tract of land upon which his first Jamaican home, Blue Harbour, was constructed.

A haven for members of high society, such luminaries as Marlene Dietrich, Katharine Hepburn, Vivien Leigh, and Laurence Olivier would flit about the two-story main house, christened Villa Grande, and its two guesthouses, Villa Rose and Villa Chica. Perhaps they inspired the name of the British bon vivant's next abode, Firefly. Coward moved up the hill to a perch with a grand view of Port Maria, constructing Firefly as an escape from the continuous commotion caused by his celebrity houseguests at Blue Harbour.

Perched on a hillside that was once the domain of Sir Henry Morgan, one of the original pirates of the Caribbean, Firefly became a peaceful retreat where the sophisticated wordsmith could pursue his passion for painting, a hobby encouraged by another famous figure who dabbled in oils, Sir Winston Churchill. Tubes of cobalt blue and vermilion lie to this day next to a set of paintbrushes in his studio, waiting to be picked up by an artist who was stilled by a heart attack in 1973.

A slab of stone, etched solely with the playwright's name and the dates of his birth and passing, marks Coward's final resting place in the garden on Firefly Hill. Perhaps, in the end, no written epitaph could sum up the life of the man dubbed "The Master." A more fitting tribute can be found in Firefly's living room, where rows of photographs grace the grand piano, each an image of a smiling celebrity face that once reveled in his company.

$$$$ ▦ **Makana.** *Vacation Rental.* Teak floors add an exotic touch to this elegant villa. Downstairs you'll find two bedrooms with lots of privacy. Upstairs, four bedrooms share a family room with a flat-screen television and a home office complete with a computer and phone service. Wi-Fi access throughout the house makes it easy to get a little work done. Outdoor amenities including an infinity pool, hot tub, gazebo with a view of the sea and nearby mountains, and a private beach with a calm lagoon. **Pros:** beautiful decor; great facilities; perfect location for families with children. **Cons:** expensive; need a car to get around; may

Ride your horse directly into the surf

be too quiet for some. ⊠ *Fortlands Rd., Discovery Bay* ⊕ *www.luxuryretreats.com* ⮢ *6 bedrooms, 6½ baths* ᴖ *In-villa: a/c (some), safe, kitchen, refrigerator, DVD, Internet, Wi-Fi, tennis court, pool, daily maid service, cook, on-site security, fully staffed, tennis court, pool, beachfront, water toys, laundry facilities* ▤ *AE, MC, V* ⦿ *EP.*

$$$$ 🖵 **Roaring Pavilion Villa and Spa.** *Vacation Rental.* A favorite with celebrities (Celine Dion, Tom Cruise, and Jack Nicholson have each stayed here), this villa is convenient to Ocho Rios, yet extremely private. The one-story house is especially noted for its on-site spa with two full-time masseuses. There's no extra charge for spa treatments if you opt for an all-inclusive package. Most bedrooms are in the main villa, but a separate bedroom in the Balinese Wing includes a luxurious private bath. Beyond the pool and well-manicured lawn is a private beach that just might look familiar: this is where Ursula Andress emerged from the surf in *Dr. No.* **Pros:** on-site spa; beautiful décor; separate wing ideal for those looking for more privacy. **Cons:** expensive; no beach view; need car to get around. ⊠ *North Coast Hwy., 3 mi (4 km) west of Ocho Rios* ⊕ *www.roaringpavilion. com* ⮢ *4 bedrooms, 6 bathrooms* ᴖ *In-villa: a/c (some), safe, dishwasher, DVD, Internet, Wi-Fi, daily maid service, cook, on-site security, fully staffed, hot tub, pool, gym, beachfront, water toys, laundry facilities* ▤ *AE, D, MC, V* ⦿ *EP.*

$$$$ ⊡ **Whispering Waters.** *Vacation Rental.* This stylish villa can accommodate 14 guests, making it perfect for large families. (For even bigger groups, there's a six-bedroom property next door.) A staff of seven keeps things immaculate with attentive butler, housekeeping, and chef service. Constructed with many local materials including breadnut floors and blackheart ceiling beams, the elegant home has individual climate control in all the bedrooms as well as a sound system throughout the grounds. A private pool and hot tub overlook a private white-sand beach. **Pros:** beautiful grounds; attentive staff; great beach; swimming cove. **Cons:** expensive; too large for some groups; need car to get around. ⊠ *Fortlands Rd., Discovery Bay* ☎ *876/670–0549* ⊕ *www.luxuryretreats.com* ⇆ *7 bedrooms, 7 baths* ♿ *In-villa: a/c (some), safe, kitchen, refrigerator, DVD, Internet, Wi-Fi, daily maid service, cook, on-site security, fully staffed, hot tub, tennis court, pool, gym, beachfront, water toys, laundry facilities* ⊟ *AE, MC, V* ⎁ *EP.*

BEACHES

Most of the big resorts in both Ocho Rios and Runaway Bay have their own beaches, some better than others. The beaches listed here are public stretches of sand accessible to all. Although it boasts no stretches as spectacular as those in Negril, Ocho Rios has many good beaches ranging from quiet to bustling, depending on the location and whether there's a cruise ship in town.

Beach World. Especially popular with cruise passengers thanks to its proximity to the pier, Beach World offers a small beach and a full array of water toys at Island Village. Admission to the beach is $5; for an extra fee, you can rent umbrellas, towels, and beach chairs. Activities include kayaking, snorkeling, scuba diving, and glass-bottom-boat rides. Changing rooms and lockers are also available. ⊠ *Island Village Shopping Complex, Main St., Ocho Rios* ☎ *876/842–9406.*

★ **Dunn's River Falls Beach.** You'll find a crowd (especially if there's a cruise ship in town) at the small beach at the foot of the falls. Although tiny—especially considering the masses of people—its got a great view, as well as a beach bar and grill. Look up from the sands for a spectacular view of the cascading water, whose roar drowns out the sea as you approach. ⊠ *Rte. A1, between St. Ann's Bay and Ocho Rios.*

Puerto Seco Beach. This public beach looks out on Discovery Bay, the place where, according to tradition, Christopher Columbus first came ashore. The explorer searched for freshwater but found none, so he named this stretch of sand Puerto Seco, or "dry port." Today the beach is anything but dry; concession stands sell bottles of Red Stripe to a primarily local crowd. Admission is $5. ⊠ *North Coast Hwy., 5 mi (8 km) west of Runaway Bay, Discovery Bay.*

Turtle Beach. One of the busiest beaches in Ocho Rios is not the prettiest, but it's usually lively and has a mix of residents and visitors. It's next to the Sunset Jamaica Grande and looks out over the cruise port. ⊠ *Main St., Ocho Rios.*

SPORTS AND THE OUTDOORS

CANOPY TOURS

With so much lush vegetation, it's no surprise that canopy tours are a popular way to enjoy the forests surrounding Ocho Rios. West of town at Cranbrook Flower Forest, canopy tours are operated by **Chukka Caribbean Adventures** (⊠ *St. Ann's Bay* ☎ *876/972–2506* ⊕ *www.chukkacaribbean. com*). A short walk takes you to the first of nine zip lines traversing the Laughlands River gorge. Participants must be 10 or older. The tour costs $89.

DIVING AND SNORKELING

These waters have been protected since 1966, which is why the Ocho Rios region is a popular diving destination. The **Ocho Rios Marine Park** stretches from Mammee Bay to Frankfort Point. Some of the top dive sites in the area include **Jack's Hall,** a 40-foot dive dotted with many types of coral, **Top of the Mountain,** a 60-foot dive near Dunn's River Falls filled with many coral heads, and the *Katryn,* a 50-foot dive to the wreck of a 140-foot minesweeper.

Five Star Watersports (⊠ *121 Main St., Ocho Rios* ☎ *876/974– 0164* ⊕ *www.fivestarwatersports.com*) operates the "Cool Runnings" catamaran cruise to Dunn's River Falls. Along with a guided climb up the falls, the trip includes a reef snorkeling excursion. Tours includes admission to Dunn's River Falls.

DOGSLEDDING

For a different kind of adventure, hitch up with the **Jamaica Dogsled Experience** (⊠ *Llandovery, St. Ann's Bay* ☎ *888/224– 8552* ⊕ *www.ckukkacaribbean.com* ✏ *$101*) offered by Chukka Caribben Adventures. This snow-less mush travels

Goodbye, Columbus

During his second voyage to the New World, rumors of a "land of blessed gold" lured Christopher Columbus to what would later be called Jamaica. Although the promise of riches turned out to be unfounded, the explorer could lay claim to discovering a tropical treasure for Spain's rulers.

Although St. Anne's Bay was to be his first glimpse of the island, Columbus first set foot on the swath of sand then known as Xaymaca, today referred to as Discovery Bay. His arrival, on May 5, 1494, marked the beginning of the end for the native Arawak people, who would be killed off by strange new diseases and the cruelties of slavery brought by those who followed in the explorer's path.

Columbus fared little better here, as a shipwreck necessitated his return to the island on his fourth voyage in 1503. Enduring an unsuccessful mutiny attempt by some of his crew, Columbus was rescued a year later, never returning to the "land of blessed gold."

the lanes and fields at Chukka Cove Farm, each wheeled dogsled pulled by a team of Jamaican dogs that have been rescued by the Jamaica Society for the Prevention of Cruelty to Animals and given a home at the farm and trained to pull the sleds. The trip takes 1½ hours and includes several stops at points of interest. If you don't have time for a tour, you can still meet the dogs in the Jamaica Dogsled Encounter ($43). Part of the proceeds are donated by Chukka to the JSPCA.

GOLF

Ocho Rios courses don't have the prestige of those around Montego Bay, but duffers will find challenges at a few lesser-known courses.

East of Falmouth, try **Breezes Rio Bueno Golf Club** Bay (⊠ *Trelawny* ☎ *876/954–0010*), between Duncans and Rio Bueno, an 18-hole executive course with lush vegetation (nonguests should call for fee information). Caddies are not mandatory on this course.

The Runaway Bay golf course is found at **SuperClubs Golf Club at Runaway** Bay (⊠ *North Coast Hwy., Runaway Bay* ☎ *876/973–7319*). This 18-hole course has hosted many championship events (green fees are $80 for nonguests; guests play for free) and is also home to an extensive golf academy.

Dolphins entertain at Dolphin Cove

The golf course at **Sandals Golf and Country Club** (*5 mi [8 km] southeast of Ocho Rios turn south at White River and continue 4 mi [6 km], Ocho Rios* ☏ *876/975–0119*) is 700 feet above sea level (green fees for 18 holes are $100, or $70 for 9 holes for nonguests; free for guests).

GUIDED TOURS
Half-day and full-day tours can be arranged with many taxi drivers. Be sure to agree on a price before heading out on the tour. **Jamaica Tours Ltd.** (☏ *876/974–6447* ⊕ *www.jamaicatoursltd.com*) offers several Ocho Rios tours with stops ranging from gardens to Dunn's River Falls.

HELICOPTER TOURS
Just west of the small fort in Ocho Rios, **Island Hoppers** (✉ *Reynolds Pier, Ocho Rios* ☏ *876/974–1285* ⊕ *www.jamaicahelicopterservices.com*) offers three helicopter tours of the region. The longest tour is the hour-long Jamaican Showcase ($1,280 for up to four persons), circling over Spanish Town, Kingston, and the Blue Mountains. The 30-minute Memories of Jamaica tour ($645 for up to four persons) travels east to Port Maria for an aerial view of Noël Coward's and Ian Fleming's former homes. For die-hard 007 fans, James Bond's Jamaica Tour ($440 for up to four persons) provides a half-hour look at the sites made famous by the movies and novels. You can also opt for a quick flight of five minutes ($25 per person) or 10 minutes ($45 per person) for a bird's-eye view of Ocho Rios

HORSEBACK RIDING

With its combination of hills and beaches, Ocho Rios is a natural for horseback excursions. Most are guided tours taken at a slow pace and perfect for those with no previous equestrian experience. Many travelers opt to pack long pants for horseback rides, especially those away from the beach.

Riders with an interest in history can combine both loves on a horseback tour at **Annandale Plantation** (✉ *4 mi [6 km] southwest of Ocho Rios, near town of Epworth* ☎ 876/974–2323). The 600-acre plantation is high above Ocho Rios and today serves as a working farm, although in its glory days it hosted dignitaries such as the Queen Mother.

In the Braco area near Trelawny, between Montego Bay and Ocho Rios, **Braco Stables** (✉ *Duncans* ☎ 876/954–0185 ⊕ *www.bracostables.com*) offers guided rides including a bareback romp in the sea. Two estate rides are offered a day for $70, and riders are matched to horses based on riding ability. The trip also includes an optional barbecue lunch. Experienced riders can also opt for a mountain ride ($84) for a more-rugged two-hour tour.

★ **Fodor's Choice** Ocho Rios has excellent horseback riding, but the best of the operations is **Chukka Caribbean Adventures** (✉ *Llandovery, St. Ann's Bay* ☎ 876/972–2506 ⊕ *www. chukkacaribbean.com*). Horse trainers at Chukka Cove originally exercised polo ponies by taking them for therapeutic rides in the sea; soon there were requests from visitors to ride the horses in the water. The company now offers a 2½-hour beach ride that ends with a bareback swim on the horses in the sea from a private beach ($76). It's a highlight of many trips to Jamaica.

Hooves (✉ *Windsor Rd., St. Ann's Bay* ☎ 876/972–0905 ⊕ *www.hoovesjamaica.com*) has several guided tours, including a popular 2½-hour beach ride ($65) for riders age 12 and up. The trip begins with a visit to the Seville Great House Museum before making its way to the beach for a ride.

Prospect Plantation (✉ *Rte. A1, about 3 mi [5 km] east of Ocho Rios* ☎ 876/994–1058 ⊕ *www.prospectplantationtours. com*) offers a 3½ hour ride for ages eight and older. The price ($70) includes use of helmets; advance reservations are required. For the adventurous, Prospect Plantation also offers guided camel rides.

JEEP AND ATV TOURS

Since most visitors to the island don't rent cars, it's not surprising that guided jeep and all-terrain vehicle tours are a popular options for travelers who want to combine some sightseeing with a little adventure travel.

Three guided jeep tours are offered in the Ocho Rios area by **Chukka Caribbean Adventures** (⊠ *Llandovery, St. Ann's Bay* ☎ *876/972–2506* ⊕ *www.chukkacaribbean.com*), each in a zebra-striped safari vehicle. The five-hour Dunn's River Safari Jeep Tour ($79) takes you to Murphy Hill for a view of the city before continuing to a cattle farm, a small coffee plantation, and the famous falls. The 4½-hour Bob Marley Jeep Tour ($73) visits the reggae star's birthplace in the community of Nine Mile. The company also has guided ATV tours for those 16 and older. The two-hour trip ($76) takes you through the farm, past a historic sugar factory, and to a local school before heading to the beach for a dip.

Wilderness ATV Tours (⊠ *Reynolds Pier, Ocho Rios* ☎ *876/382–4029* ⊕ *www.wildernessatvtours.com*) offers two different tours. One takes you to Murphy Hill, the highest point in Ocho Rios, and the other heads to Dunn's River Falls. Tours range from $60 to $80 per person. All tours, offered daily, start at Reynolds Pier, so they're popular with cruise passengers. Transportation is included if you're staying in nearby hotels.

KAYAKING

Many beachside resorts have sea kayaks available for their guests. For something more challenging, paddle up the White River on a tour with **Chukka Caribbean Adventures** (⊠ *Llandovery, St. Ann's Bay* ☎ *876/972–2506* ⊕ *www. chukkacaribbean.com*). The 1¼-hour trip is $64 per person.

MARINE-LIFE PROGRAMS

🐾 **Dolphin Cove at Treasure Reef** (⊠ *North Coast Hwy., adjacent to Dunn's River Falls, Box 21, Ocho Rios* ☎ *876/974–5335* ⊕ *www.dolphincovejamaica.com*) offers dolphin swims as well as lower-priced dolphin encounters for ages eight and up; dolphin touch programs for ages six and over; or simple admission to the grounds, which also includes a short nature walk. Programs cost between $45 and $195, depending on your depth of involvement with the dolphins. Advance reservations are required for dolphin and shark programs.

MOUNTAIN BIKING

Blue Mountain Bicycle Tours (✉ *121 Main St., Ocho Rios* ☎ *876/974–7075* ⊕ *www.bmtoursja.com*) takes travelers on guided rides in the spectacular Blue Mountains. The all-day excursion starts high and glides downhill, so all levels of riders can enjoy the tour. The trip ends with a dip in a waterfall; the package price includes transportation from Ocho Rios or Kingston, brunch, lunch, and all equipment.

TENNIS

Many hotels have tennis facilities that are free for their guests, but a few will allow nonguests to play for a fee. Fees generally run $5 to $8 per hour for nonguests; lessons generally run $30 to $65 per hour.

Breezes Runaway Bay Resort and Golf Club (✉ *North Coast Hwy., Runaway Bay* ☎ *876/973–2436* ⊕ *www.superclubs. com*) has four tennis courts.

WHITE-WATER RAFTING

White-water rafting is increasingly popular in the Ocho Rios area. For the most options, however, check out the operators in Montego Bay. **Chukka Caribbean Adventures** (✉ *Llandovery, St. Ann's Bay* ☎ *876/972–2506* ⊕ *www. chukkacaribbean.com*) offers white-water fun on the White River—an easy trip that doesn't require any previous experience. Rafters travel in a convoy along the river and through some gentle rapids. The 3½-hour tour costs $63 for adults.

SHOPPING

Thanks to the large number of cruise-ship passengers, duty-free shopping is big business in Ocho Rios. Fine jewelry and watches, rum and other liquors, and cigars are popular purchases. Most of the duty-free shops are found in the malls.

AREAS AND MALLS

Ocho Rios has several malls that draw day-trippers from the cruise ships. The best are **Soni's Plaza** and the **Taj Mahal,** two malls on the main street with stores selling jewelry, cigars, and clothing. Another popular mall on the main street is **Ocean Village.** On the North Coast Highway east of Ochos Rios are **Pineapple Place** and **Coconut Grove.**

A fun mall that also serves as an entertainment center is
★ **Island Village** (⊠ *Turtle River Rd., near cruise port, Ocho Rios*). The open-air mall includes a Margaritaville restaurant, shops selling local handicrafts, duty-free goods, and designer clothing, and a small beach area with a variety of water sports.

MARKETS

Ocho Rios is home to several interesting crafts markets, including those at Dunn's River Falls and Fern Gully. The largest craft market is the **Ocho Rios Crafts Market** (⊠ *Main St., Ocho Rios* ☎ *876/795–2286*), with stalls selling everything from straw hats to wooden figurines to T-shirts. Vendors can be aggressive, and haggling is expected for all purchases. Your best chance of getting a good price is to come on a day when there's no cruise ship in port.

The **Pineapple Craft Market** (⊠ *North Coast Hwy., Ocho Rios* ☎ *No phone*) is a small, casual market east of Ocho Rios that's operated at the site for two decades. Look for everything from carved figurines to coffee-bean necklaces.

SPECIALTY ITEMS

HANDICRAFTS

★ **Harmony Hall** (⊠ *Rte. A1, Ocho Rios* ☎ *876/974–2870*), an eight-minute drive east of the main part of town, is a restored greathouse, where Annabella Proudlock sells her unique wooden boxes (their covers are decorated with reproductions of Jamaican paintings). Also on sale—and magnificently displayed—are larger reproductions of paintings, lithographs, and signed prints of Jamaican scenes and hand-carved wooden combs. In addition, Harmony Hall is well known for its shows by local artists.

Hemp Heaven (⊠ *Taj Mahal Centre, 4 Main St., Ocho Rios* ☎ *876/675–8969*) sells apparel and accessories made of hemp.

Starfish Essentials (⊠ *Island Village, Turtle River Rd., Ocho Rios* ☎ *876/901–7113*) sells Jamaican-made candles. Don't miss the Blue Mountain candle, with whole coffee beans in the wax.

Wassi Art Pottery Works (⊠ *Bougainvillea Dr., Great Pond, Ocho Rios* ☎ *876/974–5044*) produces one-of-a-kind works of art in terra-cotta. Visitors can stroll through the studio, watching local artists produce colorful pots in an array of shapes and sizes.

Locally made carvings at the Ocho Rios Crafts Market

MUSIC

Reggae Yard & Island Life (✉ *Island Village, Turtle River Rd., Ocho Rios* ☎ *876/675–8795*), is the largest music store in Ocho Rios. The offerings include an extensive selection of reggae CDs as well as other types of Caribbean music.

NIGHTLIFE AND THE ARTS

Since many of its visitors set sail at the end of the day, Ocho Rios has a quieter after-dark scene than Negril or Montego Bay. Nonetheless, evening events range from discos to romantic cruises.

ANNUAL EVENTS

In Ocho Rios, the biggest event of the year is the **Ocho Rios Jazz Festival** (☎ *876/927–3544* ⊕ *www.ochoriosjazz. com*) held each June. The event, which started in 1991 as a one-day concert, now spans eight days and draws many top names.

BARS AND CLUBS

For the most part, the liveliest late-night happenings in Ocho Rios are at the larger resort hotels. Some of the all-inclusive resorts offer a dinner and disco pass for $50 to $100; to buy a pass, call ahead to check for availability. Pick up a copy of the *Daily Gleaner,* the *Jamaica Observer,* or the *Star* (available at newsstands throughout the island) for listings on what musicians are playing and where.

Carnival only occurs once a year, but thanks to **Five Star Watersports** (✉ *121 Main St., Ocho Rios* ☎ *876/974–0164* ∰ *www.fivestarwatersports.com*), you can experience it every Thursday aboard a special evening cruise.

In Ocho Rios, the colorful **Margaritaville Caribbean Bar and Grill** (✉ *Island Village, Turtle River Rd., Ocho Rios* ☎ *876/675–8800*) boasts a fun-loving atmosphere any night of the year. It's popular with younger travelers, reflected in a calendar of weekly nightlife activities, which includes plenty of all-night parties.

At Shaw Park Beach Hotel, **Silks** (✉ *Cutlass Bay, Ocho Rios* ☎ *876/974–2552*) is a disco with a DJ that keeps the crowd on its toes.

Port Antonio

WORD OF MOUTH

"One thing about Portland, in my own experience. it's not a sit around the beach/pool place. . . . [W]e were always checking out this or that beach, water-falls, mountains, etc."

—liza

by Paris Permenter and John Bigley

Once the darling of the Hollywood set, this eastern get-away is Jamaica's most remote resort destination. In terms of sheer distance, the town isn't that far removed—60 mi (97 km) east of Ocho Rios and 133 mi (220 km) from Montego Bay—but Port Antonio is worlds apart.

The North Coast Highway construction project that has finally improved the road from Negril all the way to Ocho Rios has finally resulted in a smoother connection between Ocho Rios and Port Antonio. Although still a long drive, it's more direct than the overland road from Kingston through the Blue Mountains, a road that received substantial damage from Hurricane Gustave in 2008 (which was only a tropical storm when it slammed into the eastern end of Jamaica, killing 11 and causing widespread destruction). Flying from Montego Bay or Kingston is another option, though Port Antonio's small airport is served only by expensive charter flights.

The best way to reach Port Antonio is by yacht—just as swashbuckling actor Errol Flynn did in the 1940s. Even if you're not among the lucky few who arrive via the high seas, you're likely to spend a good deal of time on the water. After all, Port Antonio is home to Jamaica's best marina. Anglers are attracted by the region's excellent deep-sea fishing. Dolphin (the delectable fish, not the lovable mammal) is the likely catch here, along with tuna, kingfish, and wahoo. Each October, the weeklong Blue Marlin Tournament draws crowds from around the world.

Instead of fish, you'll find that pork, chicken, and goat take center stage at Boston Beach, east of Port Antonio. This small area was the birthplace of modern jerk, dating back to the 1930s when the first roadside (locally known as wayside) stands first began offering fiery jerk. Today about half a dozen jerk stands tempt diners with modestly priced meals. Jerk may have spread throughout the island, but many aficionados still return to Boston Beach for a taste of the "real thing."

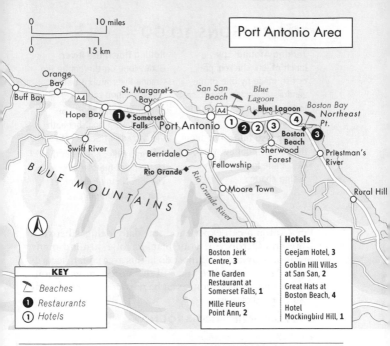

| 0 | 10 miles |
| 0 | 15 km |

Orange Bay

Buff Bay

A4

Hope Bay ● **1** ◆ Somerset Falls

St. Margaret's Bay

San San Beach

Blue Lagoon

A4 ● Blue Lagoon ◆

Boston Bay Northeast Pt.

Port Antonio ● **1** ● **2** ● **2** ● **3** ☂ ● **4**

Swift River

Berridale ○

Fellowship ○

Boston Beach

Sherwood Forest

● **3**

Priestman's River

Rio Grande ◆

Rio Grande River

Moore Town ○

Rural Hill

B L U E   M O U N T A I N S

KEY

〰 Beaches
● Restaurants
① Hotels

Restaurants	**Hotels**
Boston Jerk Centre, **3**	Geejam Hotel, **3**
The Garden Restaurant at Somerset Falls, **1**	Goblin Hill Villas at San San, **2**
	Great Hats at Boston Beach, **4**
Mille Fleurs Point Ann, **2**	Hotel Mockingbird Hill, **1**

ORIENTATION AND PLANNING

ORIENTATION

Since it's difficult to get to Port Antonio, most visitors come for a stay of a week or more. This gives them plenty of time to explore the town, its twin harbors, and the surrounding countryside. To the east of the city, the road winds beyond many beaches and bays that are waiting to be discovered. To the south, the terrain quickly turns rugged, approaching the John Crow Mountains and the Blue Mountains. This area is the home of the Windward Maroons, descendants of former slaves who sought freedom in these mountains centuries ago.

PLANNING

WHEN TO GO

Like the rest of Jamaica, Port Antonio has a high season ranging from mid-December through mid-April. The lowest prices coincide with the peak of hurricane season, September and October. As Jamaica's rainiest resort area,

TOP REASONS TO GO

Jerking Around: Enjoy a lunch of jerk chicken, pork, or fish made by one of the vendors at Boston Beach, said to be among the best jerk in Jamaica.

Telling Fish Tales: Talk about the one that got away as you cast a line for marlin on a fishing charter.

Rolling Down the River: Glide along on the gentle Rio Grande River atop a traditional bamboo raft.

Seeing the Back Side of Water: Take a boat beneath the cascade of Somerset Falls.

Taking a Hike: Follow in the footsteps of the Maroons as you visit Nanny Falls to get your blood pumping.

Port Antonio can experience near daily deluges between May and October; if your plans revolve around many outdoor activities (and most do in this area), plan accordingly. Also, access into some of the more remote regions surrounding Port Antonio can be restricted if heavy rains lead to road closures.

GETTING HERE AND AROUND

BY AIR

Limited domestic air service into the Port Antonio Aerodrome is available only via charter companies.

Airport Port Antonio Ken Jones Aerodrome (✉ *North Coast Hwy., Port Antonio* ☎ *876/923–0222*).

Air Travel Contacts City Air Charters (☎ *888/258–9247* ⊕ *www. cityaircharters.com*). **Jamaica Customized Vacations and Tours** (☎ *616/272–8257* ⊕ *www.jcvtt.com*).

BY CAR

Lighter traffic than the island's other resort areas makes driving in Port Antonio more reasonable—but incredibly rough road conditions mean a bouncy, detour-filled drive. If you rent a car, check on road conditions before heading anywhere off the beaten path. (A four-wheel-drive vehicle is recommended for many drives.)

Car-Rental Contacts Eastern Car Rentals (✉ *16 West St., Port Antonio* ☎ *876/993–2562*).

BY CRUISE SHIP

Port Antonio's Ken Wright Pier accommodates small and medium-size ships, primarily from November to March. Most arrivals are European lines.

BY TAXI

Taxi service is available in Port Antonio, but always hire a licensed taxi, indicated by the red PP license plate. The largest taxi operator is JUTA, and you can call these taxis. Taxi service in the area is expensive, and be sure to agree on a price before departure, as most taxis are not metered.

Taxi Contacts **JUTA** (☎ 876/993–2684).

RESTAURANTS

Dining options in Port Antonio range from rickety jerk stands to gourmet restaurants, with plenty of options in between. Seafood usually takes center stage, especially at upscale dining rooms where locally caught snapper and tuna are often on the menus. With Port Antonio experiencing a tourism lull, reservations usually aren't required except during peak winter months. The mood is casual at most lunch spots, but slacks or sundresses fit the bill for evening dress.

WHAT IT COSTS IN DOLLARS				
¢	$	$$	$$$	$$$$
RESTAURANTS				
under $8	$8–$12	$12–$20	$20–$30	Over $30
HOTELS*				
under $80	$80–$150	$150–$250	$250–$350	Over $350
HOTELS**				
under $125	$125–$250	$250–$350	$350–$450	Over $450

*EP, BP, CP; **AI, FAP, MAP; restaurant prices are per person for a main course at dinner and do not include the 15% V.A.T. and 10% service charge. Hotel prices are per night for a double room in high season, excluding 15% V.A.T. and 10% service charge.

HOTELS

If you've had your fill of the all-inclusive resorts in Montego Bay and Ocho Rios, then head to Port Antonio. Don't look for mixology classes or limbo dances, as the hotels here are extremely quiet. Popular with repeat customers, Port Antonio's little lodgings (many of them older and some looking a bit haggard) are also joined by some villas and even some camping options. Plans call for new, upscale hotels to join the offerings in Port Antonio, but they remain several years down the road; in the meantime, some longtime attractions have closed and are waiting for the "new" Port Antonio to emerge.

ESSENTIALS

BANKS AND CURRENCY EXCHANGE

Due to Port Antonio's relative isolation, you'll see prices marked in Jamaican dollars more often than U.S. dollars. Although you can still use U.S. currency here, your money will go further if you convert it to Jamaican dollars. Several local supermarkets contain exchange offices.

EMERGENCIES

Port Antonio has a small hospital if you have a health emergency as well as a handful of small pharmacies.

INTERNET

Internet access outside the hotels is fairly limited, especially as you travel beyond the boundaries of Port Antonio. Yachters will find high-speed access for $4 per hour at the Errol Flynn Marina. The Portland Parish Library is also a good option.

Due to Port Antonio's poor road conditions and lack of scheduled air service, if you purchase something bulky, the best way to send it home is to ship it from Kingston, Ocho Rios, or Montego Bay.

Internet Cafés Errol Flynn Marina (✉ *Ken Wright Dr., Port Antonio* ☎ *876/715–6044*). **Portland Parish Library** (✉ *Fort George St., Port Antonio* ☎ *876/993–2793*).

VISITOR INFORMATION

Port Antonio no longer has a Jamaica Tourist Board office. Along with hotel concierge staff, check with the Jamaica Tourist Board office in Montego Bay or Kingston before you head out to Port Antonio.

EXPLORING PORT ANTONIO

For most travelers, Port Antonio means an active vacation, one that involves hiking (from easy walks to multiday treks), swimming, surfing, and beachcombing. The town's few attractions are all outdoors: waterfalls, rivers, and swimming holes. With that in mind, planning a day's

Boston Beach, the birthplace of Jamaican jerk

activities can revolve around the weather, which can often be rainy. Usually morning hours are the sunniest, with afternoon heat bringing in tropical showers. During the rainy season that runs from May through October, expect longer and more frequent rainfall.

Exploring the region also means taking into account the distances between attractions. Although on the map many attractions may look easily accessible, it takes time and patience to navigate these roads. Try to group attractions and activities by region to minimize drive time.

WHAT TO SEE

Blue Lagoon. One of Port Antonio's best-known attractions is the Blue Lagoon, whose azure waters have to be seen to be believed. The colors of the spring-fed lagoon are a real contrast to the warmer waters of the ocean. Catch some rays on the floating docks, or relax on the small beach. Just how deep is the Blue Lagoon? You might hear it's bottomless, but the lagoon has been measured at a depth of 180 feet. At this writing the lagoon was closed, but was expected to reopen in 2010. Check with tourism officials for an update. ⊠ *9 mi (13 km) east of Port Antonio, 1 mi (1½ km) east of San San Beach.*

★ **Boston Beach.** A short drive east of Port Antonio is Boston Beach, a don't-miss destination for lovers of jerk pork. The recipe originated with the Arawak, the island's original inhabitants, but was perfected by the Maroons. Eating almost nothing but wild hog preserved over smoking coals enabled these former slaves to survive years of fierce guerrilla warfare with the English. Jerk resurfaced in the 1930s, and the spicy barbecue drew diners from around the island. Today a handful of small jerk stands, collectively known as the Boston Jerk Centre, offers fiery flavors cooled by some festival bread and a cold Red Stripe. ✉ *Rte. A4, east of Port Antonio, Port Antonio.*

DeMontevin Lodge. On Titchfield Hill, the DeMontevin Lodge is owned by the Mullings family. The late Gladys Mullings was Errol Flynn's cook, and you can still sample her recipes here. The lodge, and a number of structures on nearby Musgrave Street, is built in a traditional seaside style that's reminiscent of New England. ✉ *19 Fort George St., Port Antonio* ☎ *876/993–2604.*

NEED A BREAK? **Coronation Bakery** (✉ *18 West St., Port Antonio* ☎ *876/993–2710*) has served up freshly made baked goods for more than seven decades. Grab some hard-dough bread (originally brought to Jamaica by the Chinese), an unleavened bun called *bulla,* or even spicy patties.

Folly. A favorite photo stop in Port Antonio, Folly is little more than ruins these days. This structure, spanning 60 rooms in its heyday, was the home of a Tiffany heiress. The house didn't last long because seawater, rather than freshwater, was used in the cement. In July the grounds serve as the setting for the annual Portland Jerk Festival. ✉ *Folly Point, Port Antonio.*

Folly Lighthouse. Since 1888, this red-and-white-stripe masonry lighthouse has stood watch at the tip of Folly Point. Administered by the Jamaica National Heritage Trust, the lighthouse is an often-photographed site near Port Antonio's East Harbour. ✉ *Folly Point, Port Antonio.*

Rio Grande. Jamaica's river-rafting operations began here, on an 8-mi- (13-km-) long swift green waterway from Berrydale to Rafter's Rest. (Beyond that, the Rio Grande flows into the Caribbean at St. Margaret's Bay). The trip of about three hours is made on bamboo rafts pushed along by a guide who is likely to be quite a character. You can pack a picnic lunch to enjoy on the raft or on the riverbank; wherever you lunch, a Red Stripe vendor is likely

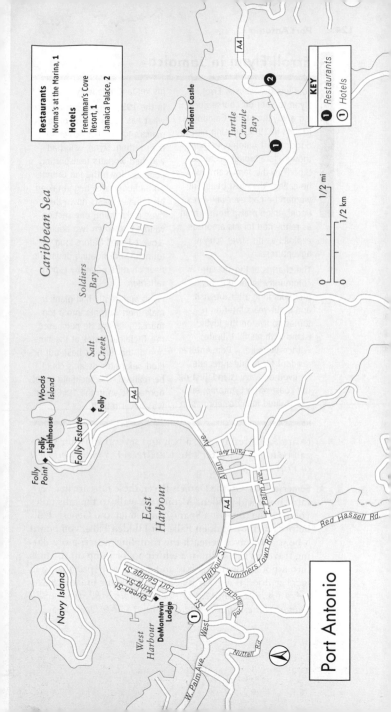

Port Antonio

Caribbean Sea

Navy Island

West Harbour

Folly Point

Folly Lighthouse

Woods Island

Folly Estate

Folly

Salt Creek

Soldiers Bay

Turtle Craule Bay

Trident Castle

East Harbour

W. Palm Ave.
Nuttall Rd.
West St.
Portland Rd.
Queen St.
King St.
Fort George St.
Harbour St.
Summers Town Rd.
Red Hassell Rd.
E. Palm Ave.
Allan Ave.
A4
A4

DeMontevin Lodge

Restaurants
Norma's at the Marina, 1

Hotels
Frenchman's Cove
Resort, 1
Jamaica Palace, 2

KEY
1 Restaurants
1 Hotels

1/2 mi
1/2 km
0

CLOSE UP

Erroll Flynn in Jamaica

Foul weather caused Errol Flynn to veer off course during a voyage to the Galápagos Islands in 1942, causing him to dock in Port Antonio. Perhaps, though, fate brought "Captain Blood" to the Jamaican town he called "the most beautiful woman he had ever laid eyes upon"—high praise from a man as renowned for his amorous exploits as his silver screen adventures.

The charms of the seaside community lingered in his thoughts long after the visit, and eight years later he returned to live on the idyllic island with his third bride, Patrice Wymore. A Port Antonio resident for nearly a decade, he lived on Navy Island, just off the coast of Port Antonio, and entertained many celebrities in his verdant hideaway.

In the 1950s, Flynn started what has become one of Jamaica's top tourist activities, river rafting. Flynn, who had watched workers transporting bananas down the Rio Grande on bamboo rafts, began taking his female guests down the river, nicknaming one section winding between two boulders "Lovers Lane." Before long, tourists were floating down the river on rafts poled by expert raftsmen.

Flynn apparently had plans to make Port Antonio into a top tourist getaway. He purchased the Titchfield Hotel, at the time one of the region's best, but he died before his dreams could be realized. The Titchfield Hotel burned down in the 1960s and was never rebuilt.

to appear. A restaurant, a bar, and several souvenir shops can be found at Rafter's Rest. ⊠ *Rte. A4, 5 mi (8 km) west of Port Antonio.*

★ **Somerset Falls.** On the Daniels River, these falls are in a veritable botanical garden. A concrete walk to the falls takes you past the ruins of a Spanish aqueduct and Genesis Falls before reaching Hidden Falls. At Hidden Falls, you board a boat and travel beneath the tumbling water; more daring travelers can swim in a whirlpool or jump off the falls into a pool of water. A bar and restaurant specializing in local seafood is a great place to catch your breath. ⊠ *Rte. A4, 13 mi (21 km) west of Port Antonio* ☎ *876/383–6970* ⊕ *www.somersetfallsjamaica.com* ⊠ *$12* ⊙ *Daily 9–5.*

BEST BETS FOR DINING

With the many restaurants to choose from, how will you decide where to eat? Fodor's writers and editors have selected their favorite restaurants in the Best Bets lists below. The Fodor's Choice properties represent the "best of the best." Find specific details about a restaurant in the full reviews.

Fodor's Choice
Boston Jerk Centre.

Best for Families: The Garden Restaurant at Somerset Falls.

Most Romantic: Mille Fleurs; Norma's at the Marina.

Best for Local Jamaican Cuisine: Boston Jerk Centre; The Garden Restaurant at Somerset Falls.

4

WHERE TO EAT

Attracting primarily European travelers, Port Antonio has slightly later dining hours than in the more Americanized resort areas of the North Coast. Dining is fairly casual, with long pants and sundresses fitting the bill for just about any establishment.

★ **Fodor's Choice** ✕ **Boston Jerk Centre.** *Jamaican.* Actually a col-
¢–$ lection of about half a dozen open-air stands, this super-casual eatery is a culinary capital in Jamaica thanks to its popular jerk pits. Stroll up to the open pits, fired by pimento logs and topped with a piece of corrugated roofing metal, locally known as zinc, and order meat by the quarter, half, or full pound; chicken, pork, goat, and fish are top options. Side dishes are few but generally include festival (a rolled bread similar to a Southern hush puppy) and rice and peas. ⊠ *Boston Beach on Rte. A4, Port Antonio, just east of Port Antonio* ☏ *No phone* ⊟ *No credit cards.*

$–$$ ✕ **The Garden Restaurant at Somerset Falls.** *Seafood.* Surrounded by tropical gardens and the flowing waters of the Daniel River, this restaurant offers lunch and dinner in a casual yet romantic setting. Seafood—including peppered shrimp, grilled lobster, and local catch such as snapper—are served daily. Some days bring Jamaican dishes such as jerk to the menu. ⊠ *Rte. A4, 13 mi (21 km) west of Port Antonio* ☏ *876/383–6970* ⊟ *MC, V.*

$–$$ ✕ **Mille Fleurs.** *Jamaican.* At this restaurant you can sit on a terrace surrounded by tropical vegetation and enjoy the sunset. The menu changes daily but always includes dishes prepared with local ingredients such as ackee-fruit soufflé

Barbecue, Jamaica-Style

Jamaica is well-known for its contributions to the world of music, but the island is also the birthplace of a cooking style known as jerk. Modern jerk originated in the 1930s along Boston Beach, east of Port Antonio. Here the first wayside stands sprang up on the side of the road, offering fiery jerk served in a casual atmosphere. Today jerk stands are everywhere on the island, but many aficionados still return to Boston Beach for the "real thing."

The historic origins of jerk are unknown (some say the Maroons brought the practice from Africa; others say the cooking style came to the island with the Caribs and the native Arawaks). The practice of cooking and preserving meat by smoking it was first recorded in 1698 by a French priest, who wrote of a jerk pit made with four forked sticks with crosspieces covered with a grill made of sticks. On the grill was placed a whole pig, stuffed with lime juice, salt, pimento, and spices that helped preserve the meat in the hot climate.

Today jerk is still cooked in a pit that contains a fire made from pimento wood. The meat, which is primarily pork but can also be chicken, goat, or fish, is marinated with jerk sauce. Every cook has his own favorite recipe, but most include allspice (pimento) berries, cloves, garlic, onion, ginger, cinnamon, thyme, and peppers. Commercial jerk sauces are also available. Once the jerk is cooked to perfection, it's served up with side dishes such as breadfruit, rice and peas, and a bread called festival.

or plantain fritters with black-bean dip. Chicken in June plum sauce is a favorite; for something more unique, try the jerk rabbit or the callaloo and goat cheese quiche. ⊠ *Hotel Mockingbird Hill, Point Ann, Box 254, Port Antonio* ☎ *876/993–7267* ⚠ *Reservations essential* ▭ *AE, MC, V.*

$–$$ ✕ **Norma's at the Marina.** *Jamaican.* Another showcase for the culinary talents of Jamaican celebrity chef Norma Shirley (her other establishments are in Kingston and Negril), this seaside restaurant serves gourmet dishes with a Jamaican twist. Start with an appetizer of smoked marlin or grilled deviled ocean crab back, then move on to entrées such as grilled shrimp in Jamaican herbs and mango salsa or pork riblets with local seasonings. ⊠ *Errol Flynn Marina, Ken Wright Dr., Port Antonio* ☎ *876/993–9510* ▭ *D, MC, V* ⊙ *Closed Mon.*

WHERE TO STAY

★ **Fodor's**Choice ⬚ **Frenchman's Cove Resort.** *Resort.* This resort
$ may be somewhat tired (a far cry from its heyday when Queen Elizabeth and her family stayed in Villa 18), but its location is pristine. Villas, definitely the best option in terms of surrounding beauty and space, are tucked back into the dense forest, and many are just steps from one of Port Antonio's best beaches. The standard rooms, many of them fairly large, are in the main building known as the greathouse. **Pros:** excellent beach; lots of privacy; large accommodations. **Cons:** somewhat dated decor; long walk to public areas and beach; no a/c in some rooms. ⊠ *Rte. A4, 5 mi (8 km) east of Port Antonio* ☎ *876/993–7270* ⊕ *www. frenchmans-cove-resort.com* ⇆ *9 rooms, 2 suites, 18 villas* ⚠ *In-room: no phone (some), a/c (some), safe, kitchen (some), refrigerator (some), Internet (some). In-hotel: restaurant, bar, beachfront, diving, water sports, bicycles, laundry service, Internet terminal* ▭ *MC, V* ⊙ *CP.*

★ **Fodor's**Choice ⬚ **Geejam.** *Vacation Rental.* Ten minutes east
$$$$ of Port Antonio, this stylish rockers' getaway (Gwen Stefani recorded an album here, and it's a favorite of Grace Jones) is part of the Island Outpost collection. Originally a music producer's hideaway, Geejam features a state-of-the-art recording studio that's available for the use of guests (assuming you're cutting your next album while on vacation here). Cell phones are provided to each guest upon arrival, and visitors have their pick of over 50 international newspapers for morning reading in their room, notable for its modern mix of high-tech and island sim-

BEST BETS FOR LODGING

Fodor's offers a selective listing of quality lodging experiences, from the island's best boutique hotel to its most luxurious beach resort. Here, we've compiled our top recommendations based on the different types of lodging found on the island. The very best properties—in other words, those that provide a particularly remarkable experience—are designated in the listings with the Fodor's Choice logo.

★ **Fodor's** Choice

Geejam; Hotel Mocking Bird Hill; Frenchman's Cove Resort.

Best Budget Stay: Great Huts at Boston Beach; Frenchman's Cove Resort.

Best Boutique Hotel: Geejam; Goblin Hill Villas at San San.

Best for Honeymooners: Geejam; Frenchman's Cove Resort.

Best for Families: Hotel Mocking Bird Hill; Frenchman's Cove Resort.

plicity. You can also rent Sanwood villa, on the property (*see* ⇨ *Sanwood in Private Villas, below*). **Pros:** with a four-night stay, rates include the transfer from Kingston; complimentary transportation to area beaches; personalized service. **Cons:** remote location; limited on-site amenities; may be too quiet for some guests. ⊠ *North Coast Hwy., San San* ☎ *876/993–7000* ⊕ *www.geejamhotel.com* ➪ *1 suite, 3 cabins* ⚹ *In-room: refrigerator, Wi-Fi. In-hotel: restaurant, room service, bar, gym, spa, Wi-Fi hotspot* ⊟ *AE, D, DC, MC, V* ⧉ *BP.*

$-$$ 🏠 **Goblin Hill Villas at San San.** *Resort.* This lush, 12-acre estate atop a hill overlooking San San Bay is best suited for travelers looking for a home-away-from-home atmosphere, not a bustling resort. Each attractively appointed villa comes with its own dramatic view, plus a staff member to do the grocery shopping, cleaning, and cooking for you. Villas come equipped with cable TV, ceiling fans (with air-conditioning in the bedrooms only), and tropical furnishings; it's sometimes possible to rent a single bedroom in one of the two-bedroom villas for a lower per-night cost. The beach is a 10-minute walk away. Excellent car-rental packages are available. **Pros:** good for guests who would like a villa experience but with the facilities of a hotel; nice bay views from villa terraces and balconies; spacious accommodations. **Cons:** long walk to beach; shared lawn and public areas with other villas at complex; some rooms in villas have no a/c. ⊠ *3 mi (5 km) east of Port Antonio on A4, San San* ☎ *876/925–8108* ⊕ *www.goblinhill.com* ⤳ *28 villas* ⚐ *In-room: no phone, kitchen, refrigerator. In-hotel: bar, tennis courts, pool* ⊟ *AE, D, MC, V* ⏻ *EP.*

¢–$ ⊠ **Great Huts at Boston Beach.** *Vacation Rental.* Port Antonio's most unique accommodation is also its most basic, aimed solely at travelers who don't mind an experience that is, as Jamaicans would say, "rootsy." Great Huts, just minutes from the jerk stands of Boston Beach, is styled like an African village and celebrates African art and culture. Accommodations range from simple huts to two-story tree houses; there are even some permanent tents planted directly on the sand for those on very tight budgets. The cheapest huts have shared baths, and these do not have access to hot water. None is air-conditioned, although all come with portable fans. The dedicated staff here can point you to out-of-the-way activities. **Pros:** good value; unique accommodations; friendly staff. **Cons:** sand floors in some rooms attract insects; no a/c due to open-air layout; some rooms are hot. ⊠ *Rte. A4, 15 mi (24 km) east of Port Antonio, Boston Beach* ☎ *876/993–8888* ⊕ *www. greathuts.com* ⤳ *2 tree houses, 7 huts, 3 tents* ⚐ *In-room: no phone, no a/c, no TV. In-hotel: restaurant, bar, Internet terminal, Wi-Fi hotspot* ⊟ *MC, V* ⏻ *BP.*

★ Fodor'sChoice ⊠ **Hotel Mocking Bird Hill.** *Hotel.* With only 10
$$–$$$ rooms, some overlooking the sea and all with views of lush hillsides, Mocking Bird Hill is much more like a cozy bed-and-breakfast than a hotel. Owners Barbara Walker and Shireen Aga run an environmentally sensitive operation, with bamboo- instead of hardwood furniture, solar-heated water, meals made with local produce in the Mille Fleurs dining terrace, locally produced toiletries and stationery sets, and 7 naturally landscaped acres. There's a free shuttle to Frenchman's Cove beach, about a five-minute drive away. Wedding packages are available, as is a meal plan offering breakfast and dinner for an additional $75 per night per person. **Pros:** numerous ecotourism options; environmentally conscious; excellent dining. **Cons:** limited on-site dining; no a/c; somewhat remote location. ⊠ *North Coast Hwy., Point Ann, Box 254, Port Antonio* ☎ *876/993–7267* ⊕ *www.hotelmockingbirdhill.com* ⤳ *10 rooms* ⚐ *In-room: no phone, no a/c, safe, no TV. In-hotel: restaurant, bar, pool, laundry service, internet terminal, Wi-Fi hotspot* ⊟ *AE, MC, V* ⏻ *EP.*

$$–$$$ ⊠ **Jamaica Palace.** *Hotel.* The Jamaica Palace might be distinctive for its Jamaica-shaped swimming pool and sur-

Hotel Mocking Bird Hill

GeeJam

rounding black-and-white pool terrace—but that's just the beginning of the unusual aspects of this Port Antonio hotel. The white building, marked with stately columns indoors and out, is designed to resemble a 17th-century Italian palace. Deemed "the art gallery hotel," the facility displays 2,000 pieces of art from paintings to sculptures, some by the hotel's owner. Inside, guest rooms are surprisingly stark, most having beds with curving footboards, flowery spreads, and little other decoration. **Pros:** uniquely decorated public areas; large poolside area with plenty of seating; good on-site dining options. **Cons:** no beach; basic guest rooms; somewhat remote location. ✉ *5 mi (8 km) east of Port Antonio on A4, Port Antonio* ☎ *876/993–7720* ⊕ *www. jamaica-palacehotel.com* ⇆ *34 rooms, 46 suites* ⚭ *In-room: safe, Internet. In-hotel: 2 restaurants, room service, bars, pool, laundry service, Internet terminal* ⊟ *MC, V* ⏀ *EP.*

PRIVATE VILLAS

$$$$ ⛫ **Belmont.** *Vacation Rental.* This luxury villa, surrounded by an acre of gardens, adjoins San San Beach. The air-conditioned master bedroom enjoys views of the beach and San San Bay as well as Pelleu Island; two other air-conditioned bedrooms feature twin beds and walk-in closets. The villa, with its airy feel and open floor plan, has a large living area with a raised wooden ceiling. For many guests, the focal point of the villa is the poolside gazebo. **Pros:** terrific views; beautiful landscaping; sizeable rooms. **Cons:** shared beach; small pool; need a car to get around. ✉ *Alligator Head, 5 mi (8 km) east of Port Antonio, San San* ☎ *876/969–8938* ⊕ *www.belmontvilla.com* ⇆ *3 bedrooms, 4 bathrooms* ⚭ *In-villa: dishwasher, Internet, daily maid service, cook, on-site security, pool, water toys, laundry facilities* ⊟ *No credit cards* ⏀ *EP.*

$$$$ ⛫ **Sanwood.** *Vacation Rental.* The original home around which Geejam hotel was later built, this villa was designed in the 1960s by British architect Anthony Wade. Decorated in a contemporary nautical theme, this three-bedroom home showcases a private pop art collection and an audio/visual library as well as plenty of relaxing options including a private pool deck and upstairs verandahs. *See* ⇨ *Geejam Hotel, above, for more information.* **Pros:** use of Geejam facilities including 24-hour room service; bedrooms can be rented separately for smaller groups; stylish amenities including an Apple TV home theater and 500-thread count linens. **Cons:** adjacent Geejam hotel means some additional traffic on property; remote location; may be too quiet for

some. ✉ *North Coast Hwy., San San* ☎ *876/993–7000*
⊕*www.geejamhotel.com* ➳*3 bedrooms, 3½ bathrooms*
⚹ *In-villa: DVD, daily maid service, on-site security, pool,*
laundry facilities, Internet terminal, Wi-Fi ⊟ *AE, D, DC,*
MC, V ⦿*BP.*

$$–$$$ ⊡**Tranquility Villa.** *Vacation Rental.* Furnishings from
Jamaica and Bali give this hillside villa a tropical feel.
From a poolside hammock you can enjoy a view of Port
Antonio's harbor; balconies off the air-conditioned bedrooms look across to the Blue Mountains. This petite villa
has many high-tech offerings, including unlimited overseas
calling with Internet phone service. **Pros:** lovely views;
nice pool area; nice amenities. **Cons:** not on beach; small
rooms; rather remote location. ✉*Richmond Hill, Port
Antonio* ☎ *786/252–7536*⊕ *www.tranquility-villa.com* ➳*2
bedrooms, 1 bathroom* ⚹ *In-villa: dishwasher, DVD, Internet, Wi-Fi, daily maid service, cook, on-site security, pool,
water toys, laundry facilities* ⊟ *No credit cards* ⦿*EP.*

BEACHES

Boston Beach. Considered the birthplace of Jamaica's famous
jerk-style cooking, this beach is a popular lunchtime spot
for locals. You can get peppery jerk pork at any of the
shacks spewing scented smoke—just follow your nose.
While you're there, you can also enjoy the small beach for
an after-lunch dip, although these waters are occasionally
rough and much more popular for surfing. ✉*11 mi (18 km)
east of Port Antonio.*

Frenchman's Cove. This picturesque, somewhat secluded
beach is petite perfection. Protected by two outcroppings
that form the cove, the inlet's calm waters are a favorite
with families. A small stream trickles into the cove. You
can find a bar and restaurant serving fried chicken right
on the beach. If this stretch of sand looks a little familiar,
you just might have seen it in the movies; it has starred
in *Club Paradise, Treasure Island* (the Charlton Heston
version), and *The Mighty Quinn.* If you're not a guest of
Frenchman's Cove Resort, admission is $4.50. ✉*Rte. A4,
5 mi (8 km) east of Port Antonio.*

San San Beach. This small beach has beautiful blue water.
Just offshore, Monkey Island is a good place to snorkel
(or even surf) and well worth the $5 admission fee. ✉*5 mi
(8 km) east of Port Antonio, San San.*

SPORTS AND THE OUTDOORS

BIRD-WATCHING

The parish of Portland is, along with the Blue Mountains and Cockpit Country, one of the top birding destinations in Jamaica. Species including the Jamaican tody, black-billed streamtail, ringtail pigeon, and many others can be spotted in this sparsely developed area.

Jamaica Explorations (☎ 876/993–7267 ⊕ www.jamaicaexplorations.com) offers several guided tours for birders including a special hummingbird tour.

BOATING

With its long history of attracting an exclusive clientele, it's not surprising that Port Antonio is the island's top yacht port. The **Errol Flynn Marina** (✉ Ken Wright Dr., Port Antonio ☎ 876/715–6044 ⊕ www.errolflynnmarina.com) is an official national port of entry, with 24-hour customs and immigrations services. The 32-berth marina, reached via a deepwater channel, includes 24-hour security, an Internet center, a swimming pool, and a 100-ton boat lift—the only one in the Western Caribbean.

DIVING AND SNORKELING

Wall diving is especially popular in the Port Antonio area. For intermediate and advanced divers, a top spot is **Trident Wall,** lined with stunning black coral. Other top spots include **Alligator Hill,** a moderate to difficult dive known for its tubes and sponges. A beginner site, **Alligator West** is prized for its calm waters.

Lady G'Diver (✉ Errol Flynn Marina, Ken Wright Dr., Port Antonio ☎ 876/995–0246 ⊕ www.ladygdiver.com) is the top dive operator in Port Antonio. Trips to interesting dive sites are offered most days except Tuesday, departing about 11 every morning for a two-tank dive.

FISHING

Port Antonio makes deep-sea-fishing headlines with its annual Blue Marlin Tournament. Licenses aren't required, and you can arrange to charter a boat at your hotel. A chartered boat (with captain, crew, and equipment) costs about $500 to $900 for a half-day or $900 to $1,500 for a full-day excursion, depending on the size of the boat.

Jamaica Deep Sea Adventures (✉ Errol Flynn Marina, Ken Wright Dr., Port Antonio ☎ 876/909–9552) offers marlin, yellowfin tuna, and wahoo fishing in a 40-foot boat with an air-conditioned cabin.

GUIDED TOURS

Along with hiking, birding, and river-rafting tours, guided sightseeing tours are a good way to get the lay of the land in Port Antonio, especially for first-time visitors. Joanna Hart of **Port Antonio Tours** (☎876/831–8434 or 876/859–3758 ⊕ www.portantoniotours.netfirms.com) leads a wide variety of guided tours. Prices range from $30 to $75 per person.

HIKING

Hiking in Port Antonio ranges from very easy to extremely difficult, with everything from hour-long strolls along riverbanks to multiday sojourns through thick rain forests. A short hike to Scatter Falls followed by a rafting trip down the Rio Grande is a good choice for those looking for a short hike; the two- to three-hour hike to Nanny Falls near Moore Town is another good option. One of the most difficult hikes is the two-day trip (and three days are generally recommended) to Nanny Town, where Nanny, Jamaica's only female national hero, led the Maroons against the British.

Jamaica Explorations (☎876/993–7267 ⊕ www.jamaicaexplorations.com) offers guided tours of varying lengths including a Reich Falls excursion and a Blue Mountain hike.

Valley Hikes (⊠ Harbour St., Port Antonio ☎876/993–3881) offers 15 different guided hikes ranging from one to four hours as well as longer hikes to Moore Town and Nanny Falls.

RAFTING

★ Fodor's Choice A relaxing trip aboard a bamboo raft poled along by a local boatman is a familiar symbol of Jamaica and represents the island's first tourist activity other than its beaches. Bamboo rafting in Jamaica originated on the **Rio Grande,** a river in the Port Antonio area. Jamaicans had long used the bamboo rafts to transport bananas downriver; decades ago actor and Port Antonio resident Errol Flynn saw the rafts and thought they'd make a good tourist attraction. Today the slow rides (taking about 2½ hours on a typical day, less time when the river's up) are a favorite with romantic travelers and anyone looking to get off the beach for a few hours. **Rio Grande Tours** (⊠ St. Margaret's Bay ☎876/993–5778 ⊕ www.jamaicatoursltd.com) guides raft trips down the Rio Grande; the cost is $75 per raft. (On top of the fee, raftsmen expect a tip of about $5 to $10.) The last raft trips

Rafting on Rio Grande, Port Antonio

depart about 3 PM, a good time to observe locals fishing and washing clothes along the riverbanks.

SHOPPING

Shopping is not a major attraction in Port Antonio, compared to the duty-free shopping of Ocho Rios and Montego Bay. With the recent addition of the marina and cruise-ship port, there is some limited shopping to be had, but it still takes a backseat to other activities.

MARKETS

Musgrave Market (✉ West St., Port Antonio ☎ 876/993–2367) is a traditional market that, unlike those in Ocho Rios and Montego Bay, is primarily aimed at locals. Although you can find some crafts here, look for luscious fruits and vegetables, household goods, and clothing in these stalls.

SPECIALTY ITEMS

HANDICRAFTS

Carricou Gallery (✉ Hotel Mocking Bird Hill, off Rte. A4, 6 mi [9½ km] east of Port Antonio, Port Antonio ☎ 876/993–7267) showcases local artists and also offers art classes.

As its name suggests, **Things Jamaican** (✉ Errol Flynn Marina, Ken Wright Dr., Port Antonio ☎ 876/715–5247) sells an assortment of local items: books, music, crafts, spices, sauces, and more.

NIGHTLIFE AND THE ARTS

ANNUAL EVENTS

For four decades, the **Port Antonio International Marlin Tournament** (✉ *Errol Flynn Marina, Ken Wright Dr., Port Antonio* ☎ *876/927–0145* ⊕ *www.errolflynnmarina.com*) has attracted anglers competing to see who can catch the biggest blue marlin in late September and early October. In addition to the fishing competition, a canoe race and lots of parties and receptions keep the action going for non-anglers.

The July **Portland Jerk Festival** (✉ *Village of St. George shopping center, Ft. George St., Port Antonio* ☎ *876/715–6553* ⊕ *www.portlandjerkfestival.com*) features the food for which Port Antonio is known: fiery jerk barbecue. The all-day festival includes jerk cook-offs (with plenty of opportunities for taste testing), live music, dominoes, and more.

BARS AND CLUBS

In Port Antonio, the hottest nightlife in town is not at the hotels, but at local joints such as the **Roof Club** (✉ *11 West St., Port Antonio* ☎ *876/715–5281*). Open Thursday to Sunday night, the somewhat rowdy second-floor club plays dance-hall hits.

Kingston and the Blue Mountains

WORD OF MOUTH

"Are there neighborhoods [in Kingston] I would avoid? Absolutely. . . . But Jamaica as a whole is no less safe a destination than any other Caribbean Island or European country, as long as you use common sense."

—Weadles

By Paris
Permenter
and John
Bigley

The "heart of the Caribbean" is what they call Jamaica, so the beating heart of Jamaica surely must be Kingston. It's the epicenter of the political and cultural life of the country as well as the home of nearly one million inhabitants, making it by far the largest city on the island.

Kingston is a big city with big-city problems, so the reactions of some visitors to the capital are not always favorable. Yet, islanders themselves are always conscious of Kingston's influence on their lives. From the slums of Trenchtown, immortalized in Bob Marley's music, to the glittering high-rise towers in New Kingston, the city is an explosion of color and sound. Despite its problems, the capital is a source of pride for all Jamaicans.

For visitors, Kingston can be intimidating. Exploring some of its dicier neighborhoods without a licensed guide is foolhardy at best. Yet, with careful planning and the normal precautions, Kingston can reward the visitor with a greater appreciation for Jamaica's unique culture. True devotees of things Jamaican can ill afford to skip this metropolis entirely.

On a clear day, when beneficial breezes have shoved some of Kingston's motor-exhaust haze out to sea, you can admire the nearby Blue Mountains from many vantage points around the city. Following your gaze across the Kingston plain into the highlands is a study in contrasts as the gritty cityscape is gradually replaced by tropical splendor.

Leaving the city far below, the highway begins to twist and turn, narrowing to an unevenly paved road as it passes panoramas of lush vegetation and soaring peaks. Rounding hairpin turns, you encounter sudden views of tiny hamlets clinging to the hillsides, their inhabitants going about their daily chores in what seems to be luxuriously unhurried fashion. The view from the top is spectacular, with Kingston's sprawl spread out before you, bounded by the harbor, the ancient stones of Port Royal and, further out, the blue Caribbean Sea glittering in the sun. As the breeze shifts, a faint hum of the frenetic human activity below may reach your ears, but no louder than the buzz of a hummingbird's wing.

ORIENTATION AND PLANNING

ORIENTATION

Kingston sprawls in every direction. Most travelers head to New Kingston, the site of many upscale hotels and several historic sites. New Kingston is bordered by Old Hope Road on the east and Half Way Tree Road (which becomes Constant Spring Road) on the west. The area is sliced by Hope Road, a major thoroughfare that connects this region with the University of the West Indies, about 15 minutes east of New Kingston.

North of New Kingston, the city gives way to steep hills and magnificent homes. East of here, the views are even grander as the road winds into the Blue Mountains. Hope Road, just after the University of the West Indies, becomes Gordon Town Road, and starts twisting up through the mountains—it's a route that leaves no room for error.

Approaching the city from the west you'll pass some of the city's worst slums in the neighborhoods of Six Miles and Riverton City. Farther south, Spanish Town Road skirts through a high-crime district that many Kingstonians avoid. In the heart of the business district, along the water, the pace is more relaxed, with lovely parks along Ocean Boulevard. From the waterfront you can look across Kingston Harbour to the Palisadoes Peninsula. This narrow strip is where you can find Norman Manley International Airport and, farther west, Port Royal, the island's former capital, which was destroyed by an earthquake.

PLANNING

WHEN TO GO

As a business destination, the demand for rooms at New Kingston hotels peak Sunday to Thursday night. During Carnival celebrations, hotels are filled with former residents who return to the island to party. One time to avoid Kingston is the period immediately before and after a national election, when security becomes more of a concern.

In the Blue Mountains, demand is fairly steady through the year, although the rainy months of May to October see a diminished number of visitors.

5

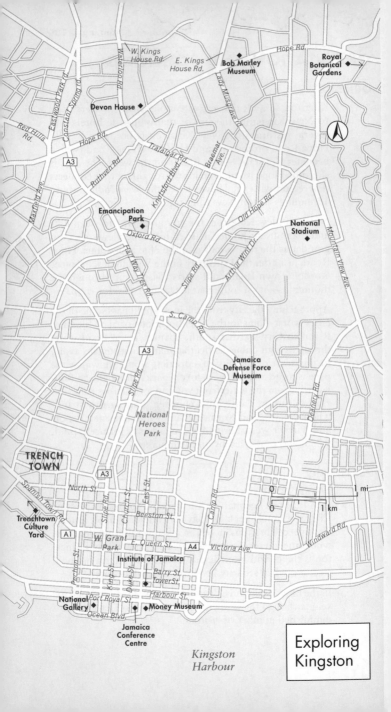

Exploring
Kingston

TOP REASONS TO GO

Get Your Heart Pumping:
Race down the Blue Mountains on a mountain bike through Holywell National Park with Blue Mountain Bicycle Tours.

Dine in Style: Enjoy Sunday brunch at Strawberry Hill with a view of Kingston in the distance. Just be sure to make reservations.

Play Pirates of the Caribbean: Explore Port Royal's pirate past at Fort Charles and check out the Maritime Museum there.

Jamaica Heritage: Explore Jamaican Art at the National Gallery, where the artists are not household names.

A Reggae Pilgrimage: Remember the legacy of the reggae legend at the Bob Marley Museum, which is housed in the singer's one-time recording studio.

5

GETTING HERE AND AROUND

BY AIR

Jamaica's second-busiest airport is Kingston's Norman Manley International Airport, about 20 minutes from the city on the Palisadoes Peninsula. From the airport, the best way into the city is by taxi; a few hotels provide hotel transfers, although most do not. The Jamaica Union of Travellers Association (JUTA) is the authorized taxi company at the Norman Manley International Airport; you'll find its desk just outside the Customs Hall in the Ground Transportation Hall.

Jamaica is well served by major airlines. From the United States, Air Jamaica, American, Continental, Northwest, Spirit, and US Airways offer nonstop and connecting service. Air Canada offers service from major airports in Canada. Air Jamaica, Virgin Atlantic and British Airways offer service from the United Kingdom. Copa has flights between Miami and Kingston. Cayman Airways connects Jamaica to Grand Cayman and Cayman Brac.

Domestic flights on TimAir are available from Kingston's Tinson Pen Aerodome to Montego Bay, Negril, Runaway Bay, Ocho Rios, and, on a limited basis, Port Antonio. Except for Skylan Airways' flights to Montego Bay, most flights are operated on a charter basis.

Contacts Norman Manley International Airport (✉ *Palisadoes Peninsula, Kingston* ☎ *876/924–8452* ⊕ *www.nmia.aero*). **Skylan Airways** (☎ *876/932–7102* ⊕ *skylanja.com*). **TimAir** (☎ *876/952–2516* ⊕ *www.timair.com*). **Tinson Pen Aerodrome** (✉ *Marcus Garvey Dr., Kingston* ☎ *876/923–3621*).

BY BUS

One option for budget-minded travelers going from Kingston to either Montego Bay ($23) or Ocho Rios ($15) is the **Knutsford Express** (☎ *876/971–1822* ⊕ *www.knutsfordexpress.com*), an air-conditioned bus with scheduled service. The bus runs at scheduled times three times daily on weekdays, Twice Daily On Weekends.

BY CAR

Renting A Car In Kingston Is Not Recommended Because Of The City's High Crime Rate And Its Tremendous Traffic Problem. It's All Too Easy To Find Yourself In One Of The Neighborhoods That Even Taxi Drivers Refuse To Visit. The Best Option For Getting Around Town Is To Hire A Licensed Taxi Driver.

BY TAXI

Some, But Not All, Of Jamaica's Taxis Are Metered. If You Accept A Driver's Offer To Serve As A Tour Guide, Be Sure To Agree On A Price Before The Vehicle Is Put Into Gear. (Note That A One-Day Tour Should Run About $150 To $180, depending on distance traveled.)

All licensed taxis display red Public Passenger license plates. In Kingston, it's preferable to have a hotel call for a taxi rather than hailing one on the street. Rates are per car, not per passenger, and a 25% surcharge is added to the metered rate between midnight and 5 AM. Licensed minivans are also available and also bear the red PP plates. The Jamaica Union for Travellers Association (JUTA) is licensed by the Jamaica Tourist Board.

Contacts JUTA (☎ *876/927–4534* ⊕ *www.jutakingston.com*).

RESTAURANTS

As home to foreign embassies and consulates, as well as many corporate headquarters, it's no surprise that Kingston offers a wide array of international cuisines, especially in the New Kingston area. Because some travelers are reluctant to venture out at night, hotel dining is often very good, although the city does have excellent independent restaurants, often with their own security. Dress is slightly more

formal than at North Coast restaurants, and reservations
for the more elegant eateries are a good idea.

HOTELS

Although it sees relatively few vacationers, Kingston is a
frequent destination for corporate travelers. The city boasts
some of the island's finest business hotels, most of these
in the New Kingston neighborhood. The hotels, primarily
high-rise towers, offer exactly what on-the-go executives
expect, from business centers to meeting rooms to concierge
services. Skirting the city are the Blue Mountains, a completely different world from the urban frenzy of the capital
city. Here you'll find mostly small, exclusive properties.

WHAT IT COSTS IN DOLLARS				
¢	$	$$	$$$	$$$$
RESTAURANTS				
under $8	$8–$12	$12–$20	$20–$30	Over $30
HOTELS*				
under $80	$80–$150	$150–$250	$250–$350	Over $350
HOTELS**				
under $125	$125–$250	$250–$350	$350–$450	Over $450

*EP, BP, CP; **AI, FAP, MAP; restaurant prices are per person for a main course at dinner
and do not include the 15% V.A.T. and 10% service charge. Hotel prices are per night
for a double room in high season, excluding 15% V.A.T. and 10% service charge.

ESSENTIALS

BANKS AND CURRENCY EXCHANGE

Currency exchange is available at Norman Manley International Airport, in larger hotels, and in local banks. However,
few Americans bother to exchange money, since American
dollars are widely accepted. Major credit cards are widely
accepted, although cash is required at gas stations, in supermarkets, and in many small stores.

EMERGENCIES

The largest hospital in Jamaica is the University Hospital
of the West Indies. There are numerous pharmacies in New
Kingston if you need to have a prescription filled.

INTERNET

Internet service is becoming far more widespread, and most hotels offer at least limited service, either at public terminals or Wi-Fi. Most Internet cafés charge between $5 and $7.50 per hour.

Internet Cafés **Cybiz Internet Cafe** (⊠ *32 King's Plaza, Kingston* ☎ *876/906–4749*). **Kingston Bookshop** (⊠ *13 Constant Spring Rd., Kingston* ☎ *876/960–5376*). **Liguanea Cybercentre** (⊠ *89½ Half Way Tree Rd., Kingston* ☎ *876/968–0323*). **Logic Internet Café** (⊠ *32 Hagley Park Rd., Kingston* ☎ *876/920–3791*).

VISITOR INFORMATION

The Jamaica Tourist Board maintains two offices in Kingston, one in New Kingston, the other in Manley International Airport. Both are good sources for information on Kingston and the Blue Mountains. They have maps and brochures, and can give recommendations for touring in the area.

Contacts **Jamaica Tourist Board** (⊠ *64 Knutsford Blvd., Kingston* ☎ *876/929–9200* ⊕ *www.visitjamaica.com*).

EXPLORING KINGSTON

Few travelers—particularly Americans—take the time to visit Kingston, although organized day trips make the city accessible from Ocho Rios and Montego Bay. That's understandable, as Kingston is a tough city to love. It's big and, all too often, bad, with gang-controlled neighborhoods that are known to erupt into violence, especially near election time.

However, if you've seen other parts of the island and yearn to know more about the heart and soul of Jamaica, Kingston is worth a visit. This government and business center is also a cultural capital, home to numerous dance troupes, theaters, and museums. It's also home to the University of the West Indies, one of the Caribbean's largest universities. In many ways, Kingston reflects the true Jamaica—a wonderful cultural mix—more than the sunny havens of the North Coast. As one Jamaican put it, "You don't really know Jamaica until you know Kingston."

North of New Kingston, the city gives way to steep hills and magnificent homes. East of here, the views are even grander as the road winds into the Blue Mountains, one of the island's least developed yet most beautiful regions.

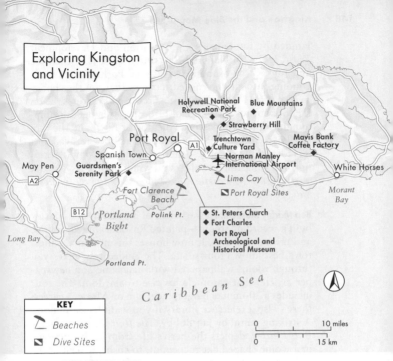

Exploring Kingston
and Vicinity

Holywell National
Recreation Park
Blue Mountains
Strawberry Hill
Port Royal
Mavis Bank
Coffee Factory
Spanish Town
Trenchtown
Culture Yard
Norman Manley
International Airport
White Horses
May Pen
Guardsmen's
Serenity Park
Lime Cay
Morant
Bay
Fort Clarence
Beach
Port Royal Sites
Portland
Bight
Polink Pt.
◆ St. Peters Church
◆ Fort Charles
◆ Port Royal
  Archeological and
  Historical Museum
Long Bay

Portland Pt.

Caribbean Sea

KEY

Beaches

Dive Sites

0   10 miles

0   15 km

WHAT TO SEE

★ **Blue Mountains.** Best known as the source of Blue Mountain
coffee, these mountains rising out of the lush jungle north
of Kingston are a favorite destination with adventure travelers, as well as hikers, birders, and anyone looking to see
what lies beyond the beach. You can find guided tours to
the mountains from the Ocho Rios and Port Antonio areas,
as well as from Kingston. Unless you're traveling with a
local, don't try to go on your own; the roads wind and
dip without warning, and hand-lettered signs blow away,
leaving you without a clue as to which way to go. It's best
to hire a taxi (look for red PPV license plates to identify a
licensed cab) or book a guided tour.

The site of Jamaica's government-owned coffee plant, the
small town of Mavis Bank is northeast of Kingston on the
main road to Blue Mountain Peak. An hour-long guided
tour of **Mavis Bank Coffee Factory** takes you through the
processing of coffee, from planting to distribution. Inquire
about tours when you arrive at the main office. ⊠ *Gordon
Town Rd., Mavis Bank* ☎ *876/977–8528* ⊕ *jablumonline.
com* ☞ *$8* ☉ *Weekdays 9–2.*

Funded by the Jamaica Conservation and Development Trust, **Holywell National Recreation Park** is in the Blue and John Crow Mountains National Park. Nature trails winding through the rugged terrain offer you the chance to spot some of the island's most reclusive creatures. Be on the lookout for the national bird, the streamer-tail hummingbird (known locally as the doctor bird) and the rare swallowtail butterfly. Rustic camping facilities are available, including showers and shelters. It's about 15 mi (25 km) north of Kingston on a slow and winding road. ⊠ *Rte. B1, northwest of Newcastle* ☎ *876/960–2849* ☜ *Free* ☉ *Tues.– Sun. 10–5.*

★ **Bob Marley Museum.** At the height of his career, Bob Marley built a recording studio—painted Rastafarian red, yellow, and green, of course. It now houses this museum, Kingston's best-known tourist site. The guided tour takes you through rooms wallpapered with magazine and newspaper articles that chronicle his rise to stardom. The tour includes a 20-minute biographical film on Marley's career; there's also a reference library if you want to learn more. A striking mural by Jah Bobby, *The Journey of Superstar Bob Marley,* depicts the hero's life from its beginnings, in a womb shaped like a coconut, to enshrinement in the hearts of the Jamaican people. ⊠ *56 Hope Rd., Kingston* ☎ *876/927–9152* ⊕ *www.bobmarley-foundation.com* ☜ *$20* ☉ *Mon.–Sat. 9:30–4.*

Devon House. Built in 1881 as the mansion of the island's first black millionaire, then bought and restored by the government in the 1960s, Devon House is filled with period furnishings, such as Venetian-crystal chandeliers and period reproductions. You can visit the two-story mansion (built with a South American gold miner's fortune) only on a guided tour. On the grounds you can find some of the island's best crafts shops, as well as one of the few mahogany trees to have survived Kingston's ambitious but not always careful development. ⊠ *26 Hope Rd., Kingston* ☎ *876/929–6602* ☜ *House tour $5* ☉ *House Mon.–Sat. 9:30–4:30.*

Emancipation Park. A 7-acre swath of greenery in the St. Andrew district of New Kingston, Emancipation Park was created in 2002. The south entrance is graced by Redemption Song, a pair of monumental statues of slaves that serve as a reminder of the island's colonial past. The park contains jogging trails and quiet spots to relax away from

A Jamaican Treasure

CLOSE UP

A sculptor, educator, and wife of one of Jamaica's most influential prime ministers, Edna Manley was born in England in 1900. As a young woman, she demonstrated considerable artistic talent and was educated at several leading art institutes. She married her cousin, Jamaican-born Norman Washington Manley, in 1921, and the pair moved to Jamaica the following year. After giving birth to her first child, Michael (himself later to be elected prime minister), Manley returned to her art, finding new inspiration in the beauty of her adopted country.

Working in mostly native wood, Manley's sculptures sought to capture the struggles of Jamaicans as they attempted to cast off the bonds of colonial rule and establish their own nation. At the same time, her husband, who was entering the political arena, began to feel the same nationalistic spirit. In 1938, he founded the People's National Party, becoming prime minister in 1955.

Over a long career, Manley's art reflected the island's culture. Although English-born, she is considered one of the founders of modern Jamaican art. A replica of one of her most famous sculptures, the monumental *Negro Aroused,* now graces the Kingston waterfront. The original, as well as many more of her works, can be seen in Kingston's National Gallery.

the buzzing city streets. ⊠ *Knutsford Blvd. at Oxford Rd., Kingston* ☎ *876/926–6312.*

Guardsmen's Serenity Park. This retreat, 20 minutes from Kingston, offers a day of outdoor activity away from the hustle and bustle of the city. There's a zoo with animals ranging from birds to buffalo, canoeing, picnicking, and more. If you catch a fish in the pond, you can have it cooked at the nearby restaurant. The park is 4 mi (6 km) west of Spanish Town. ⊠ *Off Rte. A2, Spring Village* ☎ *876/978– 5760* ☜ *$3.50* ⊙ *Thurs.–Sun. 10–5.*

Institute of Jamaica. Dating back to 1879, this natural-history museum covers the island's past starting with its early Arawak residents and continuing to modern times. Collections span art, literature, and natural history, with exhibits that range from Jamaican furniture to a display on Marcus Garvey. ⊠ *10–16 East St., Kingston* ☎ *876/922–0620* ⊕ *www.instituteofjamaica.org.jm* ☜ *$2.20* ⊙ *Mon.–Thurs. 9–4:30, Fri. 9–3:30.*

Jamaica Conference Centre. It's not often that a convention facility is also a tourist attraction, but that's the case with the Jamaica Conference Centre, which guides point out on most city tours. The facility, built in 1982, serves as headquarters for the International Seabed Authority, a division of the United Nations. The center is equipped with simultaneous translation facilities for six languages: English, Spanish, French, Chinese, Russian, and Arabic. Around-the-clock security protects the center, which includes delegates' lounges and a cafeteria and exhibition hall. ⊠ *14–20 Port Royal St., Kingston* ☎ *876/922–9160* ⊕ *www.jamaicaconference.com* ⊠ *Free* ⊙ *Weekdays 8–5.*

Jamaica Defense Force Museum. This museum is dedicated to Jamaica's military history. Exhibits include plans of the forts built around Kingston in the 18th century, as well as information, weapons, medals, and uniforms of the West Indies Regiment and the Jamaica Infantry Militia. It's north of Kingston's National Heroes Park at Arnold Road and South Camp Road. ⊠ *S. Camp Rd., Kingston* ☎ *876/926–8121* ⊕ *www.jdfmil.org* ⊠ *$2* ⊙ *Wed.–Sun. 10–4.*

Money Museum. You don't have to be a numismatist to enjoy the exhibits at this museum. In the Bank of Jamaica building on Duke Street at Nethersole Place, the museum offers a fascinating look at Jamaica's history through its monetary system. It includes everything from glass beads used as currency by the Taino Indians to Spanish gold pieces to currency of the present day. There's also a parallel exhibit on the general history of currency through world history. ⊠ *Nethersole Pl., Kingston* ☎ *876/922–0750* ⊕ *www.boj.org.jm* ⊠ *Free* ⊙ *Weekdays 10–4.*

★ **National Gallery.** The artists represented at the National Gallery may not be household names, but their paintings are sensitive and moving. You can find works by such Jamaican masters as painter John Dunkley and sculptor Edna Manley. Among other highlights from the 1920s through 1980s are works by the artist Kapo, a self-taught painter who specialized in religious images. Reggae fans should look for Christopher Gonzalez's controversial statue of Bob Marley. It was slated to be displayed near the National Arena, but was placed here because many Jamaicans felt it didn't resemble Marley. ⊠ *12 Ocean Blvd., near waterfront, Kingston* ☎ *876/922–1561* ⊠ *$2* ⊙ *Tues.–Thurs. 10–4:30, Fri. 10–4, Sat. 10–3.*

5

National Stadium. Constructed in 1962, this 35,000-seat arena (nicknamed "the Office") hosts national and international soccer matches. It's the home of Jamaica's national team, dubbed the "Reggae Boyz," which made strong showings in world competitions in recent years. Surprisingly, one of the statues in front of the main entrance honors not a soccer star, but music legend Bob Marley. Marley's monument pays homage to an iconic moment in Jamaican history. During the 1970s, Jamaica was torn by political unrest when the ruling Jamaican Labor Party met a strong challenge by the rival People's National Party. Armed gangs representing the parties engaged in open warfare in the streets. On April 22, 1978, Bob Marley and the Wailers were performing at the packed stadium. During the song "Jammin'," Marley called for the leaders of both parties to join him on the stage. As the band continued playing the song, Marley made a spirited plea for peace and unity. For the night, at least, civility and harmony prevailed in the battered streets of Kingston. ⊠ *Independence Park, Arthur Wint Dr., Kingston* ☎ *876/960–5688.*

★ **Port Royal.** Just south of Kingston, the Jamaican capital of Port Royal was once called "the wickedest city in Christendom." Jamaica's early English governors, eager to plunder treasure-laden Spanish ships, welcomed buccaneers. The city became more lawless—and more drunken. In one month alone, more than 40 new tavern licenses were issued. Rather than rein in the wild city, King Charles decided to create a royal monopoly on sales of brandy in Port Royal, using the profits to fortify and enlarge Fort Charles and to construct two smaller forts.

But brandy was not the downfall of Port Royal's residents; for most, rum was the drink of choice. A wicked drink called "kill-devil" was the pirate's preference. Jamaica's governor, Sir Thomas Modyford, wrote that "the Spaniards wondered much at the sickness of our people, until they knew of the strength of their drinks, but then they wondered more that they were not all dead."

The rollicking times came to an end on June 7, 1692, when an earthquake hit the town, plunging two-thirds of the buildings into the sea. Much of the surviving city collapsed or was hit by a tidal wave. Today this is a small fishing village, its wild ways replaced by a handful of fish stands, a couple of outdoor restaurant, a few churches, and the occasional rum shop.

CLOSE UP

Pirate of the Caribbean

Politics and piracy had close connections in early Jamaica, thanks to one of the most notorious pirates of the Caribbean: Sir Henry Morgan. Most believe the Welshman came to the West Indies as an indentured servant, eventually becoming a licensed privateer. With the government's blessing, Morgan plundered Spanish ships—as well as Spanish towns of the Caribbean, for which he did not have the approval of the crown.

Morgan's raids took him to Cuba's Puerto Principe (today's Camagüey), then to Portobello, returning to Jamaica laden with gold and silver. His raids—including his famous attack on Panama in retaliation for raids on Jamaica—earned Morgan the favor of King Charles II.

Morgan was knighted and became deputy governor of Jamaica.

It was a job change for Morgan—in many ways. Soon Charles II decided that England should enjoy better relations with Spain. Morgan was asked to persuade the privateers of Jamaica—which some historians say made up a fifth of the island's population—to give up their marauding ways. Some of those who wouldn't stop their hunt for booty were caught and sent to trial, and often to the gallows.

Morgan himself died in Jamaica—not by the sword, but by the drink. Years of alcoholism caught up to the swashbuckler in 1688. The privateer turned knight was buried in Port Royal.

Visitors usually arrive at Port Royal by taxi, traveling via Norman Manley Highway past the Norman Manley International Airport, where the highway becomes the Main Road. Driving from Kingston, you'll pass several other sights, including remains of old forts virtually hidden by vegetation, an old naval cemetery (with some intriguing headstones), and a monument commemorating Jamaica's first coconut tree, planted in 1863 (there's no tree there now, just plenty of cactus and scrub brush). Two small pubs remain in operation.

You can explore the remnants of **Fort Charles,** once the city's largest garrison. Built in 1662, this is the oldest surviving structure from the British occupation. On the grounds you can find an old artillery storehouse, called Giddy House, which gained its name after being tilted by the earthquake of 1907. Locals say its slant makes you dizzy. The Fort Charles Maritime Museum is housed in

Fort Charles, built in 1662, is Port Royal's oldest surviving British-era structure

what was once the headquarters for the British Royal Navy. Admiral Horatio Nelson served as a naval lieutenant here in 1779. The museum features a re-creation of Nelson's private quarters, as well as other artifacts from the era, including models of various sailing vessels. ⊠ *12 Long La., Port Royal* ☎ *876/967–8438* 🖃 *$5* ⊗ *Weekdays 9–5.*

The **Port Royal Archaeological and Historical Museum** displays items recovered from the ruins of Port Royal following its destruction in the 1692 earthquake. It's in the old British Naval Hospital. ⊠ *End of Morgan Rd., Port Royal* ☎ *876/922–9620* ⊕ *www.jnht.com* 🖃 *Free* ⊗ *Weekdays 9–5.*

Built in 1725 after the previous church was swept into the sea, **St. Peter's Church** was constructed by Lewis Galdy, a survivor of the 1692 earthquake. His tombstone in the church cemetery describes how "he was swallowed up in the Great Earthquake in the year 1692 and by the providence of God was by another shock thrown into the sea and miraculously saved by swimming until a boat took him up. Beloved by all and much lamented at his Death." The modest church's other treasures include an ornate organ loft, a silver candelabra, and a silver communion service that was donated, according to legend, by the notorious pirate Henry Morgan. ⊠ *Church St., Port Royal* ☎ *No phone* 🖃 *Free* ⊗ *Daily 9–5.*

Royal Botanical Gardens at Hope. The largest botanical garden in the Caribbean was originally called the Hope Estate, founded in the 1600s by an English army officer. Today it's often called Hope Gardens and features areas devoted to orchids, cacti, and palm trees. The gardens are also home to a somewhat dated zoo filled with local wildlife. ⊠ *Old Hope Rd., Kingston* ☎ *876/927–1085* ☜ *Free* ☉ *Daily 8:30–6:30.*

Spanish Town. About 12 mi (19 km) west of Kingston on A1, Spanish Town was the island's capital when it was ruled by Spain. The original name was Santiago de la Vega, meaning St. James of the Plains. The town, which has been declared a national monument by the Jamaica National Heritage Trust, has a number of historic structures, including the Jamaican People's Museum of Crafts and Technology (in the Old King's House stables), and St. James Cathedral, the oldest Anglican cathedral in the Western Hemisphere. Other historic sites include the Old Barracks Building, built in 1791 to house military personnel. Although in disrepair, its facade of brick and native stone is still imposing. The Phillippo Baptist Church honors a local hero, the Reverend James Mursell Phillippo, a missionary who led the fight for emancipation of Jamaica's slaves. His grave is in the church's graveyard. An historic cast iron bridge dates from 1801 and is said to be the oldest such bridge in the Western Hemisphere. ⊠ *Rte. A1, 13 mi (20 km) west of Kingston, Spanish Town.*

Trenchtown Culture Yard. This restored tenement building where Bob Marley spent much of his youth is now a protected National Heritage Site. Marley wrote frequently about life in the "government yard," and the area is credited with being the birthplace of reggae. The project was developed by the Trenchtown Development Association, a group dedicated to breathing new life into what had been one of Kingston's worst slums. The building contains a rudimentary museum of Marley and Wailer memorabilia. ⊠ *6–10 1st St., Kingston* ☎ *876/948–1455* ☜ *$10* ☉ *By appointment.*

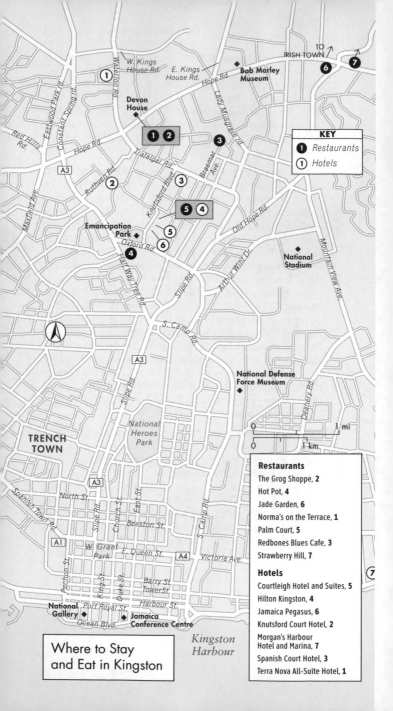

KEY

● Restaurants

① Hotels

Restaurants

The Grog Shoppe, **2**

Hot Pot, **4**

Jade Garden, **6**

Norma's on the Terrace, **1**

Palm Court, **5**

Redbones Blues Cafe, **3**

Strawberry Hill, **7**

Hotels

Courtleigh Hotel and Suites, **5**

Hilton Kingston, **4**

Jamaica Pegasus, **6**

Knutsford Court Hotel, **2**

Morgan's Harbour Hotel and Marina, **7**

Spanish Court Hotel, **3**

Terra Nova All-Suite Hotel, **1**

Where to Stay and Eat in Kingston

Kingston Harbour

TRENCH TOWN

BEST BETS FOR DINING

With the many restaurants to choose from, how will you decide where to eat? Fodor's writers and editors have selected their favorite restaurants in the Best Bets lists below. The Fodor's Choice properties represent the "best of the best." Find specific details about a restaurant in the full reviews.

Fodor's Choice

Strawberry Hill; Norma's on the Terrace.

Best Budget Eats: Hot Pot.

Best for Families: Redbones Blues Café.

Most Romantic: Strawberry Hill.

Best for Local Jamaican Cuisine: Hot Pot; Redbones Blues Café.

5

WHERE TO EAT

Kingston's varied ethnic roots—and crowds of international visitors—are clearly demonstrated by its rich array of restaurants. Although local cuisine is well represented, this city boasts the island's largest variety of restaurants, from Chinese and Indian to French and Spanish.

$–$$ ✕ **The Grog Shoppe.** *Jamaican.* At the historic Devon House, this restaurant is a bit of local history. Since 1691 it has been known for good local dishes (as well as assortment of international fare). It's pub atmosphere makes it a cool, inviting place to have a Red Stripe. ⊠ *26 Hope Rd., Kingston* ☎ *876/960–9730* ⊟ *MC, V.*

¢–$ ✕ **Hot Pot.** *Jamaican.* Jamaicans love the Hot Pot for breakfast, lunch, and dinner. Fricassee chicken is the specialty, along with other local dishes like mackerel rundown (salted mackerel cooked with coconut milk and spices) and ackee and salted cod. The restaurant's freshly squeezed juices are the best—tamarind, sorrel, coconut water, soursop, and cucumber. ⊠ *2 Altamont Terr., Kingston* ☎ *876/929–3906* ⊟ *MC, V.*

$$ ✕ **Jade Garden.** *Chinese.* On the third floor of the Sovereign Centre mall, this place has great views of the Blue Mountains. Take a seat in one of the shiny black-lacquer chairs and settle in for rave-worthy Cantonese and Thai dishes. Favorites include steamed fish in black-bean sauce, black mushrooms stuffed with shrimp, and shrimp with lychee nuts. Dim sum is served every Sunday. ⊠ *Sovereign Centre, 106 Hope Rd., Kingston* ☎ *876/978–3476* ⊟ *AE, MC, V.*

Ackee, the national fruit of Jamaica, can be poisonous unless cooked properly

★ Fodor's Choice ✕ **Norma's on the Terrace.** *Jamaican.* Jamaican
$$–$$$ food with a gourmet touch (called "fusion Jamaican" here)
is the specialty of the day at this often-lauded restaurant, the
creation of Jamaica's best-known chef, Norma Shirley. The
restaurant is a favorite with Kingstonians, although visitors
and locals alike come here for dishes like chicken thighs with
guava cream and double-smoked pork chops marinated in
Red Stripe beer. ✉ *Devon House, 26 Hope Rd., Kingston*
☎ *876/968–5488* ⊟ *AE, D, MC, V* ⊙ *Closed Sun.*

$$–$$$ ✕ **Palm Court.** *Eclectic.* On the mezzanine floor of the Hilton
Kingston, the elegant Palm Court is open for both lunch and
dinner. The dining room is furnished in rich fabrics, and
the subdued lighting creates a calm oasis in the hubbub of
New Kingston. The menu includes such favorites as rack
of lamb, snapper amandine, and grilled salmon. ✉ *Hilton
Kingston, 77 Knutsford Blvd., Kingston* ☎ *876/926–5430*
⊟ *AE, MC, V.*

$–$$ ✕ **Redbones Blues Café.** *Jamaican.* In a colonial-era residence,
this restaurant lets you choose between tables in two dining
rooms or outdoors on the terrace or in the courtyard. The
menu was created by Norma Shirley (of Norma's fame), so
look for interesting dishes like chicken breast stuffed with
callaloo and jerked cheddar or guava-glazed lamb chops.
Open for lunch on weekdays, the café really comes alive
during dinner, when meals are accompanied by live jazz or
events ranging from fashion shows to poetry readings. ✉ *21*

BEST BETS FOR LODGING

Fodor's offers a selective listing of quality lodging experiences, from the island's best boutique hotel to its most luxurious beach resort. Here are our top recommendations. The very best properties—in other words, those that provide a particularly remarkable experience—are designated in the listings with the Fodor's Choice logo.

Fodor's Choice
Strawberry Hill.

Best Budget Stay: The Knutsford Court Hotel; Morgan's Harbour Hotel and Marina.

Best Boutique Hotel: Strawberry Hill; Terra Nova.

Best All-Inclusive Resort: Morgan's Harbour Hotel and Marina.

Best for Honeymooners: Strawberry Hill.

Best for Families: Courtleigh Hotel and Suites; Jamaica Pegasus.

Braemar Ave., Kingston ☎ 876/978–6091 ⌕ *Reservations essential* ▭ *MC, V* ⊗ *Closed Sun. No lunch Sat.*

★ **Fodor's**Choice ✕**Strawberry Hill.** *Jamaican.* A favorite with
$$$– Kingstonians for its elegant Sunday brunch, Strawberry Hill
$$$$ is well worth the drive from the city. The open-air terrace has a spectacular view of Kingston and the countryside. Entrées range from steamed snapper with coconut-scented rice to jerk-marinated chicken with rice and peas. ⊠ *New Castle Rd., Irishtown* ☎ 876/944–8400 ⌕ *Reservations essential* ▭ *AE, D, MC, V.*

WHERE TO STAY

$$ ▥ **Courtleigh Hotel and Suites.** *Hotel.* This 10-story hotel is the newest of the "big three" business hotels in New Kingston. The property is aimed at business executives, but most travelers will find its rooms more than comfortable. The family-owned hotel, whose original location was a few blocks away, has one of the homiest atmospheres in the financial center. Activities range from poolside jerk buffets every Tuesday to Latin dance parties (complete with dance lessons) every Saturday. **Pros:** large rooms; lively nightlife; good business facilities. **Cons:** limited dining options; noisy location; most rooms lack balconies. ⊠ *85 Knutsford Blvd., Kingston* ☎ 876/929–9000 ⊕ *www.courtleigh.com* ➷ *88 rooms, 41 suites* ⌕ *In-room: safe, kitchens (some), refrigerator, Wi-Fi. In-hotel: 2 restaurants, bar, tennis courts,*

pools, gym, spa, laundry service, Internet terminal ⊟AE, D, DC, MC, V ⋈CP.

$$-$$$ ⊞**Hilton Kingston.** *Hotel.* With all the standard amenities travelers expect to see at a high-rise chain hotel, this property ranks as a favorite with business travelers. The expansive marble lobby, however, leads to very standard guest rooms. The concierge floors offer complimentary cocktails, hors d'oeuvres, and continental breakfast. Extras include secured-access elevators and in-room coffee and tea setups. **Pros:** good variety of restaurants; central location, nightly entertainment. **Cons:** limited leisure activities; limited in-room amenities in most room classes; no balconies in some Tower rooms. ⊠ *77 Knutsford Blvd., Box 112, Kingston* ☎ *876/926–5430* ⊕ *www.hiltoncaribbean.com* ⊸ *290 rooms, 13 suites* ♿ *In-room: safe, kitchen (some), refrigerator, Internet, Wi-Fi. In-hotel: 4 restaurants, room service, bars, pool, gym, spa, laundry service, Internet terminal, Wi-Fi hotspot* ⊟AE, D, DC, MC, V ⋈CP.

$–$$ ⊞**Jamaica Pegasus.** *Hotel.* In the heart of the financial district, this 17-story high-rise was renovated in 2008. The hotel is popular with business travelers due to its location and business amenities. Popular with locals, the hotel's restaurant offers plenty of Jamaican favorites, such as braised oxtail and grilled snapper. All rooms have balconies and large windows that face the Blue Mountains, the pool, or the Caribbean. There's an excellent business center, duty-free shops, and 24-hour room service. **Pros:** good business travel facilities; good pool area; easy access to New Kingston business district. **Cons:** limited leisure activities; 17 floors of guest rooms can mean a wait for an elevator. ⊠ *81 Knutsford Blvd., Box 333, Kingston* ☎ *876/926–3690* ⊕ *www.jamaicapegasus.com* ⊸ *300 rooms, 19 suites* ♿ *In-room: safe, refrigerator (some), Internet. In-hotel: 3 restaurants, room service, bars, tennis courts, pool, gym, spa, laundry service, Internet terminal, Wi-Fi hotspot* ⊟AE, D, DC, MC, V ⋈EP.

$ ⊞**The Knutsford Court Hotel.** *Hotel.* This modest hotel combines business services with the charm of a smaller property. Rooms are basic, most with white-tile floors and small bathrooms, but are enlivened with colorful walls or fabrics. The pool area and adjacent bar and restaurant are small but popular with the guests. **Pros:** good value; business amenities; friendly staff. **Cons:** drab decor; limited dining choices; small pool area. ⊠ *16 Chelsea Ave., Kingston* ☎ *876/929–1000* 🖷 *876/960–7373* ⊕ *www.knutsfordcourt. com* ⊸ *143 rooms* ♿ *In-room: safe, kitchen (some), Inter-*

net. In-hotel: 2 restaurants, room service, bar, pool gym, laundry service ⊟ *AE, D, DC, MC, V* ⦿ *CP.*

$ 🏨 **Morgan's Harbour Hotel and Marina.** *Hotel.* Near the entrance to Port Royal, this hotel plays up the region's swashbuckling past in everything from its seafood restaurant to its slots-filled gaming room. The accommodations feature nice touches like mahogany four-poster beds and generously sized desks; some include private balconies overlooking the sea. Although the hotel is directly on the ocean, guests rely on the pool when they want to cool off. Another alterative is heading out to Lime Cay for a day of beach fun. **Pros:** easy airport access; leisurely pace; good water sports. **Cons:** limited dining; limited nightlife; long drive to Kingston. ⊠ *Queen St., Kingston* ☎ *876/967–8040* ⇨ *54 rooms, 7 suites* ⟁ *In-room: refrigerator, Internet. In-hotel: 2 restaurants, room service, bars, golf course, tennis courts, pool, beachfront, bicycles, laundry facilities, laundry service* ⊟ *AE, D, DC, MC, V* ⦿ *AI.*

$$ 🏨 **Spanish Court Hotel.** *Hotel.* This hotel's traditional Spanish exterior surprises first-time guests with its sleekly streamlined public spaces and its modern rooms and suites aimed at the business traveler. The lobby and Gallery restaurant are the work of well-known designer Alison Antrobus. **Pros:** great business location near the city center; business center is open 24 hours; reasonable prices. **Cons:** limited dining options; executive guests may miss having a concierge. ⊠ *1 St. Lucia Ave., Kingston* ☎ *876/926–0000* ⊕ *www. spanishcourthotel.com* ⇨ *101 rooms, 7 suites* ⟁ *In-room: safe, Internet, Wi-Fi. In-hotel: restaurant, room service, bar, pool, gym, spa, Wi-Fi hotspot* ⊟ *AE, D, DC, MC, V* ⦿ *BP.*

★ **Fodor'sChoice** 🏨 **Strawberry Hill.** *Hotel.* A 45-minute drive from **$$$$** Kingston—but worlds apart in terms of atmosphere—this exclusive resort was developed by Chris Blackwell, former head of Island Records (the late Bob Marley's label). Perched in the Blue Mountains, it's where the rich and famous go to retreat and relax. The resort has an infinity pool, Aveda spa, and pure relaxation in Georgian-style cottages. This is one Jamaican property not for beach buffs but for those in search of gourmet dining thanks to its on-site restaurant which, on a clear day, offers unbeatable views over the capital city. The cottages survey the Blue Mountains from expansive porches, most with an oversized hammock. Every bed has an electric mattress pad to warm things up on chilly evenings; mosquito nets surround you—

because there's no air-conditioning, guests usually prefer to keep windows open, which can make it buggy. **Pros:** stylish accommodations with great mountain views; cool retreat from the heat; best spa in Jamaica. **Cons:** remote location a distance from the beaches; limited on-site dining options; too quiet for some guests. ⊠ *New Castle Rd., Irishtown, St. Andrew* ☎ *876/944–8400* ⊕ *www.islandoutpost.com* ⇆ *12 villas* ⚷ *In-room: no a/c, safe, kitchen, DVD, Wi-Fi. In-hotel: restaurant, room service, bar, pool, spa, bicycles, laundry service* ▭ *AE, D, MC, V* ⍩ *AI.*

$$ ⊡ **Terra Nova All-Suite Hotel.** *Hotel.* Although it's in New Kingston, this graceful hotel, a former colonial mansion, is definitely Old Jamaica. You'll agree when you encounter the white-glove service in the dining room to the afternoon tea with freshly baked scones. Tucked in a quieter part of New Kingston, a mile from the commercial district, the hotel is within walking distance of the historic Devon House as well as designer boutiques and gourmet restaurants. Rooms are decked out with classic mahogany furniture and fresh flowers. Although the hotel claims to have only suites, the standard "suites" are closer in size to hotel rooms. Rates include a daily Jamaican buffet breakfast. **Pros:** elegant atmosphere; great outdoor dining; near shopping and dining. **Cons:** fills up quickly on weekends; small rooms; dated decor. ⊠ *17 Waterloo Rd., Kingston* ☎ *876/926–2211* ⊕ *www.terranovajamaica.com* ⇆ *43 suites* ⚷ *In-room: safe, kitchen, refrigerator, Wi-Fi. In-hotel: 2 restaurants, bars, pool, gym, laundry service, Internet terminal, Wi-Fi hotspot* ▭ *AE, D, DC, MC, V* ⍩ *BP.*

BEACHES

Kingston's beaches can be packed, although rarely with tourists. The city, like much of the South Coast, doesn't boast the same beautiful beaches of the north shore but instead has stretches of sand that serve as a gathering point for groups of families and friends, especially on the weekends. If you visit local beaches, be sure to talk with your concierge first, as crime is a problem on Kingston's beaches.

The best beach getaway in the Kingston area is at **Lime Cay,** a small island just off the peninsula leading out to Port Royal. You can reach the cay by boat from Morgan's Harbour Hotel. Once there, you can swim, snorkel, or picnic on the sandy beach. There are no real facilities here, so bring what you need for the day.

Southwest of the city are some of the best-known area beaches, including **Fort Clarence,** which offers changing facilities and live entertainment. About 32 mi (52 km) east of the city lies **Lyssons Beach,** another popular choice with Kingstonians.

SPORTS AND THE OUTDOORS

BIRD-WATCHING

Some of Jamaica's best birding opportunities are found above Kingston in the misty Blue Mountains, especially in the **Blue and John Crow Mountains National Park.** You'll probably see the national bird, the streamer-tail hummingbird, a large hummingbird with a dramatic forked tail. Known locally as the "doctor bird," it's one of Jamaica's 28 endemic species. Other unique birds to watch for include the Jamaican woodpecker, Blue Mountain vireo, Rufous-tailed flycatcher, arrow-headed warbler, Jamaican stripe-headed tanager, and the yellow-shouldered grassquit. Another popular birding area is on **Lime Cay,** just offshore from Port Royal.

The **Natural History Society of Jamaica** (⊠ *Department of Life Sciences, University of the West Indies Mona, Mona Rd., Kingston* ☎ *876/927–1202*) organizes bird-watching trips into the Blue Mountains and nearby John Crow Mountains. Contact them directly for information on dates and prices.

Sun Venture Tours (⊠ *30 Balmoral Ave., Kingston* ☎ *876/960– 6685* ⊕ *www.sunventuretours.com*) specializes in ecotours.

DIVING AND SNORKELING

With its murkier waters, the southern side of the island isn't very popular for diving. A special permit is required to dive certain sites. Near Morgan's Harbour Hotel and Marina, advanced divers can explore the wreck of the *Texas,* a World War II–era ship surrounded by cool coral formations. The ship's guns are easily recognizable. Another wreck in the area is the *Cayman Trader.* A merchant ship disabled by fire, the *Trader* was sunk intentionally to make a habitat for marine life. Another favorite spot is Windward Edge, beyond Kingston's small offshore cays. After a half-hour boat ride, divers are often able to spot large fish here.

5

Jiminy Cricket!

Jamaica played host to the World Cricket Cup in 2007, welcoming teams from around the world to newly built and newly renovated stadiums scattered across the island. Kingston's Sabina Park was one of the island's top venues for the competition. With a capacity of 20,000 fans, the stadium has been the scene for many dramatic matches over the years. The World Cricket Cup, however, brought a new level of excitement to the game.

Cricket has a long history in Jamaica, not surprising given the island's history as a British colony. The first matches were held in 1895, when locals played a series of matches against a touring English team. In those early days, it was a sport played only by society's elite, so players came mainly from the island's wealthy ruling families. Gradually, the sport became more egalitarian. Indeed, Jamaican cricket achieved its greatest success only after shedding much of its colonial trappings, selecting its players by talent rather than family influence.

At present, cricket is overshadowed only by soccer in its popularity among Jamaican fans. Former players, including George Headley, who wowed fans in the 1930s, are still remembered and revered by the Jamaican public.

Buccaneer Scuba Club (⊠ *Morgan's Harbour Hotel and Marina, Queen St., Port Royal* ☎ *876/977–6938*) is home to Buccaneer divers. Buccaneer Scuba Club offers dives for different skill levels, including trips to the wreck of the *Texas*. Just offshore, the Edge offers great blue-water diving. One-tank dives give you a chance to see many of the area's rare species, including manatees.

FISHING

The waters off Jamaica's southern coast are some of the richest fishing areas around. However, much of the fishing here is done by locals, rather than visitors. There are sportfishing charters to be had from Port Royal and through local hotels such as Morgan's Harbour Hotel and Marina. Charters usually furnish bait and equipment, although typically not food and drinks. Most can be chartered for either half- or whole-day excursions. When chartering a fishing boat, be sure to discuss specifics with the captain before you set sail.

Buccaneer Scuba Club (✉ *Morgan's Harbour Hotel and Marina, Queen St., Port Royal* ☎ *876/924–8148*) charges $400 for half-day to $650 for full-day fishing trips. Evening drop-line fishing can also be arranged.

GOLF

Although golf isn't a major activity here, travelers will find two courses in the Kingston area. As in other parts of Jamaica, Kingston courses require that you hire the services of a caddy.

Caymanas Golf and Country Club (✉ *Mandela Hwy., halfway between Kingston and Spanish Town* ☎ *876/746-9773* ⊕ *www.caymanasgolfclub.com*) is about 8 mi (12 km) west of the city center. Jamaica's first major championship 18-hole course, Caymanas opened in 1957. Green fees are $45 on weekdays, $56 on weekends.

Constant Spring Golf Club (✉ *152 Constant Spring Rd., Box 743, Kingston* ☎ *876/924–1610*) dates back to 1920, when it was designed by Scotsman Stanley Thompson, mentor of Robert Trent Jones, Sr. This short course, in one of Kingston's nicest downtown neighborhoods, charges $35 per round. Rentals are available. There's a clubhouse, restaurant, bar, and pro shop.

GUIDED TOURS

Numerous operators offer tours of the Kingston area, as well as excursions into the Blue Mountains. Professional tour operators provide a valuable service, as neither destination is particularly suited to exploration without a guide. In Kingston, certain areas can be dangerous; an organized tour provides a measure of security compared with going it alone. Think twice before roaming too freely in the Blue Mountains, as roads are narrow or in poor condition, and signs are few and far between.

Typical city tours include a city overview with stops at Devon House, the Bob Marley Museum, and Port Royal. Other tour options cover the Blue Mountains. Niche operators such as Olde Jamaica Heritage Tours provide theme tours, including a churches and museums tour.

CarIbIsle Tours (✉ *5 Ellesmere Rd., Kingston* ☎ *876/755–4108* ⊕ *www.caribisletours.com*). **Jam Venture Tours and Services** (✉ *Northside Plaza, Suite 3A, Haughton Ave., Kingston* ☎ *876/960–7719*). **Jessa Tours, Ltd.** (✉ *19 Herb McKenley Dr., Kingston* ☎ *876/978–2259*). **Olde Jamaica Heritage Tours** (✉ *5 Cowper*

Kingston's Ward Theatre is a national monument

Dr., Kingston ☎ 876/371–3613 or 876/328–1385 ⊕ www.oldeja-maicatours.com). **Sun Island Tours** *(✉ 8 Bower Bank Ave., Kingston ☎ 876/931–8826).* **Sun Venture Tours** *(✉ 30 Balmoral Ave., Kingston ☎ 876/960–6685 ⊕ www.sunventuretours.com).* **Tourmarks** *(✉ 7 Leighton Rd., Kingston ☎ 876/929–5078 ⊕ www.tourmarks.com).*

HORSE RACING

In Kingston, a trip to the track is a popular afternoon activity for many residents. Although the capital city has the island's only track, you'll see more than 60 off-track betting parlors scattered across the island.

Caymanas Park *(✉ Caymanas Dr., Portmore ☎ 876/988–2523 ⊕ www.caymanasracetrack.com)* is a favorite with locals. Races are usually slated for Wednesday and Saturday afternoon. Admission to the air-conditioned lounge is $5 for adults. To enter the third-floor lounges, don't show up wearing torn jeans, shorts, or sandals. Children are welcome.

MOUNTAIN BIKING

Although you should avoid biking in Kingston, the placid Blue Mountains make a good outing for cyclists of all skill levels. The most popular outing is a downhill coast through Holywell National Park.

The Ocho Rios–based **Blue Mountain Bicycle Tours** *(✉ 121 Main St., Ocho Rios ☎ 876/974–7075 ⊕ www.bmtoursja.*

Blue Mountain Coffee

Along the misty slopes of the Blue Mountains grow some of Jamaica's most valuable plants, flourishing in a perfect microclimate of altitude, temperature, rainfall, and soil type. It's not what you might think, it's coffee—Blue Mountain coffee, to be exact. This Jamaican specialty is known throughout the world for its rich aroma and flavor.

Since 1973, the Jamaican government mandated that only coffee produced from Arabica beans grown in fields above 2,000 feet can be labeled Blue Mountain coffee. The coffee is graded by altitude, divided into lowland and high-mountain types, a distinction you'll find on every label. Most Blue Mountain coffee is exported and commands a high price. This is especially true in Japan, where the beans often sell for more than $60 per pound. On the island you'll find it for sale in many gift shops, but for the best prices, visit a local supermarket.

com) takes travelers on guided rides in the spectacular Blue Mountains. The excursion, an all-day outing, starts high and glides downhill, so all levels of riders can enjoy the tour. The trip ends with a dip in a waterfall. Children age seven and up are welcome on the trip.

SHOPPING

Unlike the communities on the island's North Coast, Kingston isn't known for its duty-free stores. Shopping here is mostly limited to shops for residents. The city's Constant Spring Road and King Street are home to a growing roster of shopping malls offering fashions, housewares, and more.

The **Shops at Devon House** (⊠ *26 Hope Rd., Kingston* ☎ *876/929–6602*) is a cluster of mostly upscale shops selling clothing, crafts, and other items. The location, at the historic Devon House, makes this a pleasant spot to spend a morning or afternoon. Prices are high, but bargains can be found.

MARKETS

Kingston Crafts Market (⊠ *Harbour St. and Ocean Blvd., Kingston* ☎ *876/922–3015*) has a large assortment of Jamaican handicrafts. Paintings, sculptures, and inexpensive jewelry can be found in the stalls. Although pickpockets have been a problem in the past, it's much safer now. Some bargaining is tolerated, but don't expect many concessions.

SPECIALTY ITEMS

The **Coffee Mill of Jamaica** (⌧ *9 Barbados Ave., Kingston* ☎ *876/929–2227*) sells Jamaica's famous Blue Mountain coffee. Enjoy a cup while shopping for herbs, spices, jellies, jams, teas, and condiments.

Starfish Essentials (⌧ *26 Hope Rd., Kingston* ☎ *876/906–8045* ⊕ *www.starfishoils.com*) specializes in aromatherapy products such as fragrant oils. Some the most popular scents include cinnamon leaf, which aids digestion and bronchitis and is said to be an aphrodisiac. Another fragrance, tea tree, is said to combat dandruff, fungal infections, and age spots.

Things Jamaican (⌧ *Devon House, 26 Hope Rd., Kingston* ☎ *876/926–1961* ⌧ *Sangster International Airport, Montego Bay* ☎ *876/971–0775*) sells some of the best Jamaican crafts—from carved wooden bowls and trays to reproductions of silver and brass period pieces.

A recording studio, **Tuff Gong Studios** (⌧ *220 Marcus Garvey Dr., Kingston* ☎ *876/923–9380*) is also a retail music shop featuring Caribbean tunes, T-shirts, and memorabilia of the reggae scene.

NIGHTLIFE AND THE ARTS

As the cultural hub of Jamaica, Kingston has the island's largest selection of nightlife options. Unlike the more tourist-oriented resort communities, nightlife here is aimed at locals, and varies from live music to discos. Because of Kingston's high crime rate, you should consult with your concierge before heading for the night's activities.

ANNUAL EVENTS

It's often said that Kingston is the heartbeat of Jamaica, and at no time does that heart beat any louder than during the annual **Carnival** (⌧ *Liguanea Park, 89 King St., Kingston* ☎ *876/922–3840* ⊕ *www.bacchanaljamaica.com*), held here in April. Parades for both children and adults fill the streets.

Carnival started in Kingston in 1990 and is now a big event

THE ARTS

Built in 1912, the **Ward Theatre** (⌧ *North Parade, between King St. and Love La., Kingston* ☎ 876/922–0453) was launched with the production of Gilbert and Sullivan's *Pirates of Penzance*. Over the years, the Ward Theatre has become one of Kingston's most cherished icons. Known not only for its prominent role in the city's cultural life, it has also hosted many important political events. Named a national monument in 2000, it continues to host year-around events ranging from classical concerts to theater.

NIGHTLIFE

Friday nights in Kingston bring on the Friday Night Jam, an impromptu street party that begins when office doors close and entrepreneurial chefs roll out oil drums transformed into jerk pits. Street corners sizzle with spicy fare, music blares, and the city launches into weekend mode.

Pick up a copy of the *Daily Gleaner,* the *Jamaica Observer,* or the *Star* (available at newsstands throughout the island) for listings on who's playing when and where.

In New Kingston, **Junkanoo Nightclub** (⌧ *Hilton Kingston, 77 Knutsford Blvd., Kingston* ☎ 876/926–5430) shakes with the sounds of everything from reggae to rock Wednesday through Sunday night.

Peppers (✉ *31 Upper Waterloo Rd., Kingston* ☎ *876/969–2421*) is a favorite with locals who start the evening with a plate of spicy jerk before working off that meal on the dance floor. The open-air restaurant and nightclub features many theme nights.

Redbones Blues Cafe (✉ *21 Braemar Ave., Kingston* ☎ *876/978–8262*) calls itself "the only juke joint in Jamaica." Although there might be plenty of other musical action in town, Redbones is well known for its live jazz as well as world music performances every Thursday night. Some events carry a cover charge ranging from $4 to $6.

PEPPER

SHRIMP

The South Coast

WORD OF MOUTH

"If . . . you're interested in something a little more off the beaten path, consider the Treasure Beach. . . . It's quiet, it's real, it's rich, it's rewarding, and it takes a little more effort to get there."

—ejcrowe

By Paris
Permenter
and John
Bigley

During the 1970s, Negril was Jamaica's most relaxed place to hang out. Now that Negril and the western end of the island have been discovered by developers, that distinction is now held by the South Coast. Many people who have visited for years consider the South Coast's Treasure Beach to be comparable to Negril Beach before the recent building boom changed it forever. Is the South Coast destined to follow Negril's pattern, trading its laid-back appeal for mass-market tourism? Only time will tell, but it's clear that change will come slowly to this region, traditionally one of island's least developed. Local business owners are keenly aware that much of the area's appeal lies in its remote feel and its lack of development.

The economy of the region is relatively diversified, with fishing and agriculture still important. You'll see small backyard gardens with clusters of banana trees and hillocks of beans and corn, as well as large commercially grown fields of citrus fruit, papayas, melons, coconuts, corn, and sugarcane, which was once the island's prime moneymaker. Some valley fields will be filled to the horizon by banana trees, some wearing their "blue dresses," plastic bags placed over the maturing fruit to protect them from insects. (It's a concession to North American consumers, who insist on blemish-free produce.)

Industry also plays a big role in the local economy, especially the mining and refining of bauxite, or aluminum ore. Since the 1940s, when the metal was first discovered here, Jamaica's South Coast has become one of the world's largest producers. The Alcan Jamaica plant, known locally as the Kirkvine Works, has operated outside the city of Mandeville since the 1950s and has become one of the city's largest employers. Another plant that processes aluminum ore is in the small town of Nain in St. Elizabeth Parish. (The bauxite industry, like others in Jamaica, was hit hard by the economic downturn, however.)

All of which means that at least for now, the South Coast, with fishing villages dotting its pristine shoreline and small agricultural towns sprinkled around the interior, is a place to experience the day-to-day life of Jamaica. It's a friendly area where locals playing dominoes under the trees still wave to passing cars. Small hotels (only one all-inclusive resort has entered the market here) cater to travelers seeking a peaceful place to unwind while exploring local communities and spending quiet evenings in local restaurants.

ORIENTATION AND PLANNING

ORIENTATION

Jamaica's South Coast spans the parishes of St. Elizabeth and Manchester and the eastern portion of Westmoreland. The terrain includes pockets of rich farmland, dry savanna, and several mountain ranges. The coastline is sparsely populated, compared to the North Coast, with small fishing villages scattered along Route A2, the coastal highway.

Another distinction of the South Coast is its ethnic diversity, with descendents of German and Scottish settlers mixing with those of Miskito Indians from Central America, brought here during colonial days to help subdue the native Maroon population. Until modern times, the South Coast remained relatively isolated from the rest of the country, contributing to the area's uniquely relaxed atmosphere.

The two major population centers in the region are Mandeville, in the Don Figuerero Mountain Range, and the coastal community of Black River. The latter is at the mouth of the Black River, Jamaica's longest, which drains one of Jamaica's most interesting natural environments, the Black River Great Morass, with its resident crocodiles paddling through mangrove thickets.

6

PLANNING

WHEN TO GO
The quiet South Coast doesn't have the spring-break crowds of Negril; this getaway is devoid of crowds whenever you choose to visit. As Jamaica's driest area, it's a good alternative from May to October, when the North Coast can be at its rainiest. Nevertheless, the South Coast, like the rest of Jamaica (and the whole Caribbean region) is vulnerable to adverse conditions during hurricane season, which runs from June to November.

GETTING HERE AND AROUND

BY AIR
There are no major airports on the South Coast. Visitors to this region can fly into international airports in Montego Bay or Kingston (or can take a charter flight into Negril). Most visitors fly into the Sangster International Airport in Montego Bay.

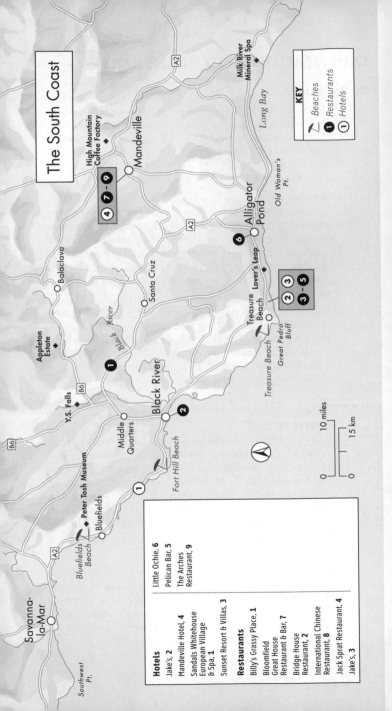

The South Coast

High Mountain Coffee Factory

Milk River Mineral Spa

Mandeville

④ ⑦ – ⑨

Long Bay

A2

Balaclava

Santa Cruz

Alligator Pond

⑥

Old Woman's Pt.

Black River

Treasure Beach

Lover's Leap

② ③

③ – ⑤

Appleton Estate

Great Pedro Bluff

Y.S. Falls

B6

Black River

Treasure Beach

Middle Quarters

①

②

Fort Hill Beach

Peter Tosh Museum

Bluefields

Bluefields Beach

A2

Savanna-la-Mar

Southwest Pt.

KEY

Beaches

① Restaurants

① Hotels

0   10 miles

0   15 km

N

Hotels

Jake's, **2**
Mandeville Hotel, **4**
Sandals Whitehouse European Village & Spa, **1**
Sunset Resort & Villas, **3**

Restaurants

Billy's Grassy Place, **1**
Bloomfield Great House Restaurant & Bar, **7**
Bridge House Restaurant, **2**
International Chinese Restaurant, **8**
Jack Sprat Restaurant, **4**
Jake's, **3**

Little Ochie, **6**
Pelican Bar, **5**
The Arches Restaurant, **9**

TOP REASONS TO GO

Getting Four for One: Spread your towel out on Treasure Beach, a series of four pristine stretches of sand.

Meeting and Greeting: This is one part of Jamaica where you'll want to mingle with the friendly welcoming locals.

Smiling at a Crocodile: Take a boat trip on the Black River, home to these amazing creatures.

Sampling the Local Vintage: This is Jamaica, so of course we mean rum, and the best place is at the Appleton Estate.

Snapping Photos: There are plenty of photo ops in this region, including the canopy of vegetation at Bamboo Avenue, between Middle Quarters and Lacovia.

BY CAR

As in the rest of Jamaica, we strongly advise against renting a vehicle to see the sights along Jamaica's South Coast. However, if you're determined to drive, this area is probably as safe as it gets, due to lighter traffic and fewer large towns. You might find it more convenient (albeit not cheaper) to take a prearranged airport transfer to your hotel, then rent a car in the area. Be aware that many roads in the south are rough and narrow, and what traffic you do encounter will whiz along at high speed.

Car Rental Contacts **Alicia Car Rental** (⌂ 44 High St., Black River ☎ 876/634–2772). **Hemisphere Car Rental** (⌂ 51 Manchester Rd., Mandeville ☎ 876/962–1921). **Mid Island Car Rental** (⌂ 1-B Caledonia Rd., Mandeville ☎ 876/961–2363). **Millinex Rental** (⌂ 3 Villa Rd., Mandeville ☎ 876/962–3542). **Moon Glow Car Rental** (⌂ 81-A Ward Ave., Mandeville ☎ 876/962–3078).

BY TAXI

Taxis are less common on the South Coast than in busier tourist areas, but are still an easy (albeit expensive) option. You'll want to call ahead for a taxi or arrange for a driver to pick you up at a designated time.

Contacts **JUTA** (☎ 876/957–9197). **Pat's Taxi** (☎ 876/918–0431 or 876/955–3335).

At Appleton Estate, sugarcane was once ground by mule power

RESTAURANTS
Dining on the South Coast is a casual affair, often enjoyed on an outdoor terrace or beside the beach. With far less hassling at than other parts of the island, visitors here enjoy dining in small establishments ranging from neighborhood hangouts to roadside eateries, all at prices far lower than those found in the major resort areas.

With many mom-and-pop eateries in this area, ingredients are always fresh and usually local—sometimes right out of the backyard. Alligator Pond and Treasure Beach are both home to fishing communities offering the freshest catch of the day, whereas the area north of Whitehouse is considered Jamaica's breadbasket, filled with farms growing the fruits and vegetables that make their way to tables across the island.

HOTELS
Until a few years ago, the South Coast was exclusively the home of a few small hotels and guesthouses, but then Sandals Whitehouse became the first all-inclusive resort in the south. Nonetheless, the South Coast is still known for its small, family-owned properties and laid-back charm, with prices generally lower than those found on the North Coast.

		WHAT IT COSTS IN DOLLARS		
¢	$	$$	$$$	$$$$
RESTAURANTS				
under $8	$8–$12	$12–$20	$20–$30	Over $30
HOTELS*				
under $80	$80–$150	$150–$250	$250–$350	Over $350
HOTELS**				
under $125	$125–$250	$250–$350	$350–$450	Over $450

*EP, BP, CP; **AI, FAP, MAP; restaurant prices are per person for a main course at dinner and do not include the 15% V.A.T. and 10% service charge. Hotel prices are per night for a double room in high season, excluding 15% V.A.T. and 10% service charge.

ESSENTIALS

BANKS AND CURRENCY EXCHANGE

Though converting U.S. dollars to Jamaican dollars may not be necessary in the tourist meccas along the North Coast, the situation is a little different on the South Coast. Here it's more likely that merchants and taxi drivers will charge Jamaican dollars, so it's handy to have some local currency on hand. You'll find banks in Mandeville, or you can change money at your hotel.

EMERGENCIES

There are no major medical facilities on the southwest coast. You'll find small local hospitals in Black River, Mandeville, and Savanna-La-Mar, and there is a hyperbaric chamber for scuba diving emergencies in the St. Ann's Bay Hospital. If you need to find a local pharmacy to fill a prescription, it's best to ask at your hotel.

INTERNET

Far fewer visitors frequent the South Coast than either the North Coast or Kingston, so you'll find that Internet access is spotty. Larger hotels have connections, but smaller ones do not.

Contacts **Cyber Lounge** (⊠ Shop 12, Empire Bldg., Mandeville ☎ 876/625–7084). **Underground High Speed Cyber Café** (⊠ Shop 2, Willowgate Plaza, Mandeville ☎ 876/625–3490).

EXPLORING THE SOUTH COAST

Visitors to Jamaica's South Coast will normally fly into Montego Bay's Sangster International Airport, then drive overland, whether by rental car, taxi, or bus through Jamaica's interior. If the nearly two-hour hour drive is done during daylight hours, you can see much of Jamaica's "breadbasket," the agricultural region where much of the nation's foodstuffs are grown.

Numbers in the margin correspond to points of interest on the South Coast map.

WHAT TO SEE

★ **Appleton Estate.** Before the rise of tourism as Jamaica's main industry, the island was highly prized for its sugarcane production. Vast fortunes were made here during colonial times, and many of the island's historic greathouses remain as reminders of that time. Much of the sugarcane was processed into molasses, the main ingredient in the production of rum. Appleton Estate, still one of the Caribbean's premier rum distillers, offers guided tours illustrating the history of rum making in the region. After a lively discussion of the days when sugarcane was crushed by donkey power, the tours move on to a behind-the-scenes tour of the modern facility. After the tour, samples flow freely, and every visitor receives a complimentary bottle of rum. There's a good restaurant here serving genuine Jamaican dishes. ⊠ *Hwy. B6, Siloah* ☎ *876/963–9215* ⊕ *www.appletonrum.com* ⊠ *$18* ⊙ *Mon.–Sat. 9–3:30.*

High Mountain Coffee Factory. Grown on nearby plantations, coffee beans are brought here for processing. Call ahead for tours, or just stop by the gift shop for a sample taste. In addition to coffee, the gift shop features other High Mountain products like spices, condiments, and scented candles. ⊠ *Winston Jones Hwy., Williamsfield* ☎ *876/963–4211* ⊠ *$3* ⊙ *Mon.–Thurs. 8–5, Fri. 8–4:30.*

Lovers' Leap. As legend has it, two slaves who were in love chose to jump off this 1,700-foot cliff rather than be recaptured by their master. Today it's a favorite stop with travelers, who enjoy a drink at the bar (try the lover's punch) and a view of the coastline. Tours of local cacti are available, and a small farm demonstrates the dry-farming technique used in this area. ⊠ *Yardley Chase, Treasure Beach* ☎ *876/365–6577* ⊠ *$1.50* ⊙ *Daily 9–5.*

Mandeville. At 2,000 feet above sea level, Mandeville is considerably cooler than the coastal areas about 25 mi (40 km) to the south. Its vegetation is also lusher, thanks to the mists that drift through the mountains. But climate and flora aren't all that separate it from the steamy coast: Mandeville seems a hilly tribute to all that's genteel in the British character. The people here live in tidy cottages with gardens around a village green; there's even a Georgian courthouse and a parish church. The entire scene could be set down in Devonshire, were it not for the occasional poinciana blossom or citrus grove. ⊠ *Rte. A2, between Black River and May Pen.*

EN ROUTE. Although the constant roar of speeding trucks keeps the site from being idyllic, **Bamboo Avenue,** a section of Route A1 between Middle Quarters and Lacovia, is an often-photographed stretch of highway because it's completely canopied with tall bamboo. Here you can see innumerable COLD JELLY signs attached to small carts. These promise jelly coconuts, young coconuts that yield a clear, sweet jelly.

Peter Tosh Mausoleum. In the small community of Belmont, this simple white-concrete building contains the grave of reggae great Peter Tosh, (nee Winston Hubert McIntosh), who was murdered in Jamaica in 1987. Together with Bob Marley and Bunny Wailer, Tosh formed the seminal reggae group the Wailers in 1967. In stark contrast to Jamaican memorials to Marley found in Kingston and Nine Mile, Tosh's burial place is quiet and uncrowded. ⊠ *Rte. A2, Belmont* ☎ *No phone* ⊡ *Donation suggested* ⊙ *Daily 9–5.*

★ **Y. S. Falls.** A quiet alternative to Dunn's River falls in Ocho Rios, the falls are tucked in a papaya plantation and reached via motorized jitney. If you aren't staying on the south coast, companies in Negril offer half-day excursions. The last tour of the day begins at 3:30. ⊠ *2 Market St., Black River, north of A2, just past town of Middle Quarters* ☎ *876/997–6360* ⊕ *www.ysfalls.com* ⊡ *$15* ⊙ *Tues.–Sun. 9:30–4:30.*

DID YOU KNOW? There's a lot of discussion in Jamaica about the origin of the name Y. S. (as in Y. S. Falls), the shortest place name on the island. Some believe it comes from the Gaelic word "wyess" (winding or twisting). Others say the name comes from a combination of the initials of the land's 1684 owners: John Yates and Lt. Col. Richard Scott.

CLOSE UP

The Black River Great Morass

One of Jamaica's most unique environments, the Black River Great Morass, near the town of Black River, covers 80,000 acres of water, marsh, and low hammocks of land. Drained by the Black River, it's named for its water, which is stained dark by natural dyes released by rotting vegetation. Largely impenetrable except by boat, the Morass's ecosystem supports a wide assortment of Jamaica's flora and fauna.

While touring upriver on one of several tours offered in the town of Black River, you have the chance to spot some of the area's wildlife such as the American Crocodile as well as a wealth of birdlife including her-

ons, ducks, and egrets. It's also common to pass small dugout canoes tied to overhanging mangrove branches while their inhabitants spearfish in the tea-color waters of the river, apparently unconcerned by sharing the river with crocodiles.

Venturing deeper into the Morass, you see other examples of Jamaica's plant life such as ackee trees, palms, and the logwood tree, a species whose dense, heavy wood was a valuable source of blue dye. The town of Black River was once an important port to export logwood, which was floated down the Black River on rafts made of more buoyant wood.

WHERE TO EAT

TREASURE BEACH AND VICINITY

¢ ✕ **Billy's Grassy Park.** *Jamaican.* A true side-of-the-road stop on the South Coast Highway, Billy's Grassy Park serves fiery Jamaican food including scorching peppered shrimp caught just behind the kitchen. Dining's mostly a grab-and-go affair although stands next door provide local desserts like fresh jelly coconut to cool the burn. ✉ *A2, about 30 mins east of Whitehouse, Middlequarters* ☎ *876/366–4182* ⊟ *No credit cards.*

$–$$ ✕ **Jack Sprat Restaurant.** *Eclectic.* It's no surprise that this restaurant shares its home resort's bohemian style (it's the beachside dining spot at Jake's). From the casual outdoor tables to the late-night dance-hall rhythm, it's a place to come and hang loose. Jerk crab joins favorites like pizzas and jerk chicken on the menu, all followed by Kingston's Devon House ice cream (try the coconut). ✉ *Jake's, Calabash Bay, Treasure Beach* ☎ *876/965–3583* ⊟ *AE, DC, MC, V.*

The Black River is an important habitat for wading birds, including cranes

★ **Fodor's**Choice × **Jake's.** *Caribbean.* The main restaurant at
$$–$$$ Jake's (there's also Jack Sprat, on the beach) offers an
authentic local menu served outdoors in a casual seaside
atmosphere. Dishes such as saltfish and ackee as well as
escovitch fish join the fresh catch of the day prepared as you
like. ⊠ *Jake's, Calabash Bay, Treasure Beach* ☎ *876/965–
3583* ⊟ *AE, D, MC, V.*

$–$$ × **Little Ochie.** *Jamaican.* This casual beachside eatery is a
favorite with locals and travelers, favored for its genuine Jamaican dishes like fish tea, escovitch fish, peppered
shrimp, jerk chicken, seapuss (octopus), and more. Most
of the seafood is brought in by fishermen just yards away.
For those staying in Treasure Beach, a favorite way to reach
Little Ochie is by boat. ⊠ *About 7 mi (11 km) south of A2
Alligator Pond* ☎ *876/610–6566 or 876/610–6567* ⊕ *www.
littleochie.com* ⊟ *AE, MC, V.*

$–$$ × **Pelican Bar.** *Caribbean.* One of the funkiest places in
Jamaica to down a cold Red Stripe, this whimsical structure
sits on stilts ½-mi (¾-km) offshore from Treasure Beach,
atop a small sandbar. It has become a local legend and a
mandatory stop for bohemian visitors to the South Coast.
The place serves fresh seafood for lunch and dinner, and
will also cook your own catch for you. The hotels of Treasure Beach can arrange boat transportation to Pelican Bar,
but these short rides can be pricey. ⊠ *Treasure Beach* ☎ *No
phone* ⊟ *No credit cards.*

BEST BETS FOR DINING

With the many restaurants to choose from, how will you decide where to eat? Fodor's writers and editors have selected their favorite restaurants in the Best Bets lists below. The Fodor's Choice properties represent the "best of the best." Find specific details about a restaurant in the full reviews.

Fodor's Choice
Jake's.

Best Budget Eats: Billy's Grassy Park; Little Ochie.

Best for Families: Jack Sprat.

Most Romantic: Bloomfield Great House Restaurant and Bar; Jake's; Jack Sprat.

Best for Local Jamaican Cuisine: Billy's Grassy Park; Little Ochie.

BLACK RIVER AND VICINITY

¢–$ × **Bridge House.** *Jamaican.* A no-nonsense eatery that's open for breakfast, lunch, and dinner, this is a popular spot with locals who come here for down-home meals of curried goat or chicken with trusty side dishes like rice and peas. It's also handy for tourists in town for the nearby Black River Safari tour. If you want to have a truly authentic Jamaican meal, skip the soda and ask for a glass of red punch. ⊠ *14 Crane Rd., Black River* ☎ *876/965–2361* ⊟ *MC, V.*

MANDEVILLE AND VICINITY

$$–$$$ × **The Arches.** *Jamaican.* Located poolside at the Mandeville Hotel, this eatery specializes in Jamaican favorites. On Wednesday evenings, the chef prepares a barbecue feast including a variety of meat and fish dishes. The Sunday breakfast is a Mandeville tradition, serving a lavish buffet of local favorites such as ackee and saltfish, mackerel rundown, escoveitch fish, fried plantains, callaloo, bammy, dumplings, and boiled green bananas. ⊠ *4 Hotel St., Mandeville* ☎ *876/962–9764* ⊟ *AE, MC, V.*

$$–$$$ × **Bloomfield Great House Restaurant and Bar.** *Jamaican.* International fare with a Caribbean twist is the order of the day at Mandeville's most lauded restaurant. It's in a plantation greathouse that dates back more than two centuries. Dining in the antiques-filled main dining room is pleasant, but the open-air verandah offers a spectacular view of the twinkling lights of Mandeville. Entrées include filet mignon with a roasted garlic and guava sauce; seafood kebabs; shrimp Creole; and grilled pork chops stuffed with

The Treasure Beach area has several good independent restaurants

tropical fruits. ✉ *8 Perth Rd., Mandeville* ☎ *876/962–7130* 🖃 *AE, MC, V.*

\$–\$\$ ✕ **International Chinese Restaurant.** *Chinese.* If you're looking for an alternative to jerk, this unassuming place offers Chinese comfort food in a casual setting. You can find many of your traditional Asian favorites like cashew chicken and sweet and sour pork. Other specialties include seafood and egg rolls. ✉ *117 Manchester Rd., Mandeville* ☎ *876/962–1252* 🖃 *MC, V.*

WHERE TO STAY

TREASURE BEACH AND VICINITY

★ Fodor'sChoice 🏨 **Jake's.** *Resort.* The laid-back, neighborly feel
\$\$–\$\$\$ of the south coast is epitomized by Jake's, a relaxed place that's fun, funky, and friendly. Co-owner Jason Henzell, now president of Island Outpost, is active in community development and encourages his guests to get out and mingle in the area, whether that means fishing with the locals or hitting a rum shop. Each villa here (designed by Jason's mother, Sally Henzell, a theatrical designer) is unique, but some are not especially roomy. **Pros:** unique accommodations; infused with south-coast friendliness; personalized service. **Cons:** some rooms can be cramped when housebound during rainy periods; no a/c in some rooms. ✉ *Calabash Bay, Treasure Beach* ☎ *876/965–3000* ⊕ *www.islandoutpost.com* ⇆ *45 villas* ♿ *In-room: no phone,*

A Helping Hand

Jason Henzell—co-owner of Jake's, president of Island Outpost, and son of the legendary movie producer Perry Henzell (The Harder They Come)—is involved in a South Coast community program called **Breds** (⊕ www.breds.org). Launched by Henzell and Peace Corps volunteer Aaron Laufer in 1998, Breds (short for Brethren, a term used by local residents to greet each other) is a nonprofit association that promotes education, cultural heritage, and environmental awareness.

The organization has coordinated the construction of homes in the Treasure Beach community, brought in doctors to train local first responders, arranged for donations of fishing boats to needy families, and helped to expand the resources of a local elementary school.

Breds raises money through donations and fund-raisers. The largest money maker for the program is the annual Treasure Beach Off-Road Triathlon.

a/c (some), safe, kitchen (some), refrigerator (some), DVD (some), no TV (some), Wi-Fi. In-hotel: 2 restaurants, room service (some), pool, beachfront, water sports, bicycles, Wi-Fi hotspot ⊟ *AE, D, MC, V* ⊠*EP.*

$–$$ 🏨 **Sunset Resort and Villas.** *Resort.* Next door to Jake's, this resort lacks the style of its attention-getting neighbor, but it still offers a friendly getaway that's lovingly owner-managed. Rooms are unique and oversized, though some of the decor strikes us as a bit too fussy and frilly. The owners are happy to advise guests about local fun and activities. The open-air restaurant serves beside a large, Astroturf-covered pool area. **Pros:** friendly staff; rooms are comfortably large; good location on Calabash Bay. **Cons:** decor is dated and fussy; remote location; pool area is dated. ⊠ *Calabash Bay, Treasure Beach* 🕾 *876/965–0143* ⊕ *www.sunsetresort.com* ⬙*14 rooms* ⚷ *In-room: no phone, refrigerator. In-hotel: restaurant, pool, beachfront* ⊟ *AE, D, MC, V* ⊠*EP.*

MANDEVILLE AND VICINITY

¢–$ 🏨 **Mandeville Hotel.** *Hotel.* This historic building, used as officers' quarters before becoming a hotel in 1875, has a homey atmosphere. Family-owned and -operated, it has a friendly feel. Tropical gardens wrap around the main building, and flowers spill onto the terrace restaurant, where breakfast and lunch are served. Basic rooms are simple and breeze-cooled; some superior rooms have a/c, as do suites, which also have full kitchens. You'll need a car to get around town, go out for dinner, and get to the beach, which is an hour away. **Pros:** quaint colonial style; great views of surrounding hills; staff helps setting up tours. **Cons:** limited nightlife; no a/c in some rooms; dated decor. ⊠ *4 Hotel St., Mandeville* ☎ *876/962–2460* ⊕ *www.mandevillehoteljamaica.com* ⇨ *60 rooms* ⚬ *In-room: a/c (some), safe, kitchen (some), refrigerator (some), Internet. In-hotel: 2 restaurants, bar, pool* ⊟ *AE, MC, V* ⑩ *EP.*

DID YOU KNOW? A fruit was developed in Mandeville: the ortanique. The combination orange and tangerine is unique to the island, hence the name.

BLACK RIVER AND VICINITY

★ Fodor's Choice ▥ **Sandals Whitehouse European Village and Spa.**
$$$$ *Resort.* The newest Sandals resort in Jamaica and the first major resort on the south coast, this property is one of the most upscale properties in the chain. The resort consists of several "villages" constructed with Italian, Dutch, and French architectural touches. The resort is surrounded by a 500-acre nature preserve and lies on a 2-mi-long (3-km-long) beach. **Pros:** great beach with no vendors; numerous dining options and an extensive all-inclusive package that includes airport shuttle; stylish accommodations in all room classes. **Cons:** some travelers won't like Disney-ish re-creation of European styles; dining at other Sandals is available as part of package, but there is no transportation to other properties due to distance; Whitehouse area can be bug-ridden and hot. ⊠ *Whitehouse* ☎ *876/957–5216* ⊕ *www.sandals.com* ⇨ *304 rooms, 54 suites* ⚬ *In-room: safe, refrigerator, Wi-Fi. In-hotel: 7 restaurants, room service, bars, tennis courts, pools, gym, spa, beachfront, diving, water sports, laundry service, Internet terminal, Wi-Fi hotspot, no kids under 18* ⊟ *AE, D, MC, V* ⚓ *2-night minimum* ⑩ *AI.*

BEACHES

If you're looking for something off the beaten path, head for Jamaica's largely undeveloped southwest coast. Because it's a sparsely populated area, these isolated beaches are some of the island's safest, with hasslers practically nonexistent. You should, however, use common sense; never leave valuables unattended on the beach, even for a few minutes. Swimming isn't recommended along the beach in the Alligator Pond area, not because of alligators (although

DID YOU KNOW?

Treasure Beach is the most atmospheric stretch of sand on the south coast, but the sand there is dark and coarse.

CLOSE UP

Helping Jamaica's Dogs and Cats

Like many islands, Jamaica has an abundance of stray dogs and cats; the economic downturn has made this situation even more acute as more animals have been abandoned. Stray dogs and beach dogs are commonplace, and many hotels report that visitors often ask how they can help. Here's how you can. The **Jamaica SPCA** (⊠ *10 Winchester Rd., Kingston* ☎ *876/929–0320* ⊕ *www.jspca. info*) welcomes volunteers, donations, and adoptions.

In Lydford, about 45 minutes from Ocho Rios, the **Animal House** (⋈ *Box 775, Ocho Rios* ☎ *876/801–8386* ⊕ *www. theanimalhousejamaica.org*) is a nonprofit, no-kill shelter.

Visitors are welcome to call and make an appointment to see the rescued cats and dogs available for adoption; volunteers are always needed. The shelter can assist with arrangements including helping travelers obtain the veterinary paperwork needed to fly home with an animal.

Chukka Caribbean (☎ *888/224–8552* ⊕ *www. ckukkacaribbean.com*) donates a portion of the proceeds of all of its dogsled tours to the Jamaica SPCA. The dogs themselves are all local rescue dogs. The company now runs dogsled tours out of the original Ocho Rios location and out of Montego Bay as well.

6

crocodiles are a concern in Black River) but because of strong currents.

Bluefields Beach Park. On the coastal road to Negril, you'll find this relatively narrow stretch of sand and rock in the town of Bluefields. A free beach, it's typically crowded only on weekends. The swimming here is good, although the sea is sometimes rough. There are some amenities, including restrooms, jerk stands, and an assortment of beach vendors. ⊠ *Bluefields.*

Font Hill Beach Park and Wildlife Sanctuary. Located between Whitehouse and Black River, this beach is part of a nature reserve that's owned by the Petroleum Corporation of Jamaica. For about a $4 entry fee, you can enjoy the day at the beach that includes restrooms, picnic tables, and plenty of golden sand. There are usually few visitors. The beach park is open Tuesday through Sunday. ⊠ *Rte. A2, near Luana Point.*

★ **Fodor'sChoice Treasure Beach.** The most atmospheric beach on the South Coast comprises four long stretches of sand as well as many small coves. Though it isn't as pretty as those to the west or north—it has more rocks and darker sand—the idea that you might be discovering a bit of the "real" Jamaica more than makes up for these small distractions. Both locals and visitors use the beaches, though you're just as likely to find it completely deserted except for a friendly beach dog. ⊠ *Treasure Beach*.

SPORTS AND THE OUTDOORS

BIRD-WATCHING

The South Coast is an excellent destination for birders who come in search of the mountain witch, jabbering crow, mango hummingbird, Jamaican oriole, and even the endangered yellow-billed parrot. The town of Bluefields was the home of the island's most famous naturalist, Englishman Philip Henry Gosse, who wrote several guides to Jamaica's birds.

Reliable Adventures Jamaica (☎ *876/955–8834* ⊕ *www. reliableadventuresjamaica.com/index.htm*) offers a guided birding tour on Monday, Wednesday, and Friday. It's aimed at serious birders with an interest in both birds and butterflies indigenous to Jamaica.

BOATING

The Black River, Jamaica's longest waterway, is named for the peat deposits that color its waters. This river is also known as the best place on the island to see crocodiles. Guided boat tours also spot local birds and point out native foliage.

South Coast Safaris Ltd. (⊠ *1 Crane St., Black River* ☎ *876/965–2513*) takes visitors on slow cruises ($16) up the river to see the birds and other animals, including crocodiles.

DIVING AND SNORKELING

The South Coast is not one of the island's top diving destinations. There's less coral here, and the visibility is so-so. Consequently, there are no independent dive outfitters in the area. Sandals Whitehouse European Village and Spa maintains its own dive shop for guests. Other South Coast resorts are happy to book dive excursions through operators in Negril.

CLOSE UP

Birding in Jamaica

Jamaica has an amazing variety of birds—nearly 300 species at last count, with a full 10% of them endemic to the island. This high rate of endemism, true for some of Jamaica's native plants as well as its wildlife, has been attributed to a number of factors, including the island's relative isolation and its varied topography.

Jamaica has been a prime birding spot since the 1800s, when the celebrated British scientist and naturalist Philip Henry Gosse reported on his travels around the Bluefields area in several books: *The Birds of Jamaica, Illustrations of the Birds of Jamaica,* and *A Naturalist's Sojourn in Jamaica.* Gosse's popular volumes are still in print, as is *Birds of the West Indies,* by James Bond. Yes, James Bond. Author Ian Fleming, writing at his home on the North Coast, needed just the right name for his new British spy hero. His eye fell on his copy of *Birds of the West Indies,* and the world's most famous fictional spy was christened.

Endemic species include the streamer-tailed hummingbird, popularly called the "doctor bird" by locals, which is also Jamaica's national bird. The yellow-billed parrot, black-billed parrot, rufous-tailed flycatcher, and Jamaican woodpecker are also species exclusive to Jamaica.

A number of tour operators, some on-island, others based in the United States, Canada, and the United Kingdom, host birding tours to Jamaica. In addition to the South Coast area, major birding hot spots include the Blue and John Crow Mountains near Kingston and the rugged Cockpit Country near Montego Bay.

There are a growing number of organizations, domestic and otherwise, dedicated to preserving and protecting Jamaica's native birds. The government, though typically slow to realize the potential value of Jamaica's birdlife, has responded in recent years by setting aside sizable areas for native flora and fauna, including the Blue and John Crow Mountains National Park, not established until 1990.

FISHING

The South Coast offers good deep-sea fishing opportunities. Half-day tours troll a few miles offshore for barracuda, kingfish, wahoo, tuna, dorado, and shark. Full-day tours can approach the Pedro Banks, where yellowtail, mutton, and redtail snapper are often caught. Hotels can often

The Incredible Peter Tosh

Peter Tosh, born Winston Hubert McIntosh, left the South Coast and headed to Kingston at the age of 15. There he met (and taught guitar to) Bob Marley and Bunny Wailer. The trio played together until the early 1970s when Tosh struck out on his own.

In 1978, Tosh performed at the One Love Peace Concert in Kingston, stopping his set to chastise the prime minister and opposition leader. A few months later, Tosh was attacked and severely beaten by local police. Although the authorities left him for dead, Tosh recovered and went on to perform with Mick Jagger and Eric Clapton and to later stage what became the longest reggae roadshow in history.

On September 11, 1987, gunmen broke into his Kingston home and killed Tosh. His funeral was held at the National Arena, where he had performed at the controversial One Love Peace Concert nearly a decade earlier.

recommend local anglers who will take travelers out on their boats for a fee.

GOLF

The South Coast is not known as a golf destination—in fact, there's only one course in the region.

In the hills, the 9-hole **Manchester Club** (⊠ *Caledonia Rd., Mandeville* ☎ *876/962–2403*) is the Caribbean's oldest golf course and charges greens fees of about $17.

GUIDED TOURS

Visitors to the South Coast can experience more of the real Jamaica through **Countrystyle Community Tourism Network** (⊠ *62 Ward Ave., Mandeville* ☎ *876/962-7758 or 876/488-7207* ⊕ *www.countrystylecommunitytourism.com*), a company that offers personalized tours of island communities.

HIKING

The terrain along the South Coast is incredibly varied, from savanna and rolling hills in the Whitehouse area to rugged mountains farther east near Mandeville. Thanks to the sparse population and light development, the area has many unspoiled hiking areas, although travelers are encouraged to hike with a local guide at all times. ⚠ Marijuana fields are hard to see until you wander upon one; these fields are closely controlled and guarded by ganja farmers.

The Black River, Jamaica's longest, is a great place to spot crocodiles

Reliable Adventures Jamaica (☎ *876/955–8834* ⊕ *www. reliableadventuresjamaica.com/index.htm*) offers half- and full-day guided hikes with no more than 20 participants.

DID YOU KNOW? Janga, a type of crayfish, are marketed locally as "hot peppered shrimp." They are sold by women along the side of the road in Middle Quarters, St. Elizabeth. They're salty, spicy, and as impossible as potato chips to stop eating.

HORSEBACK RIDING
One of the best ways to tour the South Coast's pastoral landscape is from horseback. In addition to riding along the beach, area stables offer trails through farm and pasture areas, allowing an up-close-and-personal look at some of the island's most rustic landscapes.

Paradise Park (✉ *Rte. A2, 1 mi [2 km] west of Ferris Cross* ☎ *876/955–2675*) is a working farm that has been owned and operated by the same family for more than 100 years. Visitors can rent horses to explore the farm's fields and pastures and the beaches of Bluefields Bay.

TENNIS
For about $5 per hour per person, the **Manchester Club** (✉ *Caledonia Rd., at Ward Ave., Mandeville* ☎ *876/962– 2403*) opens its tennis courts to visitors of the many small properties in the area that don't have their own facilities.

NIGHTLIFE AND THE ARTS

The nightlife on the South Coast is among the island's quietest. With its many ecotourism activities, the South Coast is very much an early-to-bed, early-to-rise destination.

ANNUAL EVENTS

In April, the **Treasure Beach Off-Road Triathlon** (☎ 876/965–3000 ⊕ *www.breds.org*) is the region's biggest annual event. The race features a 500-meter ocean swim, a 13.7-mi (25-km) mountain-bike trek, and a 4.3-mi (7-km) country run. Participation is limited to 50 Jamaicans and 50 visitors.

The **Calabash International Literary Festival** (✉ *Treasure Beach* ☎ 876/965–3000 ⊕ *www.calabashfestival.org*) offers three days and nights of both literary and musical talent at Jake's. The May festival, which in past years has featured authors including Russell Banks, Andrea Levy, and Sonia Sanchez, is the only annual literary festival in the English-speaking Caribbean.

The second Sunday in July is sure to be hot at the **Little Ochi Seafood Carnival** (✉ *7 mi [12 km] south of A2, Alligator Pond* ☎ 876/965–4449) when several thousand hungry people enjoy the best Jamaican cooking on the South Coast.

The **Treasure Beach Hook n' Line Canoe Tournament** (✉ *Treasure Beach* ☎ 876/965–0635) takes place each October. This three-day tournament pairs local fishermen with visitors. The teams compete using traditional fishing techniques.

Negril

WORD OF MOUTH

"[Negril] has a great vibe and is more for people who want to get out of the confines of their hotel to enjoy the two very different sides of Negril (beach vs. west end cliffs)."

—nunnies

By Paris
Permenter
and John
Bigley

On a winding coastal road about 55 mi (89 km) south-west of Montego Bay, Negril was once Jamaica's best-kept secret. This community, long sheltered from development by the surrounding Great Morass, was first introduced to tourism in the 1970s, when it became a haven for hippies. At first residents rented them rooms (or hammocks), but slowly mom-and-pop hotels began to spring up on the cliffs and along the beach. But even then the place had a laid-back vibe.

Today, Negril is quickly (some say *too* quickly) catching up with the rest of Jamaica. Sprawling all-inclusive resorts have appeared, with more on the horizon. One good thing: The development so far is still of the low-rise variety, as local law mandates that no building here can be taller than the tallest palm tree. The two massive Riu hotels certainly push the envelope, however.

Despite it all, Negril hangs on to its reputation as a wild vacation destination. Nudity is still common on the beaches of Bloody Bay. The infamous Hedonism II, boasting the highest repeat guest rate in the Caribbean, has been the topic of plenty of stories involving late-night hot tub parties. Reggae clubs attract some of the island's best musicians to the cliffs that overlook spectacular sunsets. And, although not as popular as it was during the '70s, more than one establishment still sells hallucinogenic teas, and freelance entrepreneurs still hawk ganja.

One thing that hasn't changed at this west-coast com-munity (whose only true claim to fame is a 7-mi [11-km] beach) is its casual approach to life. As you wander from lunch in the sun to shopping in the sun to sports in the sun, you can find that swimsuits and cover-ups are common attire. Want to dress up for a special meal? Tie a pareu over your swimsuit.

ORIENTATION AND PLANNING

ORIENTATION

Negril stretches along the coast from horseshoe-shape Bloody Bay (named when it was a whale-processing cen-ter) along the calm waters of Long Bay to the Lighthouse. Nearby, divers spiral downward off 50-foot-high cliffs into the deep green depths as the sun turns into a ball of fire and sets the clouds ablaze with color. Sunset is also the time when Norman Manley Boulevard comes to bustling bistros and ear-splitting discos.

The real wildness in Negril lies just outside the city Here, in a wide-ranging swampy area known as the Great Morass, you can see a side of the country that most visitors never glimpse. Crocodiles, not vacationers, lie in the steamy afternoon sunshine. And spectacular birds, not parasailers, fill the air with dashes of color and a cacophony of exotic sounds.

PLANNING

WHEN TO GO
Like other areas of Jamaica, Negril's high season extends from mid-December to mid-April. In late March and early April, the annual spring-break onslaught means thousands of college students, mostly from the United States and Canada, descend for days of foam parties and T-shirt contests and nights of reggae concerts and all-night disco music. The more expensive all-inclusive properties are generally devoid of the spring-break crowds because of their higher prices.

GETTING HERE AND AROUND

BY AIR
Negril has no international air service, but there is a small domestic airport across from Bloody Bay. The Negril Aerodrome has limited charter service from both Montego Bay and Kingston. Most Negril travelers arrive from Montego Bay's Sangster International Airport. Many of the larger hotels (especially the all-inclusive resorts) offer shuttle service. Transportation is also available from JCAL Tours, Jamaica Tours, and Clive's Transport Service for about $50 to $60 per person round-trip.

Contacts Clive's Transport Service (☎ 876/956–2615 or 876/869–7571 ⊕ www.clivestransportservicejamaica.com). **Jamaica Tours** (☎ 876/953–3700 ⊕ www.jamaicatoursltd.com). **JCAL Tours** (☎ 876/952–7574 ⊕ www.jcaltours.com). **Negril Aerodrome** (✉ Norman Manley Blvd., Negril ☎ 876/957–5016).

BY CAR
Driving in Negril is an easier task than in Montego Bay and Ocho Rios, but still a chore thanks to the very narrow roads (especially when the main road becomes West End Road along the cliffs). If you plan to spend the day exploring to the South Coast but don't want to travel with

7

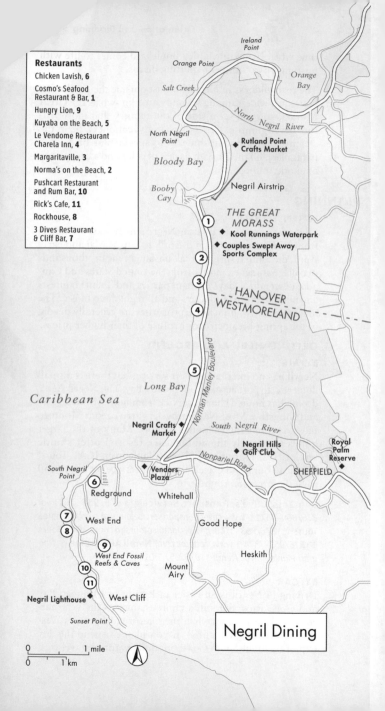

Restaurants

Chicken Lavish, **6**

Cosmo's Seafood Restaurant & Bar, **1**

Hungry Lion, **9**

Kuyaba on the Beach, **5**

Le Vendome Restaurant Charela Inn, **4**

Margaritaville, **3**

Norma's on the Beach, **2**

Pushcart Restaurant and Rum Bar, **10**

Rick's Cafe, **11**

Rockhouse, **8**

3 Dives Restaurant & Cliff Bar, **7**

Ireland Point

Orange Point

Orange Bay

Salt Creek

North Negril River

North Negril Point

Rutland Point Crafts Market

Bloody Bay

Negril Airstrip

Booby Cay

THE GREAT MORASS

Kool Runnings Waterpark

Couples Swept Away Sports Complex

HANOVER
WESTMORELAND

Norman Manley Boulevard

Long Bay

Caribbean Sea

Negril Crafts Market

South Negril River

Negril Hills Golf Club

Royal Palm Reserve

Nonpariel Road

SHEFFIELD

South Negril Point

Vendors Plaza

Redground

Whitehall

West End

Good Hope

West End Fossil Reefs & Caves

Heskith

Mount Airy

Negril Lighthouse

West Cliff

Sunset Point

Negril Dining

0   1 mile
0   1 km

TOP REASONS TO GO

Soaking Up the Sun: Stroll the chalky 7 mi (11 km) of sand along Negril Beach, one of the island's best beaches.

Dancing the Night Away: Negril is rocking all night long; catch some of the island's best nightlife at a beach bar like Alfred's Ocean Club.

Showing off Your Birthday Suit: Cast off your cares—and your clothes—at one of the west coast's clothing optional beaches.

Looking for the Green Flash: People come from all over the island to watch the sun set from Negril's cliffs; the most popular spot is Rick's.

Getting Close to Nature: Watch birds—and crocodiles—at the Royal Palm Reserve, where you can stroll on meandering wooden walkways through the palms.

an organized tour, driving can be a good choice, although signage is poor on area roads.

Car-Rental Contacts Rite Rate Car Rental (⊠ *Norman Manley Blvd., Negril* ☎ *876/957–4667*). **Vernon's Car and Jeep Rental** (⊠ *Plaza de Negril, Sheffield Rd., Negril* ☎ *876/957–4354*).

BY TAXI

Taxis are the most popular mode of transportation (although not an inexpensive one). They can be caught at any hotel or on the road. Licensed taxis have a red license plate with a PP that indicates the taxi is a Public Passenger Vehicle. Very few taxis are metered, so be sure to agree on a price with the driver before departing. Hotel staffers can let you know how much to expect to pay before you begin your negotiations.

Contacts JUTA (☎ *876/957–9197* ⊕ *www.jutatoursnegrilltd.com*).

RESTAURANTS

They call Negril the "capital of casual," and nowhere is that more true than in its restaurants. Unlike the other destinations in Jamaica, where the occasional jacket is spotted especially during the winter months, Negril is about as laid-back as you can get. Most restaurants are right on the beach, and meals are more often than not enjoyed out on the sand. Shorts and T-shirts are appropriate at many restaurants, especially for lunch; sundresses and shirts with collars make an appearance for dinner at most properties (although you can find a few of the upscale properties,

DID YOU KNOW?

Negril's lighthouse has been guiding ships since 1895. The view from the top is the best on the western end of the island.

such as Sandals Negril, that insist on "casually elegant" clothes). Reservations are rarely required or even accepted at local restaurants.

HOTELS

When it comes to hotels, there are almost two different Negrils: that of Norman Manley Boulevard and that of West End Road. Along Norman Manley, the road that leads to Negril from Montego Bay, you can find traditional hotels (including many smaller properties) as well as a growing number of all-inclusive resorts (especially along Bloody Bay).

As Norman Manley Boulevard becomes West End Road at the roundabout in town, you'll see properties best described as small and funky. This road leads along Negril's famous cliffs, an area where the mom-and-pop properties that carry on the spirit of "old" Negril live alongside a handful of more upscale boutique resorts. These lodgings are especially favored by European travelers, who often stay several weeks.

For those who would like to get out and explore the region, both the main stretch of Negril Beach on Long Bay and the cliffs area are good options. The beach properties make it easy to get out and explore on foot; the walk is lined with hotels and restaurants and just a few undeveloped areas.

7

WHAT IT COSTS IN DOLLARS				
¢	$	$$	$$$	$$$$
RESTAURANTS				
under $8	$8–$12	$12–$20	$20–$30	Over $30
HOTELS*				
under $80	$80–$150	$150–$250	$250–$350	Over $350
HOTELS**				
under $125	$125–$250	$250–$350	$350–$450	Over $450

*EP, BP, CP; **AI, FAP, MAP; restaurant prices are per person for a main course at dinner and do not include the 15% V.A.T. and 10% service charge. Hotel prices are per night for a double room in high season, excluding 15% V.A.T. and 10% service charge.

ESSENTIALS

BANKS AND CURRENCY EXCHANGE

Most of the larger hotels in Negril can exchange money and cash traveler's checks; you can also find ATMs at some of the larger properties. Scotiabank has an ATM at its Negril Square location.

EMERGENCIES

Medical care is fairly limited in Negril. All larger resorts have nurses on duty during work hours and a doctor on call and there's a medical clinic in town. The nearest hospitals are in Savannah-La-Mar and Lucea; the closest large hospitals are in Montego Bay.

INTERNET

Internet access is somewhat limited in Negril, even in hotels you might expect to see high-speed or even wireless service, due to the lower number of business travelers, the lack of cruise-ship passengers, and the difficulty of obtaining even telephone lines in Negril. However, thanks in part to its large number of spring breakers, Negril does have some Internet cafés where you can hop on a high-speed connection and check your e-mail.

Contacts **Blue Water Ice Cream Parlor and Internet** (✉ West End Rd., Negril ☎ 876/957–0125 ⊕ www.bluewaterinternetnegril.com). **Easy Rock Internet Café** (✉ West End Rd., Negril ☎ 876/957–0816 or 876/424–5481 ⊕ www.negril.com/ezrock). **Surf 'n Talk** (✉ Norman Manley Blvd., Negril).

VISITOR INFORMATION

The Negril Chamber of Commerce publishes the *Negril Guide*, a free brochure covering attractions, shopping, and dining. The organization also operates a visitor center just beyond the downtown roundabout on West End Road; you can find brochures and maps available as well as friendly assistance.

Information **Negril Chamber of Commerce** (✏ Box 3055, West End Rd., Negril ☎ 876/957–4067 ⊕ www.negrilchamberofcommerce.com).

EXPLORING NEGRIL

With lighter traffic than Montego Bay and Ocho Rios (and no cruise-ship port), Negril is fairly easy to navigate by taxi or, even better, on foot, strolling along the miles of sand on Negril Beach. This town's charms are found on its beaches, in its bars, and at its hotels—not really in area attractions, which are few and far between. The town is home to only one notable historic site, its lighthouse, and a few natural attractions such as the Royal Palm Reserve.

That said, it's an easy day trip from Negril to many attractions on the South Coast, from waterfalls to rivers, birding sites to horseback rides.

WHAT TO SEE

☺ **Kool Runnings Waterpark.** This park makes a good beach
★ alternative on days when the sea is rough or for travelers not staying at beachfront properties. Admission to the park includes 10 waterslides and a quarter-mile lazy river float ride; a go-kart track and bungee trampoline each have a separate charge. The park's newest attraction is the Kool Swamp Adventure, a 20-minute guided boat tour of the Great Morass (additional cost of $7). Kids under 48 inches tall can't use some slides so a discounted rate ($19) is charged. The park is open ⊠ *Norman Manley Blvd., Negril* ☎ *876/957–5418* ⊕ *www.koolrunnings.com* ☎ *$28* ☉ *Jan.– Mar., Wed., Sat., Sun. 11–7; Apr –Dec., Tues.–Sun. 10–7.*

7

DID YOU KNOW? Prostitution is a big problem in Negril. Along with female prostitution, male prostitution has become increasingly evident, especially during evening shows. Locally nicknamed Rent-A-Rasta, Rent-A-Dread, and Rasta-tutes, the young hustlers often approach female tourists and offer their services. (Middle-aged European women—thanks to their longer vacations—are favorite targets.) The practice is so common it became the subject of a London play called *Sugar Mommies*.

★ **Royal Palm Reserve.** On the southern side of the Great Morass, this preserve protects the wetlands and the royal palms that thrive here. Along with plenty of majestic palms, these 300 acres are also home to 113 other plant species, including 10 kinds of fern and 18 types of climbing vine. Visitors stroll on the boardwalk winding through the grounds; along the way look for crocodiles and many

Rasta for Beginners

Rastafarians, more commonly known as Rastas, are believers in the divinity of Haile Selassie, former ruler of Ethiopia. Rastafarianism remains a minority religion in Jamaica, but it is one of the most visible thanks to the popularity of Rastas such as the late reggae singer Bob Marley.

Rastafarians are usually seen wearing crocheted tams, beneath which are tucked their long dreadlocks. The Rastas do not believe in cutting their hair, citing Leviticus 21.5: "They shall not make baldness upon their head, neither shall they shave off the corner of their beard nor make any cuttings in their flesh." Rastafarian women generally wear dreadlocks as well, along with African-style clothing and headwraps.

When talking with a Rasta, you'll soon notice their distinction of speaking in the first person. "We" is substituted with "I and I," following the belief that God (known to the Rastas as *Jah*) is present in every person.

Rastas are also strict vegetarians, maintaining a salt-free diet of what is termed *Ital* food. Look for the red, green, and gold colors on restaurants as a clue to locating Ital eateries, which are often quite small.

Better known than their vegetarian diet is their use of *ganja*, or marijuana, as a part of their religion. They cite Psalm 104.14: "He causeth the grass to grow for the cattle, and herb for the service of man." Perhaps not coincidentally, Rastas are also renowned herbalists, using folk medicine and relying on the land's plants to heal many ills.

---

bird species. The Negril Royal Palm Reserve Museum has displays about the Great Morass. ⊠ *Springfield Rd., Sheffield* ☎ *876/957–3736* ⊕ *www.royalpalmreserve.com* ☞ *$10* ☉ *Daily 9–6.*

WHERE TO EAT

Dining in Negril is a casual affair, one most often enjoyed on the beach. Reservations aren't required and often aren't even accepted; many visitors just stroll down the sand until they find an eatery that appeals to them.

¢–$ ✕ **Chicken Lavish.** *Jamaican.* This longtime West End eatery serves—you guessed it—chicken prepared the way locals like it: curried, fried, jerked, and grilled. The restaurant is in a simple, green-roofed house with a porch that serves as a dining room (takeout is also popular). If you've had

Rasta cooking is strictly vegetarian

enough chicken, you can find curried goat and fried fish on the menu as well. ⊠ *Northern end of West End Rd., Negril* ☎ *876/957–4410* ▭ *MC, V.*

$$–$$$ ✕ **Cosmo's Seafood Restaurant and Bar.** *Seafood.* Owner Cosmo Brown has made this seaside open-air bistro a pleasant place to spend the afternoon—and maybe stay on for dinner. Fish is the main attraction, and the conch soup—a house specialty—is a meal in itself. You can also find lobster (grilled or curried), fish-and-chips, and the catch of the morning. Customers often drop cover-ups to take a dip before coffee and dessert and return to lounge in chairs scattered under almond and sea grape trees (there's an entrance fee of $1.50 for the beach). ⊠ *Norman Manley Blvd., Negril* ☎ *876/957–4330 or 876/957–4784* ▭ *AE, MC, V.*

$ $$ ✕ **The Hungry Lion.** *Vegetarian.* Whether you're a vegetarian, curious about the Rastafarian diet, or just looking for a good meal, the Hungry Lion has been a longtime favorite in the West End area. Traditional food cooked to Rastafarian specifications (including no salt) means dishes like meatless shepherd's pie made with lentils. Seafood such as fried snapper is another top choice (some Rastas do eat fish). You can also find a long list of freshly made juices, all enjoyed in an alfresco setting. ⊠ *Southern end of West End Rd., Negril* ☎ *876/957–4486* ▭ *AE, MC, V.*

¢–$ ✕ **Kuyaba on the Beach.** *Eclectic.* This charming thatch-roof eatery has an international menu—including curried conch, kingfish steak, grilled lamb with sautéed mushrooms, and

BEST BETS FOR DINING

With the many restaurants to choose from, how will you decide where to eat? Fodor's writers and editors have selected their favorite restaurants in the Best Bets lists below. The Fodor's Choice properties represent the "best of the best." Find specific details about a restaurant in the full reviews.

Fodor's Choice

Norma's on the Beach; The Rockhouse Restaurant.

Best Budget Eats: Chicken Lavish.

Best for Families: Margaritaville; Rick's Café.

Most Romantic: Le Vendome; Norma's on the Beach; The Rockhouse Restaurant; Rick's Café.

Best for Local Jamaican Cuisine: Chicken Lavish; The Hungry Lion; Pushcart Restaurant and Rum Bar.

several pasta dishes—plus a lively ambience, especially at the bar. There's a crafts shop on the premises, and chaise lounges line the beach; come prepared to spend some time, and don't forget a towel and bathing suit. ⊠ *Norman Manley Blvd., Negril* ☎ *876/957–4318* ☐ *AE, MC, V.*

DID YOU KNOW? With its diagonal golden cross across a black and green background, the Jamaican flag is one of the most easily distinguishable Caribbean flags. In use since 1962, each part of the flag is symbolic. The black used for the left and right triangles represents the hardship of the people. The green of the upper and lower quadrants symbolizes hope and the fertile land of Jamaica, and the gold represents wealth and sunshine.

$$–$$$ ✕ **Le Vendome.** *French.* At the middle-of-the-road Charela Inn, you might expect this place to be a simple eatery featuring standard beach fare. Le Vendome is fine dining at its best—with the added attraction of a beachside location. From fine wines to crusty bread baked fresh daily, this restaurant serves French cuisine with a hint of Jamaica (don't be surprised to see a dusting of jerk spice or ginger). The restaurant features a different five-course gourmet dinner every evening, but you can always order à la carte, and there are always dishes such as filet mignon in wine and mushroom sauce, canard à l'orange, and shrimp in garlic sauce. On Thursday and Saturday night, the mood turns distinctly Jamaican with live performances. ⊠ *Norman*

Manley Blvd., Negril 📞 *876/957–4277* ⊕ *wwu*
☆ *Reservations essential* ═ *MC, V.*

$–$$ ✕ **Margaritaville.** *Eclectic.* Like its sister p
Montego Bay and Ocho Rios, Margaritavi
Americanized menu and not-very-authentic Caribbean
experience—but with the added backdrop of Negril Beach.
Burgers are joined by a few Caribbean items like conch fritters. This restaurant–nightclub doesn't have the waterslides
of the island's other outposts, but you can find a water
trampoline and a rock-climbing wall to work off those
calories. ⊠ *Norman Manley Blvd., Negril* 📞 *876/957–4467*
═ *AE, D, MC, V.*

★ **Fodor'sChoice** ✕ **Norma's on the Beach.** *Caribbean.* Although
$–$$ it's in the modest boutique hotel Sea Splash, make no mis-
take: this is Jamaican dining at some of its finest. Norma
is Norma Shirley, one of Jamaica's best-known culinary
artists, often called the Julia Child of the Caribbean. Opt
for terrace or candlelight dining. Her dressed-up Jamaican
fare is prepared with a creative flair. Try callaloo-stuffed
chicken breast or jerk chicken pasta. ⊠ *Sea Splash Hotel,*
Norman Manley Blvd., Negril 📞 *876/957–4041* ═ *AE, D,*
MC, V.

$–$$ ✕ **Pirates Cave Bar and Restaurant.** *Eclectic.* If this place looks
just a tad familiar, it might be because the cliffs and nearby
sea cave were used as a setting in the *20,000 Leagues Under*
the Sea and other movies. Steve McQueen leaped from
the cliffs in *Papillon,* and cliff jumping continues to be the
location's top draw. The menu is hardly the stuff of pirate
lore—cheeseburgers, barbecue ribs, and fish sandwiches—
but you can find a tasty jerk chicken and rasta pasta with
ackee and vegetables to remind you you're in Jamaica.
⊠ *West End Rd., Negril* 📞 *876/957–0925* ═ *AE, MC, V.*

$–$$ ✕ **Pushcart Restaurant and Rum Bar.** *Jamaican.* At Rockhouse,
the casual Pushcart Restaurant and Rum Bar offers guests
an opportunity to enjoy traditional Jamaican street food
and authentic home cooking while sampling the Caribbean's
finest rums. One signature dish is peppered shrimp, which
recalls a traditional roadside favorite in St. Elizabeth parish.
Other favorites include "fish with bammy," a famous dish
in Port Royal and, of course, jerk sausage, a traditional
Jamaican roadside staple. Nightly live music and a stellar
sunset view add to the casual ambience. ⊠ *Rockhouse, West*
End Rd., Negril 📞 *876/957–4373* ⊕ *www.rockhousehotel.*
com ═ *MC, V* ⊘ *No lunch.*

$$–$$$ ✕ **Rick's Café.** *Caribbean.* It's hard to keep a good café–tourist
attraction down, even when a force like Hurricane Ivan

Jamaican Patois

If you feel like you're hearing a foreign tongue, you're almost right. The language of the streets is patois, a colorful combination of English, Spanish, and Portuguese, with plenty of local slang all in one. Many words are African in origin. Most are believed to come from the Twi language and other Gold Coast languages. Other influences include the language of Mendi, Igbo, Efik, Yoruba, Kongo, Kimbundu, Ewe, Mandinka and, some say, Swahili.

Here's an example of some patois you might hear on the streets:

a go foreign: to leave Jamaica

bankra: a large basket

bendung maaket: a sidewalk market, a place where you would "bend down"

bendung: to shop

boonoonunus: wonderful, beautiful

bratta: something extra

bredda: brother

chaka-chaka: messy

craven: greedy

cuss-cuss: argument with cursing

dege-dege: skinny

duppy: ghost

irie (eye-ree): all's well, good

janga: crayfish

kiss teet: sucking teeth in disapproval

ku: look

kyaan: can't

laba-laba: gossip

labrish: gossip

lilly bit: tiny, small

mash up: destroy, wreck

nyam: eat

oht fi: about to

wa mek?: why?

wagga-wagga: bountiful

winjy: sickly

yard: home

blew through in 2004, sending much of the establishment into the sea. By 2005, Rick's had been rebuilt and was bigger than ever, with two floors of dining options along with poolside cabanas for rent—as well as the cliff diving and sunset views the restaurant has been known for since 1974. Menu options range from escoveitch shrimp to jerk chicken skewers to steak. ⊠ *West End Rd., Negril* ☎ *876/957–0380* ⊕ *www.rickscafejamaica.com* ⊟ *D, MC, V.*

★ Fodor'sChoice ╳ **The Rockhouse Restaurant.** *Caribbean.* With
$$–$$$ its seaside perch, the Rockhouse restaurant would already offer a memorable dining experience—but an incredible menu makes your meal that much more special. Serving what has been deemed "new Jamaican cuisine," Rock-

house offers Jamaican fare prepared with a light touch. Top entrées include blackened mahimahi with mango chutney, Jamaican jambalaya with French bread, and even a Jamaican stir fry with callaloo, cho cho, carrot, cabbage, rice, and peas. A rich selection of international wines accompanies the menu, and the restaurant prides itself on its attentive waitstaff. ⊠ *Rockhouse, West End Rd., Negril* ☎ *876/957–4373* ⊕ *www.rockhousehotel.com* ⚓ *Reservations essential* ⊟ *AE, MC, V.*

$-$$ ✕ **3 Dives Restaurant and Cliff Bar.** *Jamaican.* This ultracasual restaurant, housed beneath a big roof and not much more, was featured on the *Amazing Race.* But before the television show, it was already tops for its amazing local cuisine. The restaurant is best known for its jerk (and its annual jerk festival), but it also serves a menu of traditional Jamaican dishes like curried goat, brown stew chicken, curried or steamed conch, and, in season, grilled lobsters. During the winter months, lunch is offered but dinner, thanks to the spectacular sunsets here, is the peak time with crowds forming well before the sun hits the horizon. ⊠ *West End Rd., Negril* ☎ *876/344–6850* ⊟ *AE, MC, V.*

WHERE TO STAY

7

$$$$ ⊞ **Beaches Negril Resort and Spa.** *Resort.* This family-friendly all-inclusive has something for everyone: a prime Negril Beach location, upscale dining for adults, and multiple attractions for kids and teens. One chief asset is its impressive water park: Pirates Island, an 18,000-square-foot theme park that is always popular. This resort also has an Xbox game room for kids (and plenty of adults, too). Sesame Street characters roam the grounds and interact with guests. Dining here can be enjoyed as a family or separately (two restaurants are reserved for adults only). There's also a supervised kids' program (and scheduled teen activities) to keep everyone happy. **Pros:** great beach; extensive water park; friendly staff. **Cons:** on major road; children's programs cancelled if too few are enrolled; some activities have a surcharge. ⊠ *Norman Manley Blvd., Negril* ☎ *876/957–9270* ⊕ *www.beaches.com* ⇆ *210 rooms* ⚹ *In-room: safe, refrigerator (some), Internet. In-hotel: 5 restaurants, room service (some), bars, tennis courts, pools, gym, spa, beachfront, diving, water sports, children's programs (ages newborn–17), laundry service, Internet terminal* ⊟ *AE, D, DC, MC, V* ⭘*AI.*

BEST BETS FOR LODGING

Fodor's offers a selective listing of quality lodging experiences, from the island's best boutique hotel to its most luxurious beach resort. Here, we've compiled our top recommendations based on the different types of lodging found on the island. The very best properties—in other words, those that provide a particularly remarkable experience—are designated in the listings with the Fodor's Choice logo.

Fodor's Choice

Breezes Grand Negril Resort and Spa; The Caves; Rockhouse; Sandals Negril Beach Resort and Spa.

Best Budget Stay: Coco La Palm, Rockhouse.

Best Boutique Hotel: The Caves; Rockhouse.

Best All-Inclusive Resort: Breezes Grand Negril Resort and Spa; Couples Swept Away Negril; Sandals Negril Beach Resort and Spa; Hedonism II.

Best for Honeymooners: Breezes Grand Negril Resort and Spa; The Caves; Couples Swept Away Negril; Sandals Negril Beach Resort and Spa; Rockhouse.

Best for Families: Beaches Negril Resort and Spa., Beaches Sandy Bay, Coco La Palm, Grand Pineapple Beach Negril.

$$$$ ⬚ **Beaches Sandy Bay.** *Resort.* This family-friendly resort is not as expansive as its sister property, Beaches Negril Resort and Spa; however, it's more economical and gives families full privileges—from the water parks to the restaurants—at its more expensive sister resort. There's even a free shuttle between the properties. You can find a wide variety of rooms here, from two-level suites with kitchenettes and living rooms to standard rooms sized for a family of four. As at other Beaches resorts, Sesame Street characters roam the grounds here and are available for special bookings such as breakfast and tuck-in service. **Pros:** moderate price; great location; airport shuttle; extensive children's program. **Cons:** smallish pools can get crowded; rooms need a face-lift; meal option somewhat limited. ⊠ *Norman Manley Blvd., Negril* ☎ *876/957–5100* ⊕ *www.beaches.com* ⇱ *128 rooms* ♿ *In-room: safe, kitchen (some), refrigerator (some), Internet. In-hotel: 3 restaurants, room service, bars, pools, gym, spa, beachfront, diving, water sports, children's programs (ages newborn–12), laundry service, Internet terminal* ⊟ *AE, D, DC, MC, V* ⦿*AI.*

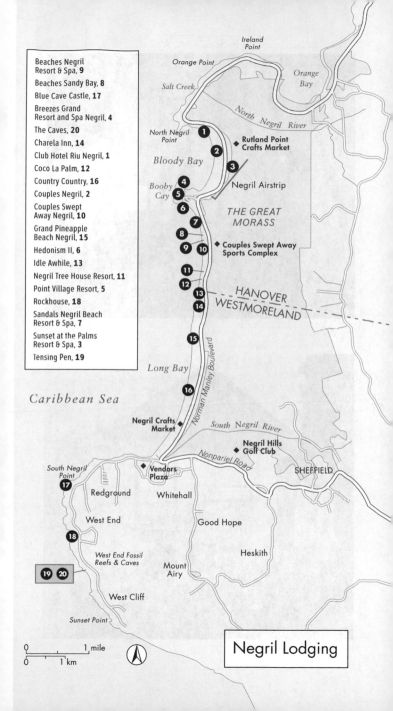

Beaches Negril
Resort & Spa, **9**

Beaches Sandy Bay, **8**

Blue Cave Castle, **17**

Breezes Grand
Resort and Spa Negril, **4**

The Caves, **20**

Charela Inn, **14**

Club Hotel Riu Negril, **1**

Coco La Palm, **12**

Country Country, **16**

Couples Negril, **2**

Couples Swept
Away Negril, **10**

Grand Pineapple
Beach Negril, **15**

Hedonism II, **6**

Idle Awhile, **13**

Negril Tree House Resort, **11**

Point Village Resort, **5**

Rockhouse, **18**

Sandals Negril Beach
Resort & Spa, **7**

Sunset at the Palms
Resort & Spa, **3**

Tensing Pen, **19**

Ireland
Point

Orange Point

Orange
Bay

Salt Creek

North Negril River

North Negril
Point

Rutland Point
Crafts Market

Bloody Bay

Negril Airstrip

Booby
Cay

THE GREAT
MORASS

Couples Swept Away
Sports Complex

HANOVER

WESTMORELAND

Norman Manley Boulevard

Long Bay

Caribbean Sea

Negril Crafts
Market

South Negril River

Negril Hills
Golf Club

Nonpariel Road

SHEFFIELD

South Negril
Point

Vendors
Plaza

Redground

Whitehall

Good Hope

West End

Heskith

West End Fossil
Reefs & Caves

Mount
Airy

West Cliff

Sunset Point

0   1 mile
0   1 km

Negril Lodging

The Caves

Breezes Grand Negril

$ ⌨ **Blue Cave Castle.** *Hotel.* One of Negril's most unique properties (and that's saying something in this land of one-of-a-kind boutique hotels), Blue Cave Castle is perched 50 feet over an actual pirate cave. A treasure is found within the walls of Blue Cave Castle, a keep towering over the cliffs of Negril. Each of the rather basic rooms boasts a seaside view—the most elaborate is the Penthouse, with its three private sunning decks. Visitors can snorkel through the grotto into a secluded garden, or just descend the flight of stairs carved into the cliff face down to the seaside, where they can sit upon stone King and Queen thrones and watch the sun sink into the cobalt-blue water of the Caribbean ocean. **Pros:** unique accommodations; good snorkeling; friendly staff. **Cons:** basic rooms; no beach; some rooms lack air-conditioning. ⊠ *West End Rd., Negril* ☎ *876/957–4845* ⊕ *www.bluecavecastle.com* ⇆ *14 rooms* ⚹ *In-room: no phone, a/c (some), refrigerator (some), no TV (some). In-hotel: bar, diving, water sports* ⊟ *D, MC, V* ⎮⚮⎮ *EP.*

★ Fodor'sChoice ⌨ **Breezes Grand Negril Resort and Spa.** *Resort.*
$$$$ Fancy touches at this resort are balanced by an expansive clothing-optional beach (including its own hot tub, bar, and grill), giving you one of Jamaica's best resorts, where it's fun to dress for dinner but equally good to strip down for a day of fun in the sun. Although a cursory look around the marble-clad lobby decorated with fine art and elegant columns might give the impression that this upscale all-inclusive (the former Grand Lido Negril) is a tad stuffy, the mood here is quiet and relaxing. And the clothed beach is one of the best strips of sand in Negril. Appealing to an upscale crowd of all stripes, you'll find a much different crowd here than at sister resort Hedonism II, which is just next door. Low-rise rooms, both oceanfront and garden suites, are stylish; many have French doors just steps from the sand. **Pros:** excellent beaches; super-inclusive package including complimentary manicure/pedicure and dry cleaning; elegant setting. **Cons:** some rooms need updating; central public area lacks view; clothing-optional pool is small. ⊠ *Norman Manley Blvd., Box 88, Negril* ☎ *876/957–5010* ⊕ *www.superclubs.com* ⇆ *210 suites* ⚹ *In-room: safe, refrigerator, Wi-Fi. In-hotel: 7 restaurants, room service (some), bars, tennis courts, pools, gym, spa, beachfront, diving, water sports, Internet terminal, Wi-Fi hotspot, no kids under 16* ⊟ *AE, D, DC, MC, V* ⚮ *3-night minimum* ⎮⚮⎮ *AI.*

★ Fodor'sChoice ⌨ **The Caves.** *Resort.* Although encompassing
$$$$ just two tiny acres, this petite resort packs a lot of punch in its cliff-side location, drawing the Hollywood set as well

as travelers looking for boutique-style pampering. Thatch-roof cottages are individually designed with vivid colors and hand-carved furniture, every one offering spectacular sunset views. The cottages are built above the natural sea caves that line the cliffs, one of which is used for private romantic dinners. TVs are available, but only if you ask. **Pros:** stylish and unique accommodations; personal service; quiet atmosphere. **Cons:** limited on-site dining options; may be too quiet for some travelers; no beach (on cliffs). ⊠ *Lighthouse Rd., Negril* ☎ *876/975–0269* ⊕ *www. islandoutpost.com* ⇆ *6 suites, 3 cottages, 1 4-bedroom villa* ⌂ *In-room: refrigerator (some), Wi-Fi. In-hotel: restaurant, pool, spa, water sports, bicycles, no kids under 16* ⊟ *AE, D, MC, V* ¶O¶ *AI.*

$$ ☶ **Charela Inn.** *Inn.* Directly on Negril Beach, this quiet hotel is understated but elegant in a simple way and has a widely praised French-Jamaican restaurant. Each quiet room has a private balcony or a covered patio. You can opt for a room-only plan if you want to explore neighboring restaurants along the beach, but most guests go all-inclusive. Children up to nine years old can stay in their parents' room for no additional charge; there's an $18 per-night charge for kids 10 to 15 years, although no children are permitted in deluxe guest rooms. The Saturday-night folkloric show draws guests from all over Negril. **Pros:** great dining; good beach location; good value for families. **Cons:** dated room decor; some guest rooms are small; facilities are not luxurious. ⊠ *Norman Manley Blvd., Box 3033, Negril* ☎ *876/957–4277* ⊕ *www.charela.com* ⇆ *49 rooms* ⌂ *In-room: safe, refrigerator, Wi-Fi. In-hotel: restaurant, bar, pool, beachfront, diving, laundry service, Internet terminal* ⊟ *MC, V* ⇆ *5-night minimum mid-Dec.–mid-Apr., 3-night minimum mid-Apr.–mid-Dec.* ¶O¶ *EP.*

$$$ ☶ **ClubHotel Riu Negril.** *Resort.* Far north of Negril on Bloody
☾ Bay, this massive resort has a decent, sandy beachfront. A lack of personalized service is balanced by good bang for the buck, decent food, and extensive activities and facilities. Rooms are attractive, but those in the second and third blocks are a *very* long walk from everything, with no resort shuttle to help your weary feet. The programs for kids are slightly better here than at the Riu Tropical Bay, which is equally large and next door. **Pros:** economical all-inclusive; family travelers find plenty of children on-site; good on-site dining. **Cons:** pools and public areas can be overcrowded with families; many rooms a long walk from public areas; long walk from attractions of Negril Beach. ⊠ *Norman*

Manley Blvd., Negril ☎ *876/957–5700* ⊕ *www.riu.com* ⤳ *402 rooms, 18 junior suites* ⚷ *In-room: safe, refrigerator. In-hotel: 4 restaurants, bars, tennis courts, pools, gym, spa, beachfront, diving, water sports, children's programs (ages 4–12), laundry facilities, laundry service, Internet terminal, Wi-Fi hotspot* ⊟ *AE, D, MC, V* ⋈ *AI.*

$–$$ ▣ **Coco La Palm.** *Inn.* This quiet, friendly hotel on the beach has oversized rooms (junior suites average 540 square feet) in octagonal buildings around the pool. Some junior suites have private patios or terraces; most of these overlook the gardens (only 11 rooms have ocean views). The resort makes a good home base from which to explore Negril Beach, or you can just relax under one of the tall coconut palms. The beachside restaurant is open-air and casual. **Pros:** good beach location; large guest rooms; good on-site dining. **Cons:** small pools; dated room decor; few ocean-view rooms. ⊠ *Norman Manley Blvd., Negril* ☎ *876/957– 4227* ⊕ *www.cocolapalm.com* ⤳ *76 rooms* ⚷ *In-room: safe, refrigerator, DVD, Internet. In-hotel: 2 restaurants, room service, bar, pools, beachfront, laundry service* ⊟ *AE, DC, MC, V* ⋈ *EP.*

$$ ▣ **Country Country.** *Inn.* Owned by Kevin and Joanne Robertson, who also own Montego Bay's Coyaba, this small hotel carries the same home-away-from-home feel of its north-coast cousin but with a distinct Negril charm. Rooms are housed in brightly painted cottages designed by Jamaican architect Ann Hodges (known for her work at Goldeneye and Strawberry Hill); the cottages come alive with country-style touches like gingerbread trim. Each oversize room has a private patio. For an additional fee, you can add a meal plan, although most guests find plenty of restaurant choices within the area. **Pros:** charming guest rooms; oversize accommodations; good location on Negril Beach. **Cons:** resort may be too small for some travelers; some rooms can be noisy at night due to nearby Margaritaville; limited on-site dining options. ⊠ *Norman Manley Blvd., Negril* ☎ *876/957–4273* ⊕ *www.countryjamaica.com* ⤳ *20 rooms* ⚷ *In-room: safe, refrigerator. In-hotel: restaurant, room service, bar, beachfront* ⊟ *AE, MC, V* ⋈ *BP.*

$$$$ ▣ **Couples Negril.** *Resort.* This couples-only resort emphasizes romance and relaxation and is a more laid-back alternative to the nearby Sandals Negril. The resort has a good beachfront along Bloody Bay, north of the funkier Negril Beach, although Negril's bohemian nature is still reflected throughout the nine low-rise buildings. The property is decorated in a rainbow of colors, and lively art by local

7

craftspeople peppers public spaces. Rooms are similarly bright and roomy but are not luxurious. All land and water activities, selected excursions, and weddings are included in the rates. **Pros:** free weddings; complimentary airport shuttle; good stretch of beach. **Cons:** minimum stay restrictive for some; doesn't include reciprocal privileges with Couples Swept Away. ✉ *Norman Manley Blvd., Negril* ⌂ *Box 35, Hanover* ☎ *876/957–5960* ⊕ *www.couples.com* ⇌ *216 rooms, 18 suites* ⚭ *In-room: safe, refrigerator, Wi-Fi (some). In-hotel: 5 restaurants, bars, tennis courts, pools, gym, spa, beachfront, diving, water sports, laundry service, Internet terminal, Wi-Fi hotspot, no kids under 18* ⊟ *AE, D, MC, V* ⚬ *3-night minimum* ⓘⒶⓁ *AI.*

$$$$ ⌖ **Couples Swept Away Negril.** *Resort.* Sports-minded couples are welcomed to this all-suites resort known for its expansive menu of sports offerings, top-notch facilities (the best in Jamaica and among the best in the Caribbean), and emphasis on healthful cuisine. If you're looking for an active vacation that is still sprinkled with a hint of romance, it's your best option in Negril. The suites are in 26 two-story tropical villas—each with a private veranda overlooking the sea or a lush garden area—spread out along a ½-mi (¾-km) stretch of gorgeous beach. Across the road lies one of Jamaica's best sports complexes, with classes and high-end equipment and instruction. A 2006 expansion added amenities ranging from new restaurants to an Internet café. **Pros:** excellent fitness and sports facilities; complimentary airport shuttle; free weddings. **Cons:** healthful emphasis not for everyone; some facilities located across the road from resort; doesn't include reciprocal privileges with Couples Negril. ✉ *Norman Manley Blvd., Negril* ⌂ *Box 3077, Westmoreland* ☎ *876/957–4061* ⊕ *www.couples. com* ⇌ *312 suites* ⚭ *In-room: safe, no TV (some), refrigerator (some), Wi-Fi (some). In-hotel: 6 restaurants, bars, tennis courts, pools, gym, spa, beachfront, diving, water sports, bicycles, laundry service, Internet terminal, Wi-Fi hotspot, no kids under 18* ⊟ *AE, D, DC, MC, V* ⚬ *3-night minimum* ⓘⒶⓁ *AI.*

$$ ⌖ **Grand Pineapple Beach Negril.** *Resort.* This low-rise resort (formerly Negril Gardens) epitomizes the relaxed and funky style for which Negril has long been known. Guests are always just a quick walk from Negril's 7-mi-long (11-km-long) beach. Rooms are fairly basic, and those on the beach side get some noise from nearby clubs until the wee hours. The resort is part of Sandals mid-price AI brand and welcomes couples, singles, and families. Children under two

Cliff diving from Rick's Café, Negril

stay free, but each room has a maximum occupancy of three persons (you wouldn't want to try to squeeze more into these rooms, either. **Pros:** good value; lovely beach; helpful staff. **Cons:** some rooms don't have balconies; nearby nightclubs can be noisy; limit of three to a room. ⊠ *Norman Manley Blvd., Box 3058, Negril* ☎ *876/957–4408* ⊕ *www.grandpineapple.com* ⇆ *65 rooms* ⚐ *In-room: safe. In-hotel: restaurant, bars, pool, beachfront, water sports* ☞ *2-night minimum* ⊟ *AE, D, MC, V* ⊚ *AI.*

$$$– 🖵 **Hedonism II.** *Resort.* Promising a perpetual spring break for
$$$$ adults, who are drawn to the legendary party atmosphere, this resort gets a lot of repeat business. Although you can find "prude" activities ranging from a rock-climbing wall to an expansive gym, it's the nude side that's perpetually sold out. Guest rooms aren't quite as spartan as they once were but don't match the opulence of those at Hedonism III; still, they include TVs, multihead showers, and (of course) mirrors over the beds. Singles must allow the resort to match them with a same-sex roommate or pay a hefty supplement. Many nude travel groups plan vacations en masse here several times a year; another peak time is Halloween, when guests celebrate the resort's anniversary with wild costumes and decorated guest rooms. **Pros:** good beaches; more economical than some adult all-inclusives; numerous activities including squash. **Cons:** spring-break atmosphere not for everyone; nude beach and pool frequently overcrowded; rooms remain fairly basic. ⊠ *Norman Manley*

Blvd., Rutland Point, Box 25, Negril ☎ *876/957–5200* ⊕ *www.superclubs.com* ⇨ *280 rooms, 15 suites* ☐ *In-room: safe, refrigerator. In-hotel: 6 restaurants, bars, tennis courts, pools, gym, spa, beachfront, diving, water sports, Internet terminal, Wi-Fi hotspot, no kids under 18* ☐ *AE, D, DC, MC, V* ⇨ *3-night minimum* ⏺ *AI.*

$$–$$$ ⊞ **Idle Awhile.** *Inn.* This boutique hotel is a far cry from the town's all-inclusives, which makes it even more surprising that Idle Awhile is owned by Lee Issa, who also owns Couples Resorts. Like its big sisters just up the beach, this property is skillfully decorated—green and brown tones with red accents provide almost a South Pacific feel. Sporting activities are limited, but all guests get complimentary access to the big sports complex at Couples Swept Away. If you book a one-bedroom suite, the resort will provide a cook for your meals for $20 per day plus groceries. **Pros:** personal service; unique accommodations; access to sports facilities. **Cons:** few on-site dining options; some rooms can be noisy at night. ⊠ *Norman Manley Blvd., Negril* ☎ *876/957–3302* ⊕ *www.idleawhile.com* ⇨ *8 rooms, 6 suites* ☐ *In-room: safe, kitchen (some), refrigerator, Wi-Fi. In-hotel: restaurant, room service, bar, beachfront, Wi-Fi hotspot* ☐ *AE, D, MC, V* ⏺ *EP.*

$$ ⊞ **Negril Tree House Resort.** *Resort.* On a wide swatch of Negril Beach, this longtime resort draws many repeat visitors, especially during the winter months. Rooms are plain, but the beach can't be beat. At the center of the complex sits a two-story rondoval; upstairs an open-air restaurant serves breakfast (included in the room rate for all guests) as well as lunch and dinner. **Pros:** great beach; friendly staff; many nearby restaurants. **Cons:** basic rooms; dated decor; limited menu at restaurant. ⊠ *Norman Manley Blvd., Negril* ☎ *876/957–4287* ⊕ *www.negril-treehouse.com* ⇨ *57 rooms, 11 suites* ☐ *In-room: safe, kitchen (some), refrigerator (some). In-hotel: restaurant, bars, pools, beachfront, diving, water sports* ☐ *MC, V* ⏺ *BP.*

$$–$$$ ⊞ **Point Village Resort.** *Resort.* Feeling more like an apartment complex than a resort hotel, Point Village can make you feel as if you're planting some roots in Negril. In fact, you have a choice of 1-, 2-, and 3-bedroom apartments here, and with both all-inclusive and room-only plans, you have the option of having it all or keeping your costs down. Kitchens help out those keeping an eye on their budget. Though it's at the north end of Negril, which is mostly adults-only (Hedonism II and Breezes Grand Negril are neighbors), this resort is friendly to families. Rooms have tile floors and basic furnishings, and each is individually decorated. The sprawling complex has two small crescent beaches, rocky grottoes to explore, and fine snorkeling offshore. One child age 13 or under stays free when sharing a room with parents. **Pros:** good value for families; large rooms; many on-site activities. **Cons:** public areas packed with kids; small beaches; outdated decor. ⊠ *Norman Manley Blvd., Box 105, Negril* ☎ *876/957–5170* ⊕ *www.pointvillage.com* ⤴ *120 apartments* ⚷ *In-room: safe, kitchen, refrigerator. In-hotel: 3 restaurants, bars, tennis court, pool, beachfront, water sports, children's programs (ages newborn–12)* ⊟ *AE, D, MC, V* ⊺◎⊺ *AI.*

★ **Fodor's**Choice ⚇ **Rockhouse.** *Hotel.* With a spectacular cliff-
$$** side location like that of the Caves—but with some viable options for avoiding the high price tag—the small and trendy Rockhouse delivers both resort comforts and funky style. Rooms and villas are built from rough-hewn timber, thatch, and stone and are filled with furniture that echoes the nature theme. Although double the price of a regular room, villas ($$$), which have outdoor showers and private sundecks above the cliffs, are worth the splurge, but they definitely change the price point. Studios have outdoor showers but are otherwise like the regular rooms, which seem pleasantly rustic. You can ask for a TV—but only to watch videos (DVDs and videos are available upon request). To be honest, you're far better off enjoying the sunsets, for which Negril is known. There's a thatch-roof Jamaican restaurant, a spa, yoga, kayaking, and a cliff-top infinity pool and bar. **Pros: excellent dining; unique accommodations; beautiful pool area. **Cons:** no beach; may be too quiet for some visitors; traditional rooms are not nearly as nice as the villas. ⊠ *West End Rd., Box 3024, Negril* ☎ *876/957–4373* ⊕ *www.rockhousehotel.com* ⤴ *14 rooms, 20 villas* ⚷ *In-room: safe, no TV, Wi-Fi. In-hotel: 2 restaurants, bars, pool, spa, water sports, laundry service, Internet terminal, no kids under 12* ⊟ *AE, MC, V* ⊺◎⊺ *EP.*

★ **Fodor's**Choice ⚇ **Sandals Negril Beach Resort and Spa.** *Resort.*
$$$$ Couples (no longer limited to male–female pairs) looking for a sports-oriented getaway and a casually elegant atmosphere (you can wear dressy shorts to dinner) flock to this resort on one of the best stretches of Negril Beach. Water sports, particularly scuba diving, are popular; the capable staff is happy to work with neophytes as well as certified veterans. Tennis, racquetball, squash, and other activities are included for landlubbers. There's a huge swim-up pool bar when you're through exerting yourself. The

range of spacious accommodations includes some two-story suites; personal butler service is available in top categories. Like other resorts in the Sandals chain, Sandals Negril offers guests the Stay at One, Dine at Six policy. If you venture into Montego Bay or Ocho Rios for a day trip, you can dine at other Sandals resorts (transportation not included, and it's a long drive, especially to Ocho Rios). **Pros:** complimentary airport shuttle; excellent beach; good restaurants; private butler service. **Cons:** on-site nightlife options limited; no transportation to sister resorts. ✉ *Norman Manley Blvd., Negril* ☎ *876/957–5216* 🌐 *www.sandals.com* ♁ *In-room: safe, refrigerator (some), Wi-Fi. In-hotel: 6 restaurants, room service (some), bars, tennis courts, pools, gym, spa, beachfront, diving, water sports, bicycles, laundry service, Wi-Fi hotspot, no kids under 18* ▭ *AE, D, DC, MC, V* 🍽 *AI.*

$$$–$$$$ **Sunset at the Palms Resort and Spa, Negril.** *Resort.* A sister property of the Sunset Resorts in Montego Bay and Ocho Rios—but far different in scale and atmosphere—this relaxed all-inclusive is a favorite with ecotourists thanks to its emphasis on environmentally sustainable tourism. Rooms here are in tree-house-like cottages amid towering royal palms. Open and airy, rooms have floral bedspreads, gauzy curtains, natural-wood floors, and high ceilings. The beach is across the street, along with activities including nonmotorized water sports. Nature enthusiasts can also take a walk with the resort's resident gardener. **Pros:** environmentally conscious hotel; beautiful grounds; unique accommodations. **Cons:** beach is across street; eco-emphasis not for everyone; not within walking distance of many Negril Beach attractions and restaurants. ✉ *Norman Manley Blvd., Box 118, Negril* ☎ *876/957–5350* 🌐 *www.sunsetatthepalms.com* ⇨ *65 rooms* ♁ *In-room: safe, Internet. In-hotel: 3 restaurants, bars, tennis court, pool, gym, spa, water sports* ▭ *AE, D, MC, V* 🍽 *AI.*

$$–$$$ **Tensing Pen.** *Inn.* Named for the inn's first dog (who was named for a famed Sherpa), this hip and casual getaway is a top choice for travelers who like to get out and explore. Hammocks throughout the property promise lazy afternoons and cliffside perches tempt visitors to sit beneath an umbrella and enjoy the sea view with a good book in hand. Rooms, and the even more appealing cottages, have a South-Seas-meets-the-Caribbean vibe, with rock accents, handmade furnishings, and big glass doors that open to the sea. The largest accommodations here are the three-bedroom units in the Long House, but even the

smaller accommodations are roomy and comfortable. The resort has some on-site activities including yoga classes. **Pros:** unique accommodations; great snorkeling; spacious rooms. **Cons:** not on beach; barking dogs and other noise; rooms without a/c can get buggy. ⊠ *West End Rd., Negril* ☎ *876/957–0387* ⊕ *www.tensingpen.com* ⇆ *16 cottages* ⚒ *In-room: a/c (some), refrigerator. In-hotel: restaurant, bar, pool, beachfront, diving, water sports* ⊟ *AE, D, DC, MC, V* ⌖ *CP.*

VILLAS RENTALS

You won't find the luxurious villas of Ocho Rios and Discovery Bay, but Negril is slowly seeing more villas for those who would like a home-away-from-home experience. Since 1967, the **Jamaica Association of Villas and Apartments** (⊕ *www. villasinjamaica.com*) has handled villas, cottages, apartments, and condos across the island. Membership requires inspection and adherence to a set of guidelines.

PRIVATE VILLAS

$$$$ ⊡ **Negril Beach Villa.** *Vacation Rental.* Booked through the reservations office at Hedonism II, this villa is on a pristine stretch of Negril Beach near Cosmo's. Staffed around the clock, the villa offers two floors of lemon-tinted rooms including a master bath with Jacuzzi tub and verandah leading out to the beach. All bedrooms are air-conditioned and include their own TVs. **Pros:** luxurious accommodations; great beach location; helpful and friendly staff. **Cons:** expensive; few on-site amenities; may be too quiet for some visitors. ⊠ *Norman Manley Blvd., Negril* ☎ *876/957–5200* ⊕ *www.superclubs.com* ⇆ *3 bedrooms, 3 bathrooms* ⚒ *In-villa: no a/c (some), safe, kitchen, refrigerator, DVD, Wi-Fi, daily maid service, cook, security on-site, fully staffed, pool, beachfront, water toys, laundry service* ⊟ *AE, DC, MC, V* ⌖ *EP.*

BEACHES

★ **Fodor's Choice** **Negril Beach.** Stretching for 7 mi (11 km), the long, white-sand beach in Negril is arguably Jamaica's finest. It starts with the white sands of Bloody Bay north of town and continues along Long Bay all the way to the cliffs on the southern edge of town. Some stretches remain undeveloped, but not many. Along the main stretch of beach, the sand is public to the high-water mark, so a nonstop line of visitors and vendors parade from end to end. The

Negril Beach, seven miles long and possibly the island's finest

walk is sprinkled with many good beach bars and open-air restaurants, some of which charge a small fee to use their beach facilities. Bloody Bay is lined with large all-inclusive resorts, and these sections are mostly private. Jamaica's best-known nude beach, at Hedonism II, is always among the busiest; only resort guests or day-pass holders may sun here. ⊠ *Norman Manley Blvd., Negril.*

DID YOU KNOW? More than at any other Jamaican destination, locals selling *ganja* (marijuana) are common throughout Negril. On Negril Beach, any pretense drops and direct (and, sometimes, frequent) offers occur. Remember, marijuana is strictly illegal throughout Jamaica. Your status as a foreign traveler won't help you if you are stopped by the police, so we strongly urge all travelers to just say no to the many offers; usually a simple no will suffice. Roadblocks, undercover agents, and drug-sniffing dogs are all used on the island.

SPORTS AND THE OUTDOORS

BIRD-WATCHING

★ About 10 minutes from Negril, **Royal Palm Reserve** (⊠ *Springfield Rd., Sheffield* ☎ *876/957–3736*) is home to some 50 bird species, including the West Indian whistling duck, which comes to feed at the park's Cotton Tree Lake. The

The Green Flash

Looking directly west, Negril's cliffs are Jamaica's best-loved sunset spot. Hundreds of visitors come every night to watch the end of another island day—and perhaps spot the rare green flash. Rick's Café has long been the island's favorite sunset spot, with a view that looks out over mile after mile of open water.

Just what is the green flash? Under the right conditions, as sunset cools into the sea, a momentary green sizzle appears on the horizon at precisely the moment that the sun sinks below the horizon. Science explains it as the refraction of sunlight through the thick lens of the Earth's atmosphere. All agree that it's a rare sight, requiring just the right combination of sun, sky, and luck. The best chances of seeing a green flash come when the horizon is slightly below you, the water is warmer than the air, and the view is unobstructed by clouds or haze.

The practice of looking for the green flash came into vogue in the late 1800s with the publication of Jules Verne's novel *Le Rayon Vert* (*The Green Ray*). The author wrote of "a green which no artist could ever obtain on his palette, a green of which neither the varied tints of vegetation nor the shades of the most limpid sea could ever produce the like! If there is a green in Paradise, it cannot be but of this shade, which most surely is the true green of Hope."

And what happens if you are lucky enough to spot the green flash? Jules Verne claimed "he who has been fortunate enough once to behold it is enabled to see closely into his own heart and to read the thoughts of others." And according to island lore, couples that witness the flash are guaranteed true love.

7

park is also home to the Jamaican woodpecker, Jamaican oriole, Jamaican parakeet, and spectacular streamertail hummingbirds, who flit among the thick vegetation. Admission to the reserve is $10.

BOATING

Negril doesn't have the marinas of Montego Bay or Port Antonio, but the larger resorts here do offer Sunfish and Hobie Cat sailing; you can also find sunset and catamaran cruises just about every day of the week.

Wild Thing Watersports Negril (✉ *Norman Manley Blvd., Negril* ☎ *876/957–9930* ⊕ *www.wildthingwatersportsnegril.*

com) offers several different types of cruises aboard its catamaran. The three-hour sunset cruise ($50) stops at Rick's Café with time to swim and watch the cliff divers. It departs daily at 3:30. The Half Moon Beach Cruise ($60) includes a snorkel stop and lunch. The Rhodes Hall Plantation Cruise ($85) includes reef snorkeling in Orange Bay, a full buffet lunch, and a horseback ride at Rhodes Hall Plantation.

DIVING AND SNORKELING

Thanks to its protected waters, Negril offers some of the best scuba diving on the island, although some sites damaged by Hurricane Ivan in 2004 still haven't recovered. There are a wide variety of dive sites to suit all levels, and you can see everything from unusual coral formations to forbidding caves to shipwrecks (and even some downed Cessna planes).

The **Negril Scuba Centre** (✉ *Mariner's Negril Beach Club, Norman Manley Blvd., Negril* ☎ *876/957–0392* ⊕ *www. negrilscuba.com*) has three locations in Negril. Along with the Marin's Negril Beach Club location, you'll find dive operations at Sunset at the Palms and Negril Escape Resort and Spa (☎ *876/957–0392*) resorts.

Wild Thing Water Sports (✉ *Norman Manley Blvd., Negril* ☎ *876/957–9930* ⊕ *www.wildthingwatersportsnegril.com*) offers several cruises from their shop in the middle of Negril Beach. Cruises include snorkeling with full use of equipment and instruction for those new to the sport.

FISHING

For less-serious anglers, Jamaica has several fishing parks. These offer lake fishing as well as nature walks, picnics, birding, and a family-friendly atmosphere. The easiest to reach is **Royal Palm Reserve** (✉ *Springfield Rd., Sheffield* ☎ *876/957–3736*), about 10 minutes from Negril. Visitors can rent gear and try their luck at catching African perch or tarpon in Cotton Tree Lake. There's an admission price of $10 to visit the park and a $5 charge for fishing; you can also purchase any fish you catch to take back to your villa or resort for the night's dinner if you like.

GOLF

Great golf, rolling hills, and a rolling "liquormobile" go hand in hand at the 18-hole **Negril Hills Golf Club** (✉ *Sheffield Rd., Negril* ☎ *876/957–4638*), the only golf course in Negril (it's east of town). Green fees are $28.75 for 9 holes or $57.50 for 18 holes.

GUIDED TOURS

Although there are tours from Montego Bay that give day-trippers a chance to experience Negril, there are few tours available to those who are staying here. One exception is waterfalls tours.

The North Coast is known for Dunn's River Falls, and the South Coast for Y. S. Falls (both accessible from Negril on a day tour), but the Negril area is home to some impressive waterfalls of its own. A top activity for travelers tired of the beach, Mayfield Falls is tucked into the Dolphin Head Mountains near Glenbrook. These falls have been the stuff of legend since the 1700s, when locals swore a mermaid lived in these mineral-rich pools. Today the "mermaids" are tourists from Negril and Montego Bay who come to enjoy the waterfalls and underwater caves. Fifty-two varieties of fern are found here, as well as many types of tropical flowers. A visit here includes a guided hike up the river with a stop at a bar and grill along the way. Several operators offer tours here, usually with transportation from nearby hotels and lunch included.

Mayfield Falls and Mineral Springs (✉ *Dolphin Head, south of Lucea* ☎ *876/957–4868* ⊕ *www.mayfieldfalls.com*) offers tours with round-trip transportation from Negril hotels, a free welcome drink, 90 minutes on the river and trail, lunch, free use of hammocks, and, twice weekly, a live heritage show. **River Walk** (☎ *876/957–3444* ⊕ *www.riverwalkatmayfield.com*) offers transportation from Negril to Mayfield Falls. **Tropical Tours** (✉ *Norman Manley Blvd., Negril* ☎ *876/957–4110 in Negril* ⊕ *www.tropicaltours-ja.com*), a Montego Bay–based company, offers Negril visitors a half-day highlights tour with a look at the Lighthouse and a stop at Rick's Café. The half-day tour is available Monday, Friday, and Saturday afternoons. Tropical Tours also offers a half-day shopping and sunset tour on Tuesday, Thursday, and Friday.

HORSEBACK RIDING

Although it doesn't have as long a history as do the horseback riding options in Ocho Rios, Negril is home to several good horseback options. Both beginning and experienced riders can be accommodated on guided rides.

Rhodes Hall Plantation (⌖ *Green Island, Hanover* ☎ *876/957–6422*) dates back to the 1700s, when it was a sugarcane plantation. Although the plantation continues to produce coconut, bananas, and mangoes, tourism is now the main draw, thanks to its location 5 mi (8 km) east of Negril. The property is home to 70 horses available for rides through a variety of terrains.

MOUNTAIN BIKING

Flanked by the marshy areas of the Great Morass, many of Negril's mountain-biking options lie along the South Coast. The fairly flat terrain makes mountain biking accessible for all levels of bikers.

The Ocho Rios–based **Blue Mountain Bicycle Tours** (☎ *876/974–7075* ⊕ *www.bmtoursja.com*) offers guided bike rides ($89) along the South Coast. The tour includes round-trip transportation from Negril hotels.

TENNIS

Couples Swept Away (⌖ *Norman Manley Blvd., Negril* ☎ *876/957–4061* ⊕ *www.couples.com*) offers 10 tennis courts as well as squash, racquetball, and many other sports.

SHOPPING

Shopping isn't one of the top activities in Negril—you'll need to go to Montego Bay or Ocho Rios for that—but some excellent duty-free shops can be found at the top shopping destination in town:

★ **Time Square** (⌖ *Norman Manley Blvd., Negril* ☎ *876/957–9263*). The mall is known for its luxury goods ranging from cigars to jewelry.

MARKETS

With its laid-back atmosphere, it's no surprise that most Negril shopping involves straw hats, woven baskets, and
★ T-shirts, all plentiful at the **Rutland Point** (⌖ *Norman Manley Blvd., Negril* ☎ *No phone*), a crafts market on the northern edge of town. The atmosphere is more laid-back than at similar establishments in Montego Bay and Ocho Rios.

Taking out a Hobie cat from Negril Beach

SPECIALTY ITEMS

CIGARS

You can also buy Cuban cigars almost everywhere, even though they can't be brought legally back to the United States.

Cigar King (✉ *7 Time Square Mall, Negril* ☎ *876/957–3315*) has a wide selection of cigars, along with a walk-in humidor.

FOOD

Java lovers will find beans and ground coffee at gift shops throughout the island as well as at the airport. The lowest prices are found in local supermarkets; check the **Hi-Lo Supermarket** (✉ *West End Rd., Negril* ☎ *876/957–4546*). But if the store is out of Blue Mountain, you may have to settle for High Mountain coffee, the locals' second-favorite brand.

NIGHTLIFE AND THE ARTS

With its many open-air beach bars and clubs, Negril has an active, if casual, nightlife scene. Most afternoons, cars with booming sound systems drive up and down Norman Manley Boulevard and West End Road, loudly promoting that night's main event. Typically every night brings a party or concert somewhere in Negril.

ANNUAL EVENTS

The **Reggae Marathon and Half Marathon Race Day** (✉ *Long Bay Beach, Negril* ☎ *876/922–8677* ⊕ *www.reggaemarathon. com*) takes place in late November or early December. Runners can test themselves on a 13.1-mi (21.1-km) or 26.2-mi (42.1-km) run along the coast. This event, which draws competitors from more than 20 countries, grows every year.

BARS AND CLUBS

Negril has some kind of event every evening, usually a beach party and live music. Some of the all-inclusive resorts (including Hedonism II) offer a dinner and disco pass for $50 to $100; to buy a pass, call ahead to check availability, and be sure to bring a photo ID with you. In Negril, trucks with loudspeakers travel through the streets in the afternoon announcing the hot spot for the evening.

★ You can find Negril's best live music at **Alfred's Ocean Palace** (✉ *Norman Manley Blvd., Negril* ☎ *876/957–4735*), with live performances right on the beach.

Bourbon Beach (✉ *Norman Manley Blvd., Negril* ☎ *876/957–4405*) is wildly popular for its live reggae music on Monday, Thursday, and Saturday nights.

★ The sexy, always packed disco at **Hedonism II** (✉ *Norman Manley Blvd., Negril* ☎ *876/957–5200*) is the wildest dance spot on the island; Tuesday (pajama night) and Thursday (toga night) are tops. For nonguests, night passes are $89 and includes meals, drinks, and use of facilities from 6 PM to 2 AM; bring a photo ID to obtain a pass, but you should call ahead for a reservation.

The **Jungle** (✉ *Norman Manley Blvd., Negril* ☎ *876/957–4005*) is the hottest nightspot in Negril, with two raised bars and a circular dance floor.

Margaritaville (✉ *Norman Manley Blvd., Negril* ☎ *876/957–4467*) is liveliest in the evening, especially for special theme nights such as the weekly Parrothead Sunset Beach Party. Call for complimentary hotel pickups.

Sunset brings the crowds to **Rick's Café** (✉ *West End Rd., Negril* ☎ *876/957–0380*) to watch live performances.

Travel Smart
Jamaica

GETTING HERE AND AROUND

We're proud of our Web site: Fodors.com is a great place to begin any journey. Scan Travel Wire for suggested itineraries, travel deals, restaurant and hotel openings, and other up-to-the-minute info. Check out Booking to research prices and book plane tickets, hotel rooms, rental cars, and vacation packages. Head to Talk for on-the-ground pointers from travelers who frequent our message boards. You can also link to loads of other travel-related resources.

Jamaica is a major hub for Caribbean flights, so there are many nonstop flights from a variety of destinations in the United States and Canada, not to mention Europe. Since most flights into Jamaica land in Montego Bay, once on the island, most tourists have to travel by road to their final destination, a trip that can take from one to three hours, depending on where they are going. Roads on the island are not generally very good, so travel is slow and car-rentals are not a good idea for the majority of travelers, who may not be comfortable navigating a confusing network of highways filled with aggressive drivers who drive on the left.

■TIP→ Ask the local tourist board about hotel and local transportation packages that include tickets to major museum exhibits or other special events.

I BY AIR

Frequently scheduled air service links Jamaica to major hub cities with the most frequent service into Montego Bay's Sangster International Airport. Flight times from Miami to Montego Bay are approximately 1 hour and 25 minutes; from Atlanta, plan on 2 hours and 40 minutes; from Chicago 3 hours; and from Los Angeles 5 hours and 30 minutes. Flights to Kingston take just minutes longer.

Airlines and Airports Airline and Airport Links.com (⊕ *www. airlineandairportlinks.com*) has links to many of the world's airlines and airports.

Airline-Security Issues Transportation Security Administration (⊕ *www.tsa.gov*) has answers for almost every question that might come up.

AIRPORTS

Most travelers will fly into Sangster International Airport in Montego Bay (MBJ); this airport offers the best access to Montego Bay, Ocho Rios, Runaway Bay, the South Coast, and Negril. The island's other major airport is Norman Manley International Airport in Kingston (KIN); fly into Kingston to more easily reach the Blue Mountains and Port Antonio. Negril has no international air service, but does have a small domestic airport across from Bloody Bay. Limited domestic air service into the Port Antonio Aerodrome is available via charter companies.

Montego Bay's Sangster International Airport has made it increasingly easy to spend your waiting time. The airport is now home to the country's largest shopping mall, with stores specializing in everything from Jamaican crafts to coffees to beachwear. Air Margaritaville, a slightly scaled-down version of the popular chain restaurant, and Jamaican Bobsled Café are both top choices for meals. Just across from the Jamaican Bobsled Café, you can also find a free exhibit featuring Jamaican art through the years including some works by Edna Manley.

International Airports Norman Manley International Airport (✉ *Kingston* ☎ *876/924-8452* ⊕ *www. nmia.aero*). **Sangster International Airport** (✉ *Montego Bay* ☎ *876/952-3124* ⊕ *www.mbjairport.com*).

Secondary Airports Negril Aerodrome (✉ *Norman Manley Blvd., Negril* ☎ *876/957-5016*). **Port Antonio Ken Jones Aerodrome** (✉ *North Coast Hwy., Port Antonio* ☎ *876/923-0222*).

GROUND TRANSPORTATION Many hotels offer shuttles to pick you up at the airport, or airport transfers may be included in the cost of a travel package. If your hotel does not offer a shuttle, the best way to your destination is by taxi, but the costs can be substantial. It's a long and expensive drive, for instance, from Norman Manley Airport in Kingston to Port Antonio.

In Montego Bay, the airport's arrivals hall is home to hotel lounges for Sandals, Beaches, SuperClubs,

> ### AIRLINE TIP
>
> If you have an afternoon flight, check in your bags early in the morning (keep a change of clothes in a carry-on), then go back to the beach for one last lunch, returning to the airport an hour before your flight departs. It makes for much easier traveling, saves time, and you get your last beach fix.

Couples, Sunset, and Half Moon resorts; check-in at the desk and relax until the bus departs. The authorized airport taxi desk is just beyond the exit past Customs.

Hotel shuttles are less likely to be provided for Kingston hotels. The Jamaica Union of Travellers Association (JUTA) is the authorized taxi company at the Norman Manley International Airport; you'll find its desk just outside the Customs Hall in the Ground Transportation Hall.

FLIGHTS
Jamaica is well served by major airlines. From the United States, Air Jamaica, American, Continental, Delta, JetBlue, Northwest, Spirit, United, and US Airways offer non-stop and connecting service.

Airline Contacts Air Canada (☎ *876/952-5160, 876/942-8211 in Kingston* ⊕ *www.aircanada.com*). **Air Jamaica** (☎ *876/940-9411* ⊕ *www. airjamaica.com*). **American Airlines** (☎ *800/744-0006* ⊕ *www.aa.com*). **British Airways** (☎ *800/247-9297* ⊕ *www.britishairways.com*). **Cayman Airways** (☎ *876/949-820* ⊕ *www. caymanairways*). **Continental Air-**

lines (☎ 800/231–0856 ⊕ www.
continental.com). **Delta Air Lines**
(☎ 876/940–1834 ⊕ www.delta.com).
JetBlue (☎ 800/538–2583 ⊕ www.
jetblue.com). **Northwest Airlines**
(☎ 800/225–2525 ⊕ www.nwa.com).
Spirit Airlines (☎ 586/971–2947
⊕ www.spiritair.com). **United Airlines**
(☎ 876/940–0711 ⊕ www.united.
com). **US Airways** (☎ 800/622–1015
⊕ www.usairways.com).

DOMESTIC CHARTER FLIGHTS

TimAir and City Air Charters offer
charter service from Montego Bay's
Sangster International Airport to
airports in Port Antonio, Ocho
Rios, Runaway Bay, Kingston, and
Negril. Scheduled service is avail-
able on Skylan Airways between
Montego Bay and Kingston. Char-
ter helicopter service is provided by
Captain John's Island Hoppers to
Ocho Rios.

**Contacts Captain John's Island
Hoppers** (☎ 876/974–1285 ⊕ www.
jamaicahelicopterservices.com). **City
Air Charters** (☎ 876/858–6551
⊕ www.cityaircharters.com). **Skylan Airways** (☎ 876/932–7102
⊕ skylanja.com). **TimAir** (☎ 876/
952–2516 ⊕ www.timair.com).

▮ BY CAR

We don't recommend renting a car
in Jamaica. Driving on the island
can be extremely frustrating. You
must constantly be on guard—for
enormous potholes and people
and animals darting out into the
street. With a narrow road encircling the island, local drivers are
quick to pass other cars. Sometimes two cars will pass simulta-

neously, inspiring the UNDERTAKERS
LOVE OVERTAKERS signs seen throughout the island.

GASOLINE

Gas stations are open daily, but
many accept only cash. Gas costs
are roughly double that in the
United States.

RENTAL CARS

Because many car renters are
returning Jamaicans, the breakdown between high season and
low season for car rentals is different than the high and low hotel
seasons. Car-rental prices are highest over the winter holidays, Easter (when Carnival brings in many
former residents), and July and
August.

To rent a car you must be between
the ages of 23 (with at least one
year possessing a valid driver's
license) and 70. Many car-rental
companies also offer cell-phone
rentals, and that's a good idea if
your phone doesn't have service
in Jamaica.

Your driver's license may not be
recognized outside your home
country. You may not be able to
rent a car without an International
Driving Permit (IDP), which can
be used only in conjunction with
a valid driver's license and which
translates your license into 10 languages. Check the AAA Web site
for more info as well as for IDPs
($15) themselves.

**Major Car Rental Companies
Alamo** (☎ 800/522–9696 ⊕ www.
alamo.com). **Avis** (☎ 800/331–
1084 ⊕ www.avis.com). **Budget**
(☎ 800/472–3325 ⊕ www.budget.

com). **Hertz** (☎ *800/654-3001* ⊕ *www.hertz.com*). **National Car Rental** (☎ *800/227-7368* ⊕ *www. nationalcar.com*).

Local Agencies Alex's Car Rentals and Tours (☎ *876/971-2615*). **Fiesta Car Rentals** (☎ *876/926-0133* ⊕ *www.fiestacarrentals.com*). **Island Car Rentals** (☎ *876/952-7225* ⊕ *www.islandcarrentals.com*). **Jamaica Car Rental** (☎ *876/952-5586*).

RENTAL CAR INSURANCE

Everyone who rents a car wonders whether the insurance that the rental companies offer is worth the expense. No one—including us—has a simple answer. If you own a car, your personal auto insurance may cover a rental to some degree, though not all policies protect you abroad; always read your policy's fine print. If you don't have auto insurance, then seriously consider buying the collision- or loss-damage waiver (CDW or LDW) from the car-rental company, which eliminates your liability for damage to the car. Some credit cards offer CDW coverage, but it's usually supplemental to your own insurance and rarely covers SUVs, minivans, or luxury models. If your coverage is secondary, you may still be liable for loss-of-use costs from the car-rental company. But no credit-card insurance is valid unless you use that card for *all* transactions, from reserving to paying the final bill. It's sometimes cheaper to buy insurance as part of your general travel insurance policy.

ROADSIDE EMERGENCIES

In case of an accident, dial 119. On the major roads such as the North Coast Highway, you can call a garage in one of the larger towns. In rural areas, you'll probably have to rely on the help of locals to get your car up and running as far as one of the larger towns.

To report a car theft, call 119. You also need to call your rental-car agency.

ROAD CONDITIONS

Many roads in Jamaica are in poor condition, so you have to be on the lookout for enormous potholes. Be sure to budget extra time on the roads; in general, you can expect to spend just about twice as long to cover a distance as you would back home.

RULES OF THE ROAD

Driving in Jamaica is on the left, British-style. Drivers and passengers in the front seat are required to wear seat belts, and motorcycle drivers are required to wear helmets. Children under age four must be in a car seat. The speed limit is 30 mph in town and 50 mph on the highways (although you'll see many local drivers going faster). Bad road conditions make it fairly easy for most drivers to remain below the speed limit, however.

Jamaica has strict drunk driving laws; drivers are prosecuted if they are found to have a blood alcohol level of more than .08%.

For U.S. drivers, Jamaica's many roundabouts or traffic circles are particularly perplexing. The rule of the road is the traffic entering the roundabout must yield to those already in it.

▌ BY TAXI

Taxis are widely available in Jamaica, but they can be expensive. Since most cabs are not metered, it's best to ask at your hotel to find out an acceptable fee, then negotiate that fee with the driver before agreeing to enter the cab. Taxis tend to congregate around hotels and attractions, and it's better to grab one there, but it's possible to flag one down on the street as well. Finally, you can call a taxi if one is not available; any restaurant or hotel can do this on your behalf.

ESSENTIALS

■ ACCOMMODATIONS

Jamaica was the birthplace of the all-inclusive beach resort, and many people still choose to stay in these large resorts, which provide all lodging, dining, drinks, activities, and entertainment for a single rate. Some of these hotels are open only to couples, so that is always a consideration when choosing an all-inclusive. But Jamaica also has many small inns and independent hotels and resorts in all price ranges—from super-budget to expensive, luxurious properties as well as business hotels. Villas, especially luxury villas, are a growing market as well with many extended families and multiple couples opting to share a villa for a home-away-from-home experience.

Be sure you understand the hotel's cancellation policy. Some places allow you to cancel without any kind of penalty—even if you pre-paid to secure a discounted rate—if you cancel at least 24 hours in advance. Others require you to cancel a week in advance or penalize you the cost of one night. Small inns and B&Bs are most likely to require you to cancel far in advance. Most hotels allow children under a certain age to stay in their parents' room at no extra charge, but others charge for them as extra adults; find out the cutoff age for discounts.

■TIP→ Assume that hotels operate on the European Plan (EP, no meals) unless we specify that they use the Breakfast Plan (BP, with full break-

FODORS.COM

Before your trip, be sure to check out what other travelers are saying in Talk on www.fodors.com.

fast), Continental Plan (CP, continental breakfast), Full American Plan (FAP, all meals), or Modified American Plan (MAP, breakfast and dinner), or are all-inclusive (AI, all meals and most activities).

For lodging price categories, consult the price charts found near the beginning of each chapter.

■ COMMUNICATIONS

INTERNET

Internet service is becoming far more common across Jamaica, and most hotels offer at least limited service, either at public terminals (sometimes free at the all-inclusive resorts) or in-room connections. High-speed cable and broadband connections are becoming more and more common at the larger resorts; expect to pay $15 to $20 per day for this option. A growing number of resorts are adding wireless service for a comparable price; some offer it only in public areas (including poolside), whereas others offer it in guest rooms as well.

PHONES

Public phones are common in Jamaica but you'll generally need to use a Cable & Wireless phone card; these are available across the island at hotels and retail stores.

Cellular service is good in the resort areas although service is spotty in the hills.

CALLING WITHIN JAMAICA

Jamaica has an efficient telephone system with direct dialing; local telephone numbers are all seven digits. All calls in Jamaica are within the 876 area code. All calls, however, are not local calls; dialing between parishes generally involves long-distance charges. To reach directory assistance on the island, dial 114.

CALLING OUTSIDE THE DESTINATION

Long-distance calls outside Jamaica can be made directly from hotels; however, calling from the hotel is the most expensive option. Some long-distance telephone companies provide calling-card service to Jamaica; others provide limited availability at only some hotels due to the high rate of fraud.

CALLING CARDS

Although used less often by visitors than cell phones and long-distance services, phone cards are very common in Jamaica, sold at the airports, retail stores, and hotels. Cable & Wireless sells phone cards in varying denominations up to $500; Cable & Wireless also sells WorldTalk cards, which can be used for international calls.

MOBILE PHONES

Good mobile-phone coverage is available in the resort areas although coverage can be spotty in rural areas. Jamaica's cellular system uses both TDMA and GSM technologies; phones that

CELL PHONE TIPS

You can purchase a cheap cell phone at numerous outlets and simply "top-up" (pay as you go). Incoming calls are free, so have your family call you to save on exorbitant island rates and huge roaming charges. Not all cell phones from home will work in Jamaica (some do, but you never know which ones until you're actually on-island), even if the phone company tells you it does.

are TDMA- or GSM-compatible will work if your provider has a roaming agreement with Lime (formerly Cable & Wireless) or Digicel Jamaica. Cell phone rates are expensive, however; rates range about $1.50 to $2 per minute for calls from Jamaica to the United States or Canada.

Cell-phone rental is available at both the Montego Bay and Kingston airports as well as from some car-rental companies. Expect to pay about $50 for a one-week rental; this includes a Jamaican SIM card. With a Jamaican SIM card, expect to pay about 14 cents per minute for local calls within Jamaica and 30 cents per minute for calls to the United States.

■TIP→ If you travel internationally frequently, save one of your old mobile phones or buy a cheap one on the Internet; ask your cellphone company to unlock it for you, and take it with you as a travel phone, buying a new SIM card with pay-as-you-go service in each destination.

Contacts **Digicel Jamaica** (☎ 888/
344–4245 ⊕ www.digiceljamaica.
com). **Lime** (☎ 888/225–5295
⊕ www.time4lime.com).

■ CUSTOMS AND DUTIES

Clearing customs is generally a fast
process at both the Montego Bay
and Kingston airports. You are
provided a customs form (often
on the airplane) that you hand to
customs officials. Arriving passengers are permitted to bring a ½
pound of tobacco, 1 quart of spirits, 6 fluid ounces of perfume, and
12 fluid ounces of cologne. Pro-
hibited items include coffee, fruits,
vegetables, fresh flowers, honey,
firearms, explosives, and illegal
drugs. Pet lovers should note that
you cannot bring any animals into
Jamaica, unlike some other Caribbean countries.

**Jamaica Information Jamaica
Customs** (⊕ www.jacustoms.gov.jm).

**U.S. Information U.S. Customs
and Border Protection** (⊕ www.
cbp.gov).

■ EATING OUT

Unless otherwise noted, the restaurants listed in this guide are open
daily for lunch and dinner.

Although a lot of people stay at
all-inclusive resorts, there is still a
good selection of independent restaurants scattered around Jamaica,
particularly in the Montego Bay
and Negril resort areas. From
beach bars that serve spicy jerk
barbecue to seafood shacks serving the catch of the day to international eateries with white-glove

service, there are plenty of dining
options. Vegetarians will favor the
meatless food at Rastafarian restaurants. As the capital, Kingston
has a very lively dining scene.

MEALS AND MEALTIMES
Jamaica maintains much the same
meals times as found in the United
States. Larger hotels serve Ameri-
can-style breakfasts; away from the
resort areas, look for a traditional
breakfast of ackee (a fruit that,
when prepared properly, resembles scrambled eggs) alongside saltfish, boiled bananas, fritters, and
fresh fruit. Lunch, served around
noon, consists of patties (turnovers
stuffed with spicy beef or chicken)
or other local dishes such as jerk
chicken or pork, often accompanied by fruit punch. Dinner is typically served at 7 or later and may
include offerings such as escovitch fish served with a vinegary
sauce and a variety of soups such
as pumpkin or callaloo. In larger
towns (especially in Kingston), it's
traditional for many families to eat
out on Friday night; restaurants

away from resorts will be busiest that night.

PAYING

Credit cards are accepted at most restaurants, but not at the more modest local spots. But you can usually pay in U.S. dollars at even the simplest establishment, though your change may be given in Jamaican currency. Most major credit cards (Visa, American Express, Diners Club, Discover, and MasterCard) are accepted in restaurants in major resort areas; outside of these areas (especially along the south coast), you may have to pay in cash.

For guidelines on tipping see Tipping, below.

RESERVATIONS AND DRESS

Although bathing suits are never appropriate for anywhere except the beach and the pool, casual dress is expected at most restaurants. In the nicest restaurants (including some hotel restaurants), long pants and collared shirt are appreciated and, at a few establishments, jackets.

We only mention reservations when they are essential (there's no other way you'll ever get a table) or when they are not accepted. We mention dress only when men are required to wear a jacket or a jacket and tie.

WINES, BEER, AND SPIRITS

There's no shortage of spirits in Jamaica; the island produces many excellent rums and beers. Local liquors are always the least expensive option (and, in some limited all-inclusives, the only options available without a surcharge). Wine is one spirit that's not made locally in Jamaica so it often demands a premium.

Bars, particularly at the all-inclusives, generally open at 10 AM and remain hopping into the early morning hours. Away from the resorts, rum shops, usually open-air bars, are very common; inquire at your hotel as to which are safe to visit.

▌ ELECTRICITY

As in North America, the current in Jamaica is 110 volts; however, unlike most of North America, which runs at 60 cycles, Jamaica's current is 50 cycles, which means some appliances may run a little hot. Outlets take two flat prongs. Some hotels provide 220-volt plugs for electric shavers. If you plan to bring electrical appliances with you, it's best to ask when making your reservation, but in general leave hair dryers and curling irons at home. Dual-voltage appliances should be OK.

▌ EMERGENCIES

Emergency Services Ambulance and Fire Emergencies (☎ 110). **Police Emergencies and Air Rescue** (☎ 119). **Hurricane Update** (☎ 116). **Scuba-Diving Emergencies** (✉ St. Ann's Bay Hospital, Seville Rd., St. Ann's Bay ☎ 876/972–2272).

▌ HEALTH

In Jamaica, tap water is generally safe to drink, especially in Negril.

Heat exhaustion and sunburn are the most common tourist ailments in Jamaica. Sunscreen is widely available in drug stores (and hotel gift stores), but is priced much higher than what you'd pay at home. Insect repellent is another handy item to pack both for mosquitoes and sand flies that generally come out at sunset.

Malaria was reported in the Kingston area in 2006. The outbreak quickly subsided, however. Another mosquito-borne disease is dengue. This disease, which causes fever and aches, is transmitted by a mosquito that, unlike malarial mosquitoes, bites during the daytime hours. A good-quality insect repellent is the best defense. Most hotels are air-conditioned, so mosquitoes are not a problem in the rooms; those that are not generally provide both mosquito netting for the bed and mosquito coils to burn to repel the insects. Also, hotel gift shops as well as local supermarkets sell mosquito repellents, although at higher prices than in the United States.

Although Jamaica has no poisonous snakes, swimmers should take care to avoid sea urchins, jellyfish, and fire coral. Wearing water shoes is the easiest way to avoid the needles of the sea urchin in shallow water.

OVER-THE-COUNTER REMEDIES

Familiar brands of pain relievers, stomach medicines, and other over-the-counter medications will be found in the resort areas, although less commonly in the small towns. All will be priced higher than in the United States.

SHOTS AND MEDICATIONS
Health Warnings National Centers for Disease Control & Prevention (*CDC* ☎ *877/394-8747 international travelers' health line* ⊕ *www.cdc.gov/travel*). **World Health Organization** (*WHO* ⊕ *www. who.int*).

▮ HOURS OF OPERATION

Banks are generally open Monday through Thursday 9 to 2, Friday 9 to 4. Post offices are open weekdays 9 to 5. Normal business hours for stores are weekdays from 8:30 to 4:30, Saturday 8 to 1. In the cruise ports of Montego Bay and Ocho Rios, stores often have extended hours to accommodate cruise-ship passengers. Expect most shops to be closed on Sunday unless a cruise ship is in port. Many bars and nightclubs close at 2 AM, but some stay open much later depending on the crowds.

HOLIDAYS
Public holidays include New Year's Day, Ash Wednesday (6 weeks before Easter), Good Friday, Easter Monday, Labor Day (May 23), Independence Day (1st Monday in August), National Heroes Day (October 15), Christmas, and Boxing Day (December 26). Along with the closure of many attractions, numerous tours do not operate on these days.

▌ MAIL

Postcards may be mailed anywhere in the world for J$50. Letters cost J$60 to the United States and Canada, J$70 to Europe, J$90 to Australia and New Zealand. Due to costly and slow air-shipping service, most travelers carry home packages, even bulky wooden carvings. As home of the island's busiest international airport, you can find international courier services in Montego Bay for shipping extremely large purchases. A number of shipping companies, both international and domestic, also operate out of Kingston. Call around for the best rates and to confirm pickup options. Your hotel should be able to help.

▌ MONEY

The official currency is the Jamaican dollar. At this writing the exchange rate was about J$89 to US$1. Prices quoted throughout this chapter are in U.S. dollars, unless otherwise noted.

The U.S. dollar is widely accepted, and few Americans bother to exchange money—especially if they stay in an all-inclusive resort for their entire trip. As long as you're in a resort area, you can almost be assured of being able to pay in U.S. dollars (though your change may be given in Jamaican currency). You can exchange money at the airport or your hotel, and you'll get a fairly good exchange rate regardless of where you go.

Prices throughout this guide are given for adults. Substantially reduced fees are almost always available for children, students, and senior citizens.

ATMS AND BANKS

Not all ATMs in Jamaica accept American cards, although a growing number in the resort areas do. Travelers often find themselves having to try more than one machine. Some ATMs dispense either Jamaican or U.S. dollars. NCB ATMs offer U.S. dollars using debit or credit cards.

CREDIT CARDS

Throughout this guide, the following abbreviations are used: **AE**, American Express; **D**, Discover **DC**, Diners Club; **MC**, MasterCard; and **V**, Visa.

It's a good idea to inform your credit-card company before you travel, especially if you're going abroad and don't travel internationally very often. Otherwise, the credit-card company might put a hold on your card owing to unusual activity—not a good thing halfway through your trip. Record all your credit-card numbers—as well as the phone numbers to call if your cards are lost or stolen—in a safe place, so you're prepared should something go wrong. Both MasterCard and Visa have general numbers you can call (collect if you're abroad) if your card is lost, but you're better off calling the number of your issuing bank, since MasterCard and Visa usually just transfer you to your bank; your bank's number is usually printed on your card.

If you plan to use your credit card for cash advances, you'll need to apply for a PIN at least two weeks before your trip. Although it's usually cheaper (and safer) to use a credit card abroad for large purchases (so you can cancel payments or be reimbursed if there's a problem), note that some credit-card companies *and* the banks that issue them add substantial percentages to all foreign transactions, whether they're in a foreign currency or not. Check on these fees before leaving home, so there won't be any surprises when you get the bill.

Reporting Lost Cards American Express (📧 800/528–4800 in U.S., 336/393–1111 collect from abroad ⊕ www.americanexpress.com). **MasterCard** (📧 800/627–8372 in U.S., 636/722–7111 collect from abroad ⊕ www.mastercard.com). **Visa** (📧 800/847–2911 in U.S., 410/581–9994 collect from abroad ⊕ www.visa.com).

▌ PACKING

Because of its British heritage, Jamaica can seem a little formal at times. Some resorts still require guests to dress for dinner (often with a jacket, though rarely with a tie). And in Kingston in particular, guests tend to dress up a little more at better establishments. Negril in particular is more laid back.

Bring loose-fitting clothing made of natural fabrics to see you through days of heat and humidity. Pack a beach cover-up, both to protect yourself from the sun and to provide something to wear to and from your hotel room. Bathing suits and immodest attire are frowned upon away from the beach. A sun hat is advisable. For shopping and sightseeing, bring walking shorts, jeans, T-shirts, long-sleeve cotton shirts, slacks, and sundresses. Nighttime dress can range from very informal to casually elegant, depending on the establishment. A tie is practically never required, but a jacket may be appropriate in fancy restaurants. You may need a light sweater or jacket for evening.

▌ PASSPORTS AND VISAS

A valid passport is required to enter or reenter the United States from Jamaica.

▌ SAFETY

Jamaica has a reputation as a dangerous destination thanks to a murder rate that consistently ranks among the world's highest. Much of the violence is centered on gang conflicts in Kingston, but it does occasionally spill over into other communities. The weeks before and after general elections are particular hazardous, as political tensions have been known to spark gunfire and killings.

Beyond murder, road safety is another prime concern. Jamaica is plagued by one of the world's highest auto fatality rates. Excessive speed and reckless driving are commonplace, so travelers should always be conscientious about taking licensed taxicabs.

Theft is also a problem, everything from wallets left on beach blankets to items from parked cars. Most hotels provide in-room safes, so be sure to use them for all valuables that aren't necessary during the day. It's best to leave jewelry at home, although costume jewelry is generally fine. Pickpocketing and snatch-and-run thefts are not much as problem in the resort areas (although they can be a worry in crowded markets), but they are concerns in Kingston.

■TIP→ Distribute your cash, credit cards, IDs, and other valuables between a deep front pocket, an inside jacket or vest pocket, and a hidden money pouch. Don't reach for the money pouch once you're in public.

Contact **Transportation Security Administration** (*TSA* ⊕ *www.tsa.gov*)

▌ TAXES

A departure tax of $20 must be paid in cash if it's not added to the cost of your airline tickets; this policy varies by carrier, although most tickets now include the departure tax. Jamaica has replaced the room occupancy tax with a V.A.T. of 15% on most goods and services, which is already incorporated into the prices of taxable goods. Since 2005, incoming air passengers are charged a $10 tourism enhancement fee; incoming cruise passengers pay a $2 fee. Both these fees are almost always included in the price of your ticket.

▌ TIME

Jamaica is in the eastern time zone (GMT-5). The island does not observe daylight saving time.

▌ TIPPING

Most hotels and restaurants add a 10% service charge to your bill. When a service charge isn't included, a 10% to 20% tip is expected. Tips of 10% to 20% are customary for taxi drivers as well. However, many all-inclusives have a strict no-tipping policy; ask if there is any doubt.

▌ TRIP INSURANCE

Comprehensive travel policies typically cover trip-cancellation and interruption, letting you cancel or cut your trip short because of a personal emergency, illness, or, in some cases, acts of terrorism in your destination. Such policies also cover evacuation and medical care. Some also cover you for trip delays because of bad weather or mechanical problems as well as for lost or delayed baggage. Another type of coverage to look for is financial default—that is, when your trip is disrupted because a tour operator, airline, or cruise line goes out of business. Generally you must buy this when you book your trip or shortly thereafter, and it's only available to you if your operator isn't on a list of excluded companies.

At the very least, consider buying medical-only coverage. Neither Medicare nor some private insurers cover medical expenses anywhere outside of the United States (including time aboard a cruise ship, even if it leaves from a U.S. port). Medical-only policies typically reimburse you for medical care (excluding that related to preexisting conditions) and hospitalization abroad, and provide for evacuation. You still have to pay the bills and await reimbursement from the insurer, though.

Another option is to sign up with a medical-evacuation assistance company. A membership in one of these companies gets you doctor referrals, emergency evacuation or repatriation, 24-hour hotlines for medical consultation, and other assistance. International SOS Assistance Emergency and AirMed International provide evacuation services and medical referrals. MedjetAssist offers medical evacuation.

Expect comprehensive travel insurance policies to cost about 4% to 7% or 8% of the total price of your trip (it's more like 8%–12% if you're over age 70). A medical-only policy may or may not be cheaper than a comprehensive policy. Always read the fine print of your policy to make sure that you are covered for the risks that are of most concern to you. Compare several policies to make sure you're getting the best price and range of coverage available.

■TIP→ OK. You know you can save a bundle on trips to warm-weather destinations by traveling in rainy season. But there's also a chance that a severe storm will disrupt your plans. The solution? Look for hotels and resorts that offer storm/hurricane guarantees. Although they rarely allow refunds, most guarantees do let you rebook later if a storm strikes.

Insurance Comparison Sites
Insure My Trip.com (☎ 800/487–4722 ⊕ www.insuremytrip.com).
Square Mouth.com (☎ 800/240–0369 or 727/490–5803 ⊕ www.squaremouth.com).

Medical Assistance Companies
AirMed International Medical Group (⊕ www.airmed.com).
International SOS (⊕ www.internationalsos.com). **MedjetAssist** (⊕ www.medjetassist.com).

Medical-Only Insurers **International Medical Group** (☎ 800/628–4664 ⊕ www.imglobal.com). **Wallach & Company** (☎ 800/237–6615 or 540/687–3166 ⊕ www.wallach.com).

Comprehensive Travel Insurers
Access America (☎ 866/729–6021 ⊕ www.accessamerica.com). **AIG Travel Guard** (☎ 800/826–4919 ⊕ www.travelguard.com). **CSA Travel Protection** (☎ 800/873–9855 ⊕ www.csatravelprotection.com). **HTH Worldwide** (☎ 610/254–8700 ⊕ www.hthworldwide.com). **Travelex Insurance** (☎ 888/228–9792 ⊕ www.travelex-insurance.com). **Travel Insured International** (☎ 800/243–3174 ⊕ www.travelinsured.com).

▌ VISITOR INFORMATION

At Montego Bay's Sangster International Airport, arriving passengers will find a Jamaica tourist Board booth in the customs hall. This desk can help with a limited number of brochures and maps and can also make hotel arrangements for travelers who arrive with reservations. The airport information desk is open 6 AM TO 10 PM daily.

Jamaica Information **Jamaica Tourist Board** (☎ *800/233–4582* ⊕ *www.visitjamaica.com*).

▮ WEDDINGS

Thanks to its accommodating marriage laws, tropical beauty, and bountiful couples-only resorts, Jamaica is one of the top wedding destinations in the Caribbean. Several all-inclusives offer free wedding ceremonies, including the officiant fee, marriage license, tropical flowers, a small wedding cake, champagne, and more; typically couples pay government fees.

Most couples work with their resort's wedding coordinator in advance of their visit to handle the legal paperwork. You can marry after only 24 hours on the island if you've applied for your license and supplied all necessary forms beforehand. You need to supply proof of citizenship (a passport or certified copy of your birth certificate signed by a notary public), written parental consent for couples under age 18, proof of divorce with the original or certified copy of the divorce decree if applicable, and copy of the death certificate if a previous marriage ended in death. Blood tests are not required.

INDEX

A

Airports, 234–235
Air travel, 12, 234–236
charter flights, 236
flights, 235–236
Kingston and the Blue
  Mountains, 141, 144
Montego Bay, 27, 29
Negril, 199
Ocho Rios and Runaway
  Bay, 73
Port Antonio, 118
South Coast, 175
Alcoholic drinks, 13, 242
Alfred's Ocean Palace, 232
Amusement parks, 205
Appleton Estate, 180
Art galleries and
  museums
Kingston and the Blue
  Mountains, 151
Montego Bay, 67
ATMs, 32–33, 244
ATV tours. ⇨See Jeep
  and ATV tours

B

Bamboo Avenue, 181
Banks, 244
hours of operation, 243
Kingston and the Blue
  Mountains, 145
Montego Bay, 32–33
Negril, 204
Ocho Rios and Runaway
  Bay, 77
Port Antonio, 120
South Coast, 179
Beaches
Kingston and the Blue
  Mountains, 164–165
Montego Bay, 56–57
Negril, 223–224
Ocho Rios and Runaway
  Bay, 105–106
Port Antonio, 121, 122,
  132
South Coast, 189,
  191–192

Bellefield Great House,
  35
Biking. ⇨See Mountain
  biking
Bird-watching, 17
Kingston and the Blue
  Mountains, 165
Montego Bay, 37, 40, 57
Negril, 205–206,
  224–225
Port Antonio, 133
South Coast, 192, 193
Black River, 16
Black River Great
  Morass, 184
Blue Lagoon, 121
Blue Mountain coffee, 169
Blue Mountains, 147,
  148. ⇨See also Kingston and the Blue
  Mountains
Boating
Negril, 225–226
Port Antonio, 133
South Coast, 192
Bob Marley Centre &
  Mausoleum, 35, 80
Bob Marley Museum,
  148
Bobsled team of
  Jamaica, 43
Boston Beach, 121,
  122
Boston Jerk Centre ⊠,
  125
Breds community program, 188
Breezes Grand Negril
  Resort & Spa ✕, 215
Breezes Runaway Bay
  ✕, 99–100
Bus travel
Kingston and the Blue
  Mountains, 144
Montego Bay, 29
Ocho Rios and Runaway
  Bay, 75
Business hours, 243

C

Canopy tours
Montego Bay, 57
Ocho Rios and Runaway
  Bay, 106
Car rentals, 236–237
Car travel, 12, 236–238
Kingston and the Blue
  Mountains, 144
Montego Bay, 30
Negril, 199, 201
Ocho Rios and Runaway
  Bay, 75
Port Antonio, 118
roadside emergencies,
  237
South Coast, 177
Cash, Johnny, 66
Casinos, 70
Caves
Ocho Rios and Runaway
  Bay, 82
Caves, The ✕, 215–216
Charter flights, 236
Children's attractions
Montego Bay, 46–49,
  52, 54
Negril, 205, 216–217
Ocho Rios and Runaway
  Bay, 92, 98, 100, 110
Chukka Caribbean
  Adventures, 109
Churches, 154
Climate, 18
Cockpit Country, 36
Coffee factories
Kingston and the Blue
  Mountains, 147
South Coast, 180
Columbus, Christopher,
  107
Coward, Noël, 82, 103
Coyaba River Garden &
  Museum, 80
Cranbrook Flower Forest, 81
Credit cards, 7, 244–245
Cricket, 166

Cruises
Montego Bay, 31
Ocho Rios and Runaway Bay, 76
Port Antonio, 119
Cuisine of Jamaica, 13, 44
Culture, 22–24
Customs, 241

D

DeMontevin Lodge, 122
Dengue fever, 243
Devon House, 148
Dining, 241–242. ⇨ *Also specific locations*
cuisine of Jamaica, 13, 44
jerk cooking style, 126
meal plans, 239
price categories, 13, 32, 76, 119, 145, 179, 203
symbols related to, 7
tipping, 246
Diving and snorkeling
Kingston and the Blue Mountains, 165–166
Montego Bay, 57–58
Negril, 226
Ocho Rios and Runaway Bay, 106
Port Antonio, 133
South Coast, 192
Doctor's Cave Beach, 56
Dogsled tours, 59, 106–107
Dolphin swims, 59
Dunn's River Falls, 81
Dunn's River Falls Beach, 105
Duties, 241

E

Electricity, 13, 242
Emancipation Park, 148, 150
Emergencies, 242
Kingston and the Blue Mountains, 145
Montego Bay, 33
Negril, 204

Ocho Rios and Runaway Bay, 77
Port Antonio, 120
roadside emergencies, 237
South Coast, 179
Evita's Italian Restaurant 🍽, 87
Exchange services
Kingston and the Blue Mountains, 145
Montego Bay, 32–33
Negril, 204
Ocho Rios and Runaway Bay, 77
Port Antonio, 120
South Coast, 179

F

Faith's Pen, 81
Fern Gully, 82
Festivals and annual events
Kingston and the Blue Mountains, 170
Montego Bay, 15, 69
Ocho Rios and Runaway Bay, 113
Port Antonio, 136
South Coast, 196
Firefly, 82
Fisherman's Cove Resort 🍽, 127
Fishing
Kingston and the Blue Mountains, 166–167
Montego Bay, 59–60
Negril, 226
Ocho Rios and Runaway Bay, 133–134
Port Antonio, 226
South Coast, 193–194
Flag of Jamaica, 208
Fleming, Ian, 91
Flynn, Erroll, 124
Folly, 122
Folly Lighthouse, 122
Fort Charles, 153–154
Forts
Kingston and the Blue Mountains, 153–154
Ocho Rios and Runaway Bay, 83–84

G

Gardens
Kingston and the Blue Mountains, 155
Ocho Rios and Runaway Bay, 80, 84
Gasoline, 236
Geejam 🍽, 127–128
Goldeneye, 91
Golf, 17
Kingston and the Blue Mountains, 167
Montego Bay, 34, 60–61
Negril, 227
Ocho Rios and Runaway Bay, 107–108
South Coast, 194
Golf at Half Moon, 60
Green flash, 14, 225
Green Grotto Caves, 82
Greenwood Great House, 36
Guardsmen's Serenity Park, 150

H

Half Moon 🍽, 48
Half Moon golf course, 60
Half Moon Village, 66
Harmony Hall, 112
Health concerns, 242–243
Hedonism II disco, 232
Helicopter tours
Montego Bay, 62
Ocho Rios and Runaway Bay, 108
High Mountain Coffee Factory, 180
Hiking
Port Antonio, 134
South Coast, 194–195
History, 22–24
Holiday Inn SunSpree Resort 🍽, 48–49
Holidays, 243
Holywell National Recreation park, 148
Horseback riding, 16
Montego Bay, 62–63
Negril, 230

Ocho Rios and Runaway Bay, 109
South Coast, 195
Horse racing, *168*
Hospitals. ⇨See Emergencies
Hotel Mocking Bird ✕, *129*
Hours of operation, *243*
Houses of historic interest
Kingston and the Blue Mountains, 148
Montego Bay, 35, 36, 40
Ocho Rios and Runaway Bay, 82, 103

I
Iberostar Rose Hall Beach ✕, *49*
Institute of Jamaica, *150*
Insurance
car-rental insurance, 237
trip insurance, 246–247
Internet access, *239*
Kingston and the Blue Mountains, 146
Montego Bay, 33
Negril, 204
Ocho Rios and Runaway Bay, 77
Port Antonio, 120
South Coast, 179
Island Village, *112*
Itineraries, *19*

J
Jake's 🖭, *185*
Jake's ✕, *187–188*
Jamaica Conference Centre, *151*
Jamaica Defense Force Museum, *151*
Jamaican Inn ✕, *96*
James Bond-related sites, *91*
Jeep and ATV tours
Montego Bay, 63–64
Ocho Rios and Runaway Bay, 110
Jerk cooking style, *126*

K
Kayaking, *110*
Kingston and the Blue Mountains, *10, 137–172*
beaches, 164–165
dining, 144–145, 157–159
emergencies, 145
exploring, 146–155
lodging, 145, 159–161, 164
nightlife & the arts, 170–172
price categories, 145
shopping, 169–170
sports and the outdoors, 164–169
transportation, 141, 144
visitor information, 146
when to go, 139
Kool Runnings Water Park, *205*

L
Language, *210*
Leeward Maroons, *37*
Lighthouses
Port Antonio, 122
Lodging, *13, 239* ⇨See also Villa rentals; specific locations
all-inclusive resorts, 16
meal plans, 239
price categories, 13, 32, 76, 119, 145, 179, 203
symbols related to, 7
tipping, 246
Lovers' Leap, *180*

M
Mahoe Waterfall, *80*
Mail and shipping, *244*
Malaria, *243*
Mandeville, *181*
Manley, Edna, *150*
Marijuana, *224*
Marine-life programs, *110*
Marley, Bob, *35, 80, 148*
Maroon people, *37*
Martha Brae River, *36*
Mavis Bank Coffee Factory, *147*

Meal plans, *239*
Meals and mealtimes, *241–242*
Medical insurance, *246–247*
Medical services. ⇨See Emergencies
Mobile phones, *240–241*
Money matters, *13, 244–245*
Money Museum, *151*
Montego Bay, *10, 25–70*
beaches, 56–57
dining, 31–32, 40–46
emergencies, 33
exploring, 33–40
lodging, 32, 46–56
nightlife, 69–70
price categories, 32
shopping, 65–68
sports and the outdoors, 34, 56–65
transportation, 27, 29–31
visitor information, 33
when to go, 27
Morgan, Sir Henry, *153*
Mountain biking
Kingston and the Blue Mountains, 168–169
Negril, 230
Ocho Rios and Runaway Bay, 111
Museums
history, 80, 154
in Kingston, 148, 150, 151, 153–154
maritime history, 153–154
Marley, 148
military history, 151
money, 151
natural history, 150
in Ocho Rios, 80
Port Royal, 153–154
Mystic Museum, *83*

N
National Gallery, *151*
National Stadium, *152*
Negril, *11, 197–232*
beaches, 223–224
dining, 201, 203, 206–211

emergencies, 204
exploring, 205–206
lodging, 203, 211–223
nightlife & the arts,
231–232
price categories, 203
shopping, 230–231
sports and the outdoors,
223–227, 230
transportation, 199, 201
visitor information, 204
when to go, 199
Negril Beach, 223–224
Norma's on the Beach
☒, 158, 209

O

Ocho Rios and Runaway
Bay, 10, 71–114
beaches, 105–106
dining, 76, 85–91
emergencies, 77
exploring, 80–85
lodging, 76, 77, 91–105
nightlife & the arts,
113–114
price categories, 76
shopping, 111–113
sports and the outdoors,
105–111
transportation, 73,
75–76
visitor information, 77
when to go, 73
Ocho Rios Fort, 83–84

P

Packing, 245
Parks, 148, 150
Passports, 245
Patois of Jamaica, 210
Peter Tosh Mausoleum,
181
Pharmacies. ⇨See
Emergencies
Phones, 239–241
Pirates, 153
Pork Pit ☒, 43
Port Antonio, 10,
115–136
beaches, 121,122, 132
dining, 119, 125, 132
emergencies, 120
exploring, 120–124

lodging, 119–120,
127–132
nightlife & the arts, 136
price categories, 119
shopping, 134
sports and the outdoors,
132–135
transportation, 118–119
visitor information, 120
when to go, 117–118
Port Royal, 152–154
Port Royal Archaeolog-
ical and Historical
Museum, 154
Price categories, 13
Kingston and the Blue
Mountains, 145
Montego Bay, 32
Negril, 203
Ocho Rios and Runaway
Bay, 76
Port Antonio, 119
South Coast, 179
Prospect Plantation, 84
Prostitution, 205

R

Rafting. ⇨See also
White-water rafting
Port Antonio, 134–135
Rastafarians, 206
Reggae music, 69
Reggae Sumfest, 15, 69
Rio Grande, 122, 124,
134–135
Ritz-Carlton Golf & Spa
Resort, Rose Hall, 60
River Head Adventure
Trail, 81
Road conditions, 237
Rockhouse Hotel ☒, 221
Rockhouse Restaurant
☒, 210–211
Rocklands Bird Sanctu-
ary & Feeding Sta-
tion, 37, 40
Rose Hall, 14, 34, 40
Royal Botanical Gardens
at Hope, 155
Royal Palm Reserve,
205–206, 224–225
Rum distillers, 180

Runaway Bay. ⇨See
Ocho Rios and Run-
away Bay
Rutland Point, 230

S

Safety, 13, 245–246
Sailing, 64
St. Peter's Church, 154
Sandals Negril Beach
Resort and Spa ☒,
221–222
Sandals Royal Carib-
bean Resort & Private
Island ☒, 53–54
Sandals Whitehouse
European Village &
Spa ☒, 189
Scotchie's Too ☒, 90
Shaw Park Gardens and
Waterfalls, 84
Shopping, 17 ⇨ Also
specific locations
hours of operation, 243
Snorkeling. ⇨See Diving
and snorkeling
Somerset Falls, 124
South Coast, 11,
173–196
beaches, 189, 191–192
dining, 178, 184–186
emergencies, 179
exploring, 180–184
lodging, 178, 187–189
nightlife & the arts, 196
price categories, 179
sports and the outdoors,
189–195
transportation, 175,
177
when to go, 175
Spanish Town, 155
Sports and the out-
doors, 12 ⇨ Also spe-
cific locations; specific
activities
Strawberry Hill ☒, 159
Strawberry Hill ☒, 161,
164
Stray dogs and cats,
191
Symbols, 7

T

Taxes, 246
Taxis
*Kingston and the Blue
    Mountains,* 144
Montego Bay, 31
Negril, 201
*Ocho Rios and Runaway
    Bay,* 76
Port Antonio, 119
South Coast, 177
tipping, 246
Tennis
Montego Bay, 64
Negril, 230
*Ocho Rios and Runaway
    Bay,* 111
South Coast, 195
Three Palms Restaurant
    🖂, 45–46
Time, 246
Times Square (mall), 230
Tipping, 246
Tosh, Peter, *181, 194*
Tour options
*Kingston and the Blue
    Mountains,* 167–168
Montego Bay, 61–62

Negril, 227
*Ocho Rios and Runaway
    Bay,* 108
Port Antonio, 134
South Coast, 194
Treasure Beach, *191,
    192*
**Trenchtown Culture
    Yard,** *155*
Trip insurance, 246–247
Tryall Club golf course,
    61

V

Villa rentals
Montego Bay, 55–56
Negril, 223
*Ocho Rios and Runaway
    Bay,* 101–105
Port Antonio, 131–132
Visas, 245
Visitor information,
    247–248
*Kingston and the Blue
    Mountains,* 146
Montego Bay, 33
Negril, 204

*Ocho Rios and Runaway
    Bay,* 77
Port Antonio, 120

W

**Walkerswood Fac-
    tory,** *85*
Waterfalls
*Ocho Rios and Runaway
    Bay,* 80, 81, 84
Port Antonio, 124
South Coast, 181
Weather information, *18*
**Weddings & honey-
    moons in Jamaica,** *16,
    20–21, 83, 248*
When to go, *18*
White-water rafting
Montego Bay, 64–65
*Ocho Rios and Runaway
    Bay,* 111
Wildlife preserves,
    205–206

Y

Y. S. Falls, *181*

Photo Credits

1, Martin Kreuzer / age fotostock. 2-3, Heeb Christian / age fotostock. 6, Franz Marc Frei / age fotostock. Chapter 1 Experience Jamaica: 8-9, Stuart Pearce / age fotostock. 10, Jamaica Tourist Board. 11 (top left), Miranda van der Kroft/Shutterstock. 11 (top right), Chee-Onn Leong/Shutterstock. 11 (bottom), Torrance Lewis/Jamaica Tourist Board/Fotoseeker.com. 14 (left), Jamaica Tourist Board. 14 (right), Breezes Runaway Bay. 15 (top left), Rickís Café. 15 (right), Psycler/wikipedia.org. 15 (bottom left), Island Outpost. 16 (left), Sandals Resorts. 16 (top right), Sergio Pitamitz / age fotostock. 16 (bottom right), Julian Love/Jamaica Tourist Board/Fotoseeker.com. 17 (top left), Steve Sanacore/Sandals Resorts. 17 (right), LT Media Group, LLC. 17 (bottom left), LT Media Group. 18, Jamaica Tourist Board. 19, Torrance Lewis/Jamaica Tourist Board/Fotoseeker.com. 21, Sandals Resorts/ Ingalls. 22, Torrance Lewis/Jamaica Tourist Board/Fotoseeker.com. 23, Julian Love/Jamaica Tourist Board/Fotoseeker.com. 24, Greenwood Great House. Chapter 2 Montego Bay: 25, Ian Cumming / age fotostock. 30, Paris Permenter and John Bigley. 35, terry harris just greece photo library / Alamy. 38-39, M. Timothy O'Keefe / Alamy. 45, Robert Fried / Alamy. 50, Sandals Resorts. 55, Sylvain Grandadam / age fotostock. 58, Chee-Onn Leong/Shutterstock. 63, piero guerrini / age fotostock. 67, Richard Cummins / Alamy. 68, Brittany Somerset. Chapter 3 Ocho Rios and Runaway Bay: 71, Doug Pearson / age fotostock. 78-79, Ian Cumming / age fotostock. 84, Roderick Chen / age fotostock. 89, Jamaica Inn. 94 (top), Breezes Runaway Bay. 94 (bottom), Jamaica Inn. 99, Peter Phipp / Travels / age fotostock. 104, Ian Cumming / age fotostock. 108, Peter Phipp / age fotostock. 113, Travelshots / age fotostock. Chapter 4 Port Antonio: 115, Ken Welsh / age fotostock. 121, travelstock44 / Alamy. 126, Nico Tondini / age fotostock. 130 (top), Heeb Christian / age fotostock. 130 (bottom), Island Outpost. 135, Sergio Pitamitz / age fotostock. Chapter 5 Kingston and the Blue Mountains: 137, Ian Cumming / age fotostock. 142–43, Ian Cumming / age fotostock. 149, JTB Photo / age fotostock. 154, Ken Welsh / age fotostock. 158, Roderick Chen / age fotostock. 162–63, Island Outpost. 168, Ken Welsh / age fotostock. 171, Ian Cumming / age fotostock. Chapter 6 The South Coast: 173, Torrance Lewis/Jamaica Tourist Board/Fotoseeker.com. 178, Held Jürgen / age fotostock. 182–83, Sergio Pitamitz / age fotostock. 185, Johannes49/wikipedia.org. 187, Heeb Christian / age fotostock. 190, Paul Hackett / age fotostock. 195, Sergio Pitamitz / age fotostock. Chapter 7 Negril: 197, Doug Pearson / age fotostock. 202, WellyWelly/Shutterstock. 207, Brittany Somerset. 214 (top), Island Outpost. 214 (bottom), Breezes Grand Negril. 219, LT Media Group. 224, DU BOISBERRANGER Jean / age fotostock. 228–29, Peter Phipp / age fotostock. 231, Travelshots.com / Alamy.

NOTES

Negril: Royal Palm Preserve

Kool Runnings waterpark

food: Norma's On the Beach

cliffs

ABOUT OUR WRITERS

John Bigley and Paris Permenter fell in love with the Caribbean two decades ago and have turned their extensive knowledge of the region into an occupation. As professional travel writers and photographers, the husband-wife team contributes to many consumer and trade publications. From their home base in the Hill Country near Austin, Texas, Paris and John also edit Lovetripper.com, an online romantic travel guide for honeymooners and romantic travelers. Both Paris and John are members of the Society of American Travel Writers.